Language learning and professionalization in higher education: pathways to preparing learners and teachers in/for the 21st century

Edited by Béatrice Dupuy and Muriel Grosbois

Published by Research-publishing.net, a not-for-profit association
Contact: info@research-publishing.net

© 2020 by Editors (collective work)
© 2020 by Authors (individual work)

Language learning and professionalization in higher education: pathways to preparing learners and teachers in/for the 21st century
Edited by Béatrice Dupuy and Muriel Grosbois

Publication date: 2020/11/16

Rights: the whole volume is published under the Attribution-NonCommercial-NoDerivatives International (CC BY-NC-ND) licence; **individual articles may have a different licence**. Under the CC BY-NC-ND licence, the volume is freely available online (https://doi.org/10.14705/rpnet.2020.44.9782490057757) for anybody to read, download, copy, and redistribute provided that the author(s), editorial team, and publisher are properly cited. Commercial use and derivative works are, however, not permitted.

Disclaimer: Research-publishing.net does not take any responsibility for the content of the pages written by the authors of this book. The authors have recognised that the work described was not published before, or that it was not under consideration for publication elsewhere. While the information in this book is believed to be true and accurate on the date of its going to press, neither the editorial team nor the publisher can accept any legal responsibility for any errors or omissions. The publisher makes no warranty, expressed or implied, with respect to the material contained herein. While Research-publishing.net is committed to publishing works of integrity, the words are the authors' alone.

Trademark notice: product or corporate names may be trademarks or registered trademarks, and are used only for identification and explanation without intent to infringe.

Copyrighted material: every effort has been made by the editorial team to trace copyright holders and to obtain their permission for the use of copyrighted material in this book. In the event of errors or omissions, please notify the publisher of any corrections that will need to be incorporated in future editions of this book.

Typeset by Research-publishing.net
Cover photo by Linus Nylund on Unsplash (https://unsplash.com/license)
Cover layout by © 2020 Raphaël Savina (raphael@savina.net)

ISBN13: 978-2-490057-75-7 (Ebook, PDF, colour)
ISBN13: 978-2-490057-76-4 (Ebook, EPUB, colour)
ISBN13: 978-2-490057-74-0 (Paperback - Print on demand, black and white)
Print on demand technology is a high-quality, innovative and ecological printing method; with which the book is never 'out of stock' or 'out of print'.

British Library Cataloguing-in-Publication Data.
A cataloguing record for this book is available from the British Library.

Legal deposit, France: Bibliothèque Nationale de France - Dépôt légal: novembre 2020.

Table of contents

v   Notes on contributors

xi   Acknowledgements

1   Introduction – language learning and professionalization in higher education: where we are, where we need to be, and how we get there
Béatrice Dupuy and Muriel Grosbois

Part I. Curriculum design and professionalization

11   Language learning in the 21st century: current status and future directions
Betül Czerkawski and Margherita Berti

37   Needs analysis for the design of a professional English curriculum: insights from a French lifelong learning context
Naouel Zoghlami

71   Questioning the notion of 'professionalisation': LANSOD contexts and the specific case of a musicology undergraduate programme
Aude Labetoulle

99   Graduate student teacher voices: perception of and apprenticeship in multiliteracies-oriented teaching
Tara Hashemi

Part II. (Multimodal) communication and professionalization

137 Digital storytelling for developing students' agency through the process of design: a case study
Elyse Petit

167 Telling stories multimodally: what observations of parent-child shared book-reading activities can bring to L2 kindergarten teachers' training
Pauline Beaupoil-Hourdel

Table of contents

199 Informing language training with multimodal analysis: insights from the use of gesture in tandem interactions
Camille Debras

229 The social dimension of learner autonomy in a telecollaborative project: a Russian course for apprentice engineers
Elsa Chachkine

263 Coda – opportunities and challenges in language learning and professionalization in higher education: the road ahead
Béatrice Dupuy and Muriel Grosbois

269 Author index

Notes on contributors

Editors

DUPUY Béatrice (PhD, University of Southern California, USA)
bdupuy@email.arizona.edu
Béatrice Dupuy is Professor of French and Applied Linguistics at the *University of Arizona*. She is co-Director of the *Center for Educational Resources in Culture, Language, and Literacy* (CERCLL), a Language Resource Center funded by the US Department of Education under Title VI. She is affiliated with the interdisciplinary PhD program in Second Language Acquisition and Teaching (SLAT). Her research primarily focuses on language teacher professional development and literacy-based approaches to teaching and learning. She has authored and co-authored books, book chapters, and articles which have appeared in numerous journals including *Foreign Language Annals, Canadian Modern Language Review, System,* and *L2 Journal.*

GROSBOIS Muriel (PhD, Sorbonne Nouvelle Université, FRANCE)
muriel.grosbois@lecnam.net
Muriel Grosbois is Professor of English and Applied Linguistics at the *Conservatoire National des Arts et Métiers* (Cnam), Paris, France. She is the Director of the language department and a member of the FoAP (*Formation et Apprentissages Professionnels*, EA 7529) research unit. Her research focuses on foreign language learning in a technology-enhanced context (computer-assisted language learning and computer-mediated communication). She has published widely in both French and English on the use of digital technologies for language learning and teaching. Her research interests also include curriculum design (course development in online settings), second language acquisition, and teacher education.

Authors

BEAUPOIL-HOURDEL Pauline (PhD, Sorbonne Nouvelle Université, FRANCE)
pauline.beaupoil-hourdel@espe-paris.fr
Pauline Beaupoil-Hourdel is Assistant Professor of Linguistics at *Sorbonne*

University, INSPE-Paris. She has developed a multimodal approach to child language development combining quantitative and qualitative analyses in her research on children's negations. Her research interests include first and early second language acquisition, multimodality, and interaction. She is Principal Investigator of the IMAAJEE project, funded by the RREEFOR-INSPE and focused on the role of embodied cognition in second-language-learning kindergartners in Paris, France.

BERTI Margherita (PhD candidate, University of Arizona, USA)
berti@email.arizona.edu
Margherita Berti is a PhD candidate in the interdisciplinary PhD program in Second Language Acquisition and Teaching (SLAT) at the *University of Arizona*. In her research, she investigates the use of 360-degree virtual reality videos for foreign language teaching and learning. Margherita has five years of experience in language teaching at the university level in various languages, and she contributes to various organizations that promote applied linguistics research and language education. Margherita has presented at national and international conferences, and has published articles and chapters addressing open educational resources, innovative technologies, and Italian pedagogy.

CHACHKINE Elsa (PhD, Université Aix-Marseille 1, FRANCE)
elsa.chachkine@lecnam.net
Elsa Chachkine is Assistant Professor at the *Conservatoire National des Arts et Métiers* (Cnam), Paris, France, and a member of the FoAP (*Formation et Apprentissages Professionnels*, EA 7529) research unit. Her research focuses on the development of distance-learning language courses and of combined distance and in-person language courses that are aimed at enhancing learners' language skills but also skills that are highly valued in the professional world such as learner autonomy, social communication skills, or cooperation skills. This is achieved by setting up experimental socially stimulating learning environments (through telecollaboration in particular) that provide significant freedom of choice and strong individual and collective support to learners. Active for four years in redesigning the Abbé Grégoire Doctoral School's program, her research has been extended to include skills of young researchers throughout the course

of their doctoral studies (environments favorable to their skills development and helpful in identifying their skills).

CZERKAWSKI Betül (PhD, Hacettepe Üniversitesi, TURKEY)
bcozkan@email.arizona.edu
Betül Czerkawski is Professor of educational technology in the College of Applied Science and Technology at the University of Arizona. She is also Associate faculty in the interdisciplinary PhD program in Second Language Acquisition and Teaching (SLAT). She has taught and conducted research in higher education contexts in a variety of roles, as Professor, Program Director, Fulbright Grant Manager, Fulbright Specialist, Fulbright Scholar, Post-Doctoral Researcher, Distance Education Mentor, Course Designer, and Journal Editor for two decades. Her research interests include learning experience design, emerging educational technologies, and design of foreign language instruction. She has presented and published over 90 papers on these subjects. Currently, she is the editor of *Issues and Trends in Learning Technologies* (ITLT).

DEBRAS Camille (PhD, Sorbonne Nouvelle Université, FRANCE)
cdebras@parisnanterre.fr
Camille Debras is Assistant Professor of English Linguistics at Université Paris Nanterre. In her research on the multimodality of spoken interactions, she studies how speakers integrate speech and gesture to construct meaning intersubjectively, in various contexts such as adult interactions, native-learner interactions, first language acquisition, or political addresses. Her research interests include interactional linguistics, linguistic anthropology, discourse analysis, and visual communication.

HASHEMI Tara (PhD, University of Arizona, USA)
tarahashemi@csufresno.edu
Tara Hashemi is Assistant Professor of French in the Department of Modern and Classical Languages and Literatures at California State University, Fresno. She graduated with a PhD from the interdisciplinary PhD program in Second Language Acquisition and Teaching (SLAT) at the University of Arizona. Her research and scholarly work focus on multilteracies pedagogies, language

Notes on contributors

instructor professional development, textbooks, and technology in language teaching. She is also Assistant Editor of *Contemporary French Civilization* by Liverpool University Press.

LABETOULLE Aude (PhD, Université de Lille, FRANCE)
aude.labetoulle@lecnam.net
Aude Labetoulle was trained at the Ecole Normale Supérieure of Paris Saclay. She is Assistant Professor of English at the *Conservatoire National des Arts et Métiers* (Cnam) in Paris, a leading higher education and research institution dedicated to adult continuing education. She is a member of the FoAP (*Formation et Apprentissages Professionnels*, EA 7529), a research unit where she conducts research that examines the links between professional learning and activity in the workplace. She previously taught English both in France and abroad, in the public and private sectors, and in French universities and elite institutions. Her research focuses on (1) educational engineering involving technology-enhanced English learning and teaching, (2) the characterization of the LANSOD sector, and (3) specialized forms of English (such as musicology).

PETIT Elyse (PhD, University of Arizona, USA)
elyse.b.petit@vanderbilt.edu
Elyse Petit is Assistant Professor of the Practice of French and serves as the French Language Program Director (LPD) at Vanderbilt University. Prior to receiving her PhD, she taught French as a foreign language in K-12 contexts in France and the United States. Her research interests focus on the implementation of innovative pedagogical frameworks supported by technological tools and authentic resources that foster the development of students' 21st century skills and new literacies including media productions and digital storytelling, and promote intercultural competence and social justice awareness. She is also interested in designing classroom activities around the representation and production of French language and culture in movies, documentaries, and on social media platforms. As LPD, she is currently working on the development of a lower-level French curriculum grounded in multiliteracies, further enhanced through the integration of slow teaching and ecopedagogical approaches.

ZOGHLAMI Naouel (PhD, Université Paris 8, FRANCE)
naouel.zoghlamiterrien@lecnam.net
Naouel Zoghlami has extensive international experience of language teaching and learning (Tunisia, England, France). She is Assistant Professor of English and Program Coordinator at the *Conservatoire National des Arts et Métiers* (Cnam) in Paris, a unique higher education public institution exclusively dedicated to lifelong learning, and a member of the FoAP (*Formation et Apprentissages Professionnels*, EA 7529) research unit. She is an applied linguist with a particular focus on English as a foreign language teaching practices and individual learning paths, curriculum design, and online course development for professional adult learners. Her other research interests and publications revolve around the cognitive processes of L2 listening and reading comprehension, and developing successful training methods for these skills.

x

Acknowledgements

We thank the editorial team at Research-publishing.net for their interest in this book. We are particularly grateful to Sylvie Thouësny for her support and timely guidance in the editorial process.

We also extend our thanks to the Conservatoire National des Arts et Métiers, the FoAP (*Formation et Apprentissages Professionnels*, EA 7529) research unit, the *Communication en Langues Étrangères* Department, and the Interdisciplinary PhD in Second Language Acquisition and Teaching program at the University of Arizona for their financial support.

Our gratitude also goes to the following colleagues who kindly accepted our invitation to review the chapters submitted for this publication and provided invaluable feedback to the authors:
- José A. Alvarez Valencia (University del Valle, Colombia),
- Carl Blyth (University of Texas at Austin, United States),
- Linda Bradley (University of Gothenburg, Sweden),
- Marco Capellini (Aix-Marseille Université, France),
- Catherine Caws (University of Victoria, Canada),
- Euline Cutrim Schmid (University of Education Schwäbisch Gmünd, Germany),
- Sébastien Dubreil (Carnegie Mellon University, United States),
- Marie-Josée Hamel (University of Ottawa, Canada),
- Mirjam Hauck (The Open University, United Kingdom),
- Emily Hellmich (The University of Arizona, United States),
- Heather Hilton (Université Lumière Lyon 2, France),
- Phil Hubbard (Stanford University, United States),
- Neil Johnson (The University of Sunderland, United Kingdom),
- Paul Lyddon (University of Shizuoka, Japan),
- Kristen Michelson (Texas Tech University, United States),
- Müge Satar (University of Newcastle, United Kingdom),
- Ursula Stickler (The Open University, United Kingdom),
- Joshua Thoms (Utah State University, United States),
- Shona Whyte (Université Côte d'Azur, France), and
- Ciara Wigham (Université Clermont Auvergne, France).

Acknowledgements

We also want to recognize Nina Conrad (PhD candidate in Second Language Acquisition and Teaching program, The University of Arizona, United States) who assisted the editors of the book by carefully copy editing the chapters.

Finally, our thanks go to the authors of the eight chapters included in this book. We believe that their contributions will generate interest and give rise to conversation among professionals in the field. Thank you for your dedication to rethinking language learning and teaching in/for the 21st century.

Béatrice Dupuy and Muriel Grosbois
Editors

Introduction – language learning and professionalization in higher education: where we are, where we need to be, and how we get there

Béatrice Dupuy[1] and Muriel Grosbois[2]

Institutions of higher education worldwide are facing the challenges of responding to global changes that sit at the junction of science and society today and of informing new modes of knowing and learning to know for the purpose of developing professionals who will be able to problem-solve these challenges successfully (Aspin, Chapman, Evans, & Bagnall, 2011; Milana et al., 2018; Slowey & Schuetze, 2012).

To meet these social and economic requirements, institutions of higher education have been called on to address the need for enhanced soft skills, which are now as valued as hard skills in the workplace. As a result, fostering learners' intercultural competence, critical thinking, problem-solving abilities, and capacity to communicate in multiple Foreign Languages (FLs) and to fully participate in today's networked communication practices has become a strategic focus with the goal to develop a globally competent workforce (ACTFL, 2011).

While broad recognition exists for the need to develop proficient intercultural multilingual speakers who can "negotiate complex demands and opportunities for varied, emergent competencies across their languages" (The Douglas Fir Group, 2016, p. 19), a discrepancy exists between current needs and current

---

1. University of Arizona, Tucson, Arizona, United States; bdupuy@email.arizona.edu; https://orcid.org/0000-0003-1122-4264

2. Conservatoire National des Arts et Métiers (Cnam), Paris, France; muriel.grosbois@lecnam.net; https://orcid.org/0000-0003-2258-8733

How to cite: Dupuy, B., & Grosbois, M. (2020). Introduction – language learning and professionalization in higher education: where we are, where we need to be, and how we get there. In B. Dupuy and M. Grosbois (Eds), *Language learning and professionalization in higher education: pathways to preparing learners and teachers in/for the 21st century* (pp. 1-7). Research-publishing.net. https://doi.org/10.14705/rpnet.2020.44.1099

outcomes (AAAS, 2017; European Commission, 2012) and calls into question not only the ways in which FLs continue to be taught and learned (Chancelade et al., 2016) but also the content of FL courses.

Furthermore, in this globalized world, it is becoming increasingly evident that a paradigm shift from education to lifelong learning needs to take place. Lifelong learning now tends to be understood as a response to societal trends and improved understandings of how humans develop knowledge and skills. In response to this, the European Universities' *Charter on Lifelong Learning* (EUA, 2008) underscores the necessity to provide relevant programs, flexible learning paths, assessment, and recognition of prior learning, in a learner-centered approach. While there is recognition for lifelong learning opportunities for professionals across all academic areas and for people at all stages of their careers, the larger question remains whether institutions of higher education can see beyond the completion of a degree and consider the degree as a milestone that binds the student, the learning community, and the institution on the lifelong learning journey. With a view to investigating higher education modes of knowing and learning – in FLs in particular – and their link to professionalization, the following questions are explored.

- How can institutions of higher education expand FL teaching and learning offerings and help ensure that graduates continue to thrive in work environments shaped by accelerating change?

- What kinds of programs can institutions of higher education actively develop and implement to best serve continuing FL learning in professional contexts?

- Which processes can best facilitate this learning?

Language learning for professional purposes is here explored through themes related to postsecondary students' experiences and professional integration, (multimodal) communication, and (online) instructional design principles, and language teacher education.

Each chapter seeks to focus on how research results could/should inform training design in higher education (research-based recommendations, implications for pedagogy) so as to promote learning and sustain the link between FL education and professionalization in today's and tomorrow's society.

The present volume

The eight chapters of the volume are grouped into two interrelated parts: *Curriculum design and professionalization* and *(Multimodal) communication and professionalization.*

Part I, Curriculum design and professionalization, opens with a general reflection on key issues related to the teaching and learning of FLs relevant to the needs of the 21st century in Chapter 1. These various perspectives are echoed in the remaining contributions included in this section. Chapters 2, 3, and 4 coalesce around the challenge of designing a curriculum for professional FL courses so as to bridge the gap between institutional learning and workplace requirements, and the questioning of teachers' professional development in a context where FL programs are undergoing curricular changes to meet today's needs.

In **Chapter 1**, "Language learning in the 21st century: current status and future directions", **Betül Czerkawski** and **Margherita Berti** focus on the challenges higher education faces when coping with new realities. How do learners acquire the skills necessary for effective cross-cultural communication? What professional learning opportunities do universities offer to language learners? What are some present practices found in universities today, and how are these practices shaping tomorrow's FL language education? The key issues raised in this chapter center on the need to go beyond just language and focus more broadly on technology-supported communication in multicultural settings, the importance of better language teacher preparation, the necessity of FL curricula so they foster 21st century skills and lifelong learning, and the importance of instructional design to develop meaningful learning experiences that help people navigate complex realities and constantly evolving environments. The authors offer possible ways in which these issues can be addressed and end with a discussion of future trends.

Introduction

In **Chapter 2**, "Needs analysis for the design of a professional English curriculum: insights from a French lifelong learning context", **Naouel Zoghlami** draws on needs analysis as a fundamental approach to inform the design of a professional English curriculum at the Cnam, a unique French research institution of higher education dedicated to lifelong learning. While needs analysis is still not widely used in the development of English for specific purposes programs in French higher education contexts, this study attempts to fill this gap by revealing the kinds of tasks adult professional learners studying at the Cnam say they need to perform in English at work. One of the strengths of this study thus lies in relying on data provided by domain insiders rather than assumptions held by the researcher-teacher about what adults need to learn to inform a professional English curriculum. Study data provide the information needed to improve the existing syllabus and the basis on which to build relevant pedagogical tasks.

In **Chapter 3**, "Questioning the notion of 'professionalization': LANSOD contexts and the specific case of a musicology undergraduate program", **Aude Labetoulle** addresses the challenge of designing courses that meet the needs of learners whose major is not languages in French universities – a sector usually referred to as 'LANSOD' (LANguages for Students of Other Disciplines). University language requirements are typically related to the increased importance of 'mobility' and 'employability'. Yet, French universities seem to struggle with the design of language courses that are relevant to the future professional needs of learners. To explore this issue, Aude Labetoulle first investigates how 'professionalization' has been progressively defined and implemented by French universities and stresses the tensions underlying the various interpretations of the ongoing movement toward the 'professionalization' of university courses in France. She then analyzes the specific case of a LANSOD undergraduate course at the University of Lille (France) and demonstrates how complex it can be to design an undergraduate English curriculum relevant to learners' future professional needs when learners have different disciplinary backgrounds and professional aspirations. This study provides LANSOD course designers with an approach to curriculum design and evaluation that addresses these challenges and offers transferable tools to, generally underprepared, LANSOD teachers.

In **Chapter 4**, "Graduate student teacher voices: perception of and apprenticeship in multiliteracies-oriented teaching", **Tara Hashemi** examines Graduate Student Teachers' (GSTs') perceptions of their professionalization in FL programs which have adopted a literacy-based approach to teaching French in the United States. Findings show that while some clear efforts are being made by language program directors to provide GSTs with a large panoply of tools, GSTs wish they had more opportunities for direct and personalized feedback on their teaching as well as more demonstrations of concrete lessons in which the concepts of the literacy-based framework are instantiated. It cannot be expected that GSTs will understand and apply complex notions of the multiliteracies framework and multiliteracies pedagogy without relevant, adapted, and ongoing professional development.

Part II, (Multimodal) communication and professionalization, provides case examples of how practices are sustained and enriched by the multifaceted nature of 21st century communications and the multiliteracies approach, thus informing instructional design principles in return.

In **Chapter 5**, "Digital storytelling for developing students' agency through the process of design: a case study", **Elyse Petit** compares two case studies that illustrate the potential of using a multimodal project (i.e. digital storytelling) in the FL classroom to enhance students' 21st ccentury skills and support their understanding of how their selection and orchestration of semiotic resources construct layers of meaning, promote multiliteracies, and foster language use and appropriateness. Findings suggest that students' selection of semiotic resources and the ways in which they arrange them reveal their ability to face and find solutions to circumvent challenges brought on by language and culture to convey their stories.

In **Chapter 6**, "Telling stories multimodally: what observations of parent-child shared book-reading activities can bring to L2 kindergarten teachers' training", **Pauline Beaupoil-Hourdel** presents multimodal and plurisemiotic analyses of storytelling activities in adult-child dyadic interactions at home in France and analyzes the extent to which this context can inform the professionalization of teachers in the 21st century. Findings show that spontaneous adult-child interactions during storytelling and shared book reading at home provide valuable insights for kindergarten and primary school teachers to teach an L2, as well as new multimodal perspectives on fostering linguistic, narrative, and communication skills in young children at school.

In **Chapter 7**, "Informing language training with multimodal analysis: insights from the use of gesture in tandem interactions", **Camille Debras** explores face-to-face tandem interactions between undergraduate university students who are native speakers of French and English and the role multimodality plays in these. Drawing from linguistics research on the multimodality of tandem interactions, four multimodal interactional linguistics studies based on the annotation and/or qualitative analysis of data from a corpus made of audio- and video-recorded face-to-face tandem interactions provide evidence for the crucial communicative functions of gesture during exolingual interactions. Findings underscore the need to involve the nonverbal dimension in language learning and teaching and professionalization in higher education, so as to prepare L2 learners for the (international) workplace.

In **Chapter 8**, "The social dimension of learner autonomy in a telecollaborative project: a Russian course for apprentice engineers", **Elsa Chachkine** explores the social turn in autonomous learning through a telecollaborative project based on teletandems and the use of social media in a self-study Russian course whose aim is to familiarize future engineers with the Russian language and culture and to develop their autonomy as learners before their work placement in Russia. This research contributes to our understanding of the ways in which the social dimension manifests itself and its potential role in the development of autonomy, language and culture, and other skills valued in the world of work.

References

AAAS. (2017). *America's languages: investing in language education in the 21st century*. American Academy of Arts & Sciences. https://www.amacad.org/publication/americas-languages

ACTFL. (2011). *ACTFL 21st Century Skills Map*. American Council on the Teaching of Foreign Languages. https://www.actfl.org/sites/default/files/resources/21st%20Century%20Skills%20Map-World%20Languages.pdf

Aspin, D., Chapman, J., Evans, K., & Bagnall, R. (2011). *Second international handbook of lifelong learning*. Springer. https://doi.org/10.1007/978-94-007-2360-3

Chancelade, C., Janissin, P., Giret, J. F., Guégnard, C., Benoit, P., & Vogt, A. (2016). *Analyse des besoins des employeurs français au regard des compétences en langues vivantes étrangères : synthèse d'enquête* [Research report]. https://pdfs.semanticscholar.org/8059/cbe14a6ffd0f73c4bfeba8e65cd94d0b6ba9.pdf

EUA. (2008). *European universities' charter on lifelong learning*. European University Association. https://eua.eu/downloads/publications/european%20universities%20charter%20on%20lifelong%20learning%202008.pdf

European Commission. (2012). *First European survey on language competences. Final report*. http://www.surveylang.org/media/ExecutivesummaryoftheESLC_210612.pdf

Milana, M., Webb, S., Holford, J., Waller, R., & Jarvis, P. (2018). *The Palgrave international handbook on adult and lifelong education and learning*. Palgrave Macmillan. https://doi.org/10.1057/978-1-137-55783-4

Slowey, M., & Schuetze, H. (2012). *Global perspectives on higher education and lifelong learners*. Routledge. https://doi.org/10.4324/9780203122495

The Douglas Fir Group. (2016). A transdisciplinary framework for SLA in a multilingual world. *The Modern Language Journal, 100*(S1), 19-47. https://doi.org/10.1111/modl.12301

Part I

Curriculum design and professionalization

1. Language learning in the 21st century: current status and future directions

Betül Czerkawski[1] and Margherita Berti[2]

1. Introduction

In today's interconnected world, higher education institutions are challenged with new realities: how to effectively assist students in advancing their professional development, gain skills for successful 21st century interactions, and start new careers. In the context of Foreign Language (FL) education, some have argued that language proficiency and oral communication have been favored, while the integration of higher-order and critical thinking skills with language learning has been peripheral especially in lower-level language courses (Correa, 2011; Garrett-Rucks, 2013; Yamada, 2010). The lack of meaningful activities that engage students beyond vocabulary and grammatical structures has become an issue in a world where students need to navigate complex realities and constantly evolving environments. Problem-solving, critical thinking, and digital literacy, which fall under the umbrella term of 21st-century skills, are only some examples of abilities necessary to succeed in today's rapidly changing global economy. In this chapter, 21st century skills are defined as the knowledge and skills necessary to enter and succeed in today's workforce. The 21st century skills have been emphasized by the American Council on the Teaching of Foreign Languages (ACTFL, 2011), which designed a 21st century skills map to provide educators, administrators, and policymakers with concrete examples of how to integrate such skills in language courses. Lifelong learning – that is,

---

1. University of Arizona, Tucson, Arizona, United States; bcozkan@email.arizona.edu; https://orcid.org/0000-0002-4189-4042

2. University of Arizona, Tucson, Arizona, United States; berti@email.arizona.edu; https://orcid.org/0000-0002-6572-921X

How to cite this chapter: Czerkawski, B., & Berti, M. (2020). Language learning in the 21st century: current status and future directions. In B. Dupuy and M. Grosbois (Eds), *Language learning and professionalization in higher education: pathways to preparing learners and teachers in/for the 21st century* (pp. 11-35). Research-publishing.net. https://doi.org/10.14705/rpnet.2020.44.1100

self-initiated education for either professional or personal reasons – is another important skill that should be instilled in language learners.

In 2009, the decline in the number of students enrolled in collegiate FL courses led to a reconsideration of the role and value of language education in the United States (Lomicka & Lord, 2018). In many cases, students abandon their language studies unless they choose to major in a language or literature program, which primarily consists of literary and cultural studies. According to the 2016 Modern Language Association (MLA) report (Looney & Lusin, 2018), undergraduate and graduate enrollments in languages other than English dropped by 9.2% between fall 2013 and fall 2016. At this point, universities assume an important role in assisting students while they undertake or continue learning a FL in the context of higher education. Since many beginning FL offerings continue to often privilege linguistic aspects of language learning over others, followed by more advanced courses with cultural emphasis oftentimes offered in English, the options for students to study a language for professional purposes, develop 21st century skills, and extend their chosen career options through developing linguistic knowledge are lacking. Furthermore, although the MLA explains that the causes of this trend are beyond the scope of their enrollments reports (Looney & Lusin, 2018), it is possible that one reason for the decrease is linked to the fact that grammar and vocabulary are still major learning foci in beginning FL courses. In other words, after a couple of semesters of courses with a grammar and vocabulary emphasis, students might lose interest in languages and choose to end their language-learning journey.

The purpose of this chapter is twofold. First, we will explore the status of FL learning in higher education institutions in the United States, including language learning for professional purposes, which historically concerns "helping students meet their immediate linguistic needs in professional contexts, as observed on a global scale in programs created to teach English for specific and academic purposes" (King de Ramírez & Lafford, 2018, p. 2). Today there is a need to go beyond just language and look at how language studies can help students in their future professions and in multicultural settings. Second, the need for 21st century skills will be discussed, and pedagogical suggestions will be provided as solutions to the sole focus on linguistic structures and the transmission-oriented teaching model still present in FL teaching. Following that, recommendations for the integration of 21st century skills in FL courses with the aid of technology and Instructional Design (ID) guidelines for creating highly effective learning environments will be discussed. The chapter closes with a discussion of future directions for professional language learning considering developments in the fields of learning technologies and design.

2. FL learning in higher education: current status in the United States

The need for an approach that emphasizes language from a critical and dynamic perspective in the context of FL education has been stressed by organizations and professional associations. For example, in 2007, a report published by the MLA Ad Hoc Committee on FLs highlighted translingual and transcultural competence as the primary goal of language education (MLA, 2007). This competence emphasizes students' abilities to operate between languages and cultures, while also being able to reflect on the world and themselves through a critical lens. In light of the decline of enrollments in collegiate FL courses in the United States (Lomicka & Lord, 2018) and the alarming survey reports published by the 2016 MLA (Looney & Lusin, 2018), scholars and language educators have called for changes in curricula to engage students with FLs and cultures in new and relevant ways (Pascual y Cabo & Prada, 2018; Pufahl & Rhodes, 2011). For example, Richards (2015) suggested the use of the Internet, technology, and the media to foster students' communicative skills. Blattner, Dalola, and Lomicka (2016) discussed how Twitter can be used to facilitate the cultural enrichment of beginner French learners, by enhancing sociopragmatic awareness and developing multiliteracy skills. Cox and Montgomery (2019) proposed project-based language learning for organizing curricular tasks that develop students' 21st century skills and enable engagement with authentic learning resources.

Chapter 1

In 2017, the Commission on Language Learning created by the American Academy of Arts and Sciences (AAAS) published a report aimed at addressing questions related to the influence of language education on economic growth, cultural diplomacy, and the productivity of future generations (AAAS, 2017). The report states that the United States has neglected FL in educational curricula, and this oversight has had "adverse and often unforeseen consequences at home and abroad – in business and diplomacy, in civic life, and in the exchange of ideas" (AAAS, 2017, p. 1). The report has also found that K-12 schools have struggled to identify qualified language instructors that meet the current and future needs of multicultural societies within the United States. The Commission on Language Learning recommended better preparation of language teachers and pointed out that cultural understanding is key in language education. In fact, if language is often taught in terms of grammar and vocabulary, students might miss out on acquiring how to effectively function and communicate across cultures (Cutshall, 2012). Despite the numerous calls for changes in FL pedagogical practices, there still appears to be a lack of focus on 21st century skills in language education. Both reports published by the Commission on Language Learning (AAAS, 2017) and the MLA (2007) Ad Hoc Committee on Foreign Languages emphasize the importance of study abroad experiences to connect with other cultures and to learn how to appropriately interact in diverse environments. Although sojourns abroad are certainly valuable, they are not accessible to most college students.

According to another study conducted by Open Doors in 2017, in the 2016-2017 academic year, about 300,000 students, not exclusively enrolled in FL courses, traveled abroad to study, which represents only a fraction of students enrolled in collegiate courses. In fall 2016, 1,417,921 students were enrolled in higher education courses other than English (Looney & Lusin, 2018), meaning that universities cannot rely on study abroad to be the major vehicle to promote intercultural skills. Rather, it is fundamental to consider how FL teaching strategies as well as FL curricula need to evolve to foster 21st century skills and lifelong learning. The landscape of professional language learning, also called language for specific purposes, has begun to expand on these needs by proposing curricular innovations and meaningful learning opportunities for students and their future professions. Research has explored how professional language learning might contribute to better preparing students for their future careers. Crouse (2013) claimed that professional language learning courses "offer students real-world opportunities to practice language and navigate culture in the context of a specific field" (p. 33). For example, Martinsen (2015) explored how student-centered teaching in a lower-division Spanish course could increase university language learners' motivation and willingness to communicate through reflections on personal goals and the identification of contexts in which students might use Spanish in their professional lives. Students also sought opportunities to foster their own language and culture learning in relation to their own future careers. Although a marginal increase in motivation to continue studying Spanish was reported, the author concluded that student-centered teaching and studying languages for specific purposes can be an effective means to fill students' unmet needs in their transition toward the workplace. In another study, López (2015) argued for community engagement and service learning in language studies for specific purposes to better meet the needs of students and society. Altstaedter (2016) described the development and improvement of students' perceptions of a Spanish for specific purposes course aimed at helping future healthcare professionals develop their linguistic proficiency and intercultural abilities. Connecting professions with language learning has now become of central importance, and higher education institutions should continue to further explore how students' professional and 21st century skills can be fostered in the collegiate setting.

Some universities have developed undergraduate majors, certificates, and courses that integrate language learning with other disciplines. For example, in 2019, Montclair State University launched a new major in language, business, and culture, to combine languages (i.e. Arabic, French, German, Italian, or Spanish) and culture studies with essential business skills with the aim of preparing students for careers in the United States and abroad. Similarly, Bentley University is to offer a language, culture, and business major with a concentration in Chinese, French, Italian, or Spanish starting fall 2020. Emmanuel College offers a Spanish for health care professionals certificate for students planning a career in a health-related field, which guides them through an exploration of the culture of Latino communities in the United States. Another example is the establishment of a specific residence hall for Italian students at Mount Holyoke College with the objective of creating a community of language learners through extracurricular activities. These initiatives show an important turn in collegiate FL education in the United States. Nevertheless, although research trends suggest that there is a strong demand for employees with high levels of linguistic proficiency and cultural competence in a variety of fields (Cox & Montgomery, 2019; Damari et al., 2018), more needs to be done, especially in basic FL courses, to foster 21st century skills and engage students in meaningful lifelong learning practices. The examples described just above are only a handful, and most FL courses in the United States still rely on traditional language teaching and learning.

3. Possible solutions

Language learning and teaching in the professional context is a complicated and multifaceted matter. There are various ways to improve current practices, although these ways change constantly in our ever-changing educational landscape. After conducting a comprehensive literature review, the authors propose the following solutions. These solutions should not be viewed as a complete list, as they are some of the highlights and outcomes arising from the literature.

We suggest that 21st century skills should be the main conceptual framework used to create up-to-date curricula so that learning goals can be aligned with the demands of the labor market. In addition, the use of ID practices is emphasized because, as a holistic field, ID can help create consistent, meaningful, and effective learning experiences while also utilizing important findings of learning sciences. Finally, the use of technology to support learning experiences and ways of taking advantage of nonformal learning experiences are discussed as complementary activities to 21st century skills and ID. Taken together, these solutions provide a solid effort to alleviate some of the major issues experienced today in the context of language education.

3.1. 21st century skills in education

In 2002, the Partnership for 21st century skills (P21) was founded by the National Education Association, the United States Department of Education, and other organizations interested in supporting schools, districts, and states in the integration of 21st century skills and technology into education, while also providing resources to facilitate such efforts. In 2008, the P21 proposed a framework[3] for 21st century learning to ensure student success in a constantly changing world. In this framework, it was argued that 21st century skills are an indispensable currency for participation, competitiveness, and achievement in today's global economy, and suggestions for promoting such skills were provided. First, the P21 proposes that students think critically (i.e. assessing accuracy, analyzing, and making reasoned decisions) about information in its various forms, whether it is presented on the web, at school, or anywhere else. Next, the framework suggests creative thinking and solving complex and multidisciplinary problems, which usually do not come in a multiple-choice format and do not have a single correct solution for fostering 21st century skills. Haley, Steeley, and Salahshoor (2013) provided an example of how teachers of Arabic and Chinese can be prepared to connect 21st century skills to instructional practices through specific training. In their study they explained that the teacher training, provided in the form of blended learning activities, better equipped and prepared students for a global community, as participants grasped the salient concepts and adapted them to their instructional practices. Takeda (2016) described a project-based learning course at the University of California San Diego called 'Japanese for professional purposes', in which students conduct research, develop a feasible project, and put it into action through the use of the Japanese language. McKeeman and Oviedo (2013) discussed the use of web 2.0 tools (i.e. VoiceThread, Poll Everywhere, Animoto, and Xtranormal) to foster 21st century skills, with a focus on communicative competence. In their action research project, they used individual and collaborative assignments to review, reinforce, and practice concepts integrating technology tools and incorporating 21st century skills. For example, with VoiceThread, students were asked to

---

3. https://files.eric.ed.gov/fulltext/ED519337.pdf

respond to a series of questions regarding the differences between their family and a Latino or Hispanic family based upon their interpretation of an embedded video. The collaborative nature of VoiceThread supported critical thinking, and students negotiated meaning and understanding from comments made by their classmates in the target language. Communicating and collaborating with people across language and cultural boundaries and making innovative use of knowledge can help learners become well-rounded global citizens. Although some courses for professional language learning, as described above, are contributing to the development of such skills, it is important to include the framework described above and related guidelines in the design of basic language courses where students can start engaging in higher-order and critical thinking practices.

Saavedra and Opfer (2012) argued that 21st century skills require 21st century teaching, calling for a definition and practical teaching guidelines. In an interconnected global ecosystem, they explain, the 'teaching as transmission' model (i.e. where the teacher transmits factual knowledge to students) has become outdated. From the transmission perspective, the role of the teacher is to prepare and transmit information to learners, while learners' role is to receive and store information (Tishman, Jay, & Perkins, 1993). Freire (1970) called this the "banking model" of education, where "knowledge is a gift bestowed by those who consider themselves knowledgeable upon those whom they consider to know nothing" (p. 72). Under this view, the teacher talks, and the students listen as passive receivers of knowledge with no creative power. This model is problematic since learners are not asked to think critically, but rather information is memorized for the purpose of being rehearsed to the teacher or repeated in a test, whereas opportunities to communicate in complex ways and apply what is learned to new and meaningful contexts are lacking. The transmission or banking model is not the most effective way to teach 21st century skills (Saavedra & Opfer, 2012). In today's world, skills sought by employers go beyond the memorization of basic information. Higher-order thinking skills, including creative thinking, decision-making, and problem-solving, are strongly valued capacities necessary to thrive in increasingly complex working environments and societies. Laurillard (2002) points out that academics have been arguing for a shift from the standard transmission model of university teaching to a reflective practicum, with the aim of preparing students for their future professional careers. Yet, the transmission model, consisting of the lecture, the book, and the marked assignment, remains the dominant approach in the formal education landscape. Thus, learners are not developing 21st century skills since these skills are not being fostered (Schleicher, 2012).

Furthermore, since such skills are more difficult to assess compared to the repetition of knowledge as in the transmission model, educators may choose to continue with pedagogical practices that see students as 'empty containers' to be filled with 'prefabricated' knowledge.

On the other hand, meaningful learning views education "as knowledge construction in which students seek to make sense of their experiences" (Mayer, 2002, p. 227). From this constructivist perspective, students are engaged in active cognitive processes, such as organizing incoming information and integrating it with existing knowledge, and are able to move beyond factual knowledge. Constructivism refers to the idea that knowledge is built by the learner, rather than being transmitted from the teacher to the student (Schwienhorst, 2002). As opposed to behaviorist theories, which emphasize imitation and knowledge reproduction, constructivism is a cognitive theory that focuses on the combination of existing knowledge and novel information to develop new meaning and understanding through active, authentic, and reflective learning activities (Chen, 2009). Building on a constructivist approach, in the classroom setting, students can be regarded as individuals "with different experiences and prior knowledge, [diverse] cultural backgrounds, and different learning trajectories" (Mellis, Carvalho, & Thompson, 2013, p. 6). Bearing in mind that students are actual individuals who can construct their own understandings, the teacher's role shifts from preacher to facilitator. The teacher helps students connect their prior knowledge to the new knowledge and contributes to learning experiences that are long-lasting. From this constructivist perspective, 21st century skills can be developed as teachers and students participate in solving authentic and complex learning tasks that have real-life connections and offer opportunities to transfer what is learned in the formal instructional context to experiences beyond the classroom and authentic settings.

Chapter 1

Concerning 21st century skills, learning scientists have proposed various guidelines for their development in educational contexts. For example, the curriculum needs to be relevant to the students, who should also be aware of the bigger picture and understand the value of the subject matter. Students should participate in lower-order as well as higher-order thinking exercises. While lower-order activities are common in existing curricula, higher-order thinking exercises are less common (Saavedra & Opfer, 2012), yet they are much needed to engage students in deeper learning. Other recommendations for the promotion of 21st century skills include encouraging students to apply skills and knowledge gained in one discipline to other areas of their lives, fostering creativity, and exploiting technology to support learning and collaboration. These types of activities can foster lifelong learning (Koper & Tattersall, 2004) and the acquisition of skills necessary to thrive in adult and professional contexts.

3.2. Incorporating technology in FL education

The current need to prepare students for the 21st century has also led to the use of more technology in the classroom (Ruggiero & Mong, 2015). Technology is constantly changing, and while the literature on its affordances and limitations for language learning is extensive (e.g. Al-Ali, 2014; Borau, Ullrich, Feng, & Shen, 2009; Chang, Wu, & Ku, 2004; Golonka et al., 2014; Reinhardt & Ryu, 2014; Schmerbeck & Lucht, 2017), it is important to purposefully and effectively implement technology tools in educational contexts for best outcomes. It has also been argued that teachers should move "from singular use of the traditional classroom to a more blended or hybrid form of education that combines traditional classroom instruction with computer-based language learning" (Meurant, 2010, p. 229). Eaton (2010) explained that in addition to the technology tools that help foster learning outcomes, there are also technologies that facilitate student learning. These technologies can be synchronous (in real time), such as Skype, Moodle, chat-based platforms, or virtual live classes, or they can be asynchronous (not occurring in real time), such as podcasts, discussion boards, and blogs. Technology tools can be implemented in language education to connect students with users of the target language and help them engage in multimodal learning and learn how to express themselves through new means. Eaton (2010) also posited that in the future, Mobile-Assisted Language Learning (MALL) will likely play a central role in educational contexts, and perhaps replace the traditional textbook. As mobile technologies become more and more ubiquitous, it is possible that language courses will see increasing use and integration of mobile devices.

The other dimension of technology use in language education is digital literacy. Digital literacy involves more than the ability to operate a digital device or use specific software; it includes a variety of complex skills (e.g. effective virtual communication and collaboration, ability to find and select information, cultural and social understanding) needed to function effectively in digital environments (Eshet, 2004). Digital literacy is now an essential ability for participation in digital spaces, and students should acquire these skills through practice in instructional contexts. Harris (2015) suggested addressing four aspects of digital literacy with adult language learners: using basic digital skills (i.e. those needed to operate digital devices), creating and communicating information, finding and evaluating information, and solving problems in technology-rich environments. According to Ollivier (2018), digital literacy results from the intertwining of three sets of competencies: technology literacy, meaning-making literacy, and interaction literacy. Lotherington and Jenson (2011) talked about multimodal and digital literacy and reported on innovative pedagogical approaches for language learners. They explained that language instruction "continues to resist digitized multimedia and multimodal literacy practices as optional or secondary to flat textual practices" (Lotherington & Jenson, 2011, p. 239). This resistance might be linked to the complexities of the educational system, teachers' professional expectations, and assessment paradigms. Thus, Lotherington and Jenson argued for wider use of MALL in teaching practices to enable a more agentive and participatory learning, digital storytelling to promote mode-switching activities (e.g. students translating textbook materials into comic strips), and digital games to move from the controlled spaces of the classroom to less controlled learning environments. Nevertheless, although multimodal and digital literacy-based learning can expand students' skills and experiences, more empirical evidence is needed to understand the "depth in which students develop their linguistic repertoire when moving across digital modes" (Ware, 2008, p. 49). Furthermore, it is important to consider how digital literacy is being fostered in FL courses and how it can help students develop skills useful to their adult lives.

3.3. ID to learning design

Designing effective professional learning and creating meaningful learning experiences are among the major functions of higher education institutions. In order to develop pedagogically sound learning, scholars use ID guidelines. In the broader sense of the word, the aim of ID is to "make the learning more efficient and effective" (Morrison, Ross, Kalman, & Kemp, 2011, p. 2) so learners will have fewer difficulties.

In recent years, many scholars have come to prefer the term *learning design* rather than ID in order to emphasize the importance of learner-centeredness of the design process. ID refers to a broader focus, such as designing courses, programs, assessments, and curriculum plans to test the overall consistency, coherence, and effectiveness of instructional processes and procedures. Learning design, on the other hand, is about the instructor or trainers' day-to-day efforts to create learning experiences for their students at the micro level. Learning design is more specific and purposeful in its attention to meet learner needs. To add to the confusion, a quick search on job forums will show that private businesses and higher education institutions are hiring 'learning experience designers', learning architects, and engineers. In the end, broad or specific, all these terms refer to the same activities and are used interchangeably.

Regardless of the level of instruction/training or the micro or macro levels of developing instruction, ID principles married with the most recent learning theories provide clarity about instructional or performance-related issues so that solutions can be offered while saving time and money. ID forces us to define the goals of our efforts as instructors while making us better equipped to create high-quality experiences for our students. Most modern ID models start with an analysis of the learners so that truly learner-centered training for students can be provided. In the context of professional language learning, such an approach can be beneficial for capturing the needs of learners, as they change over time.

Various ID models over the years have presented instructors with options depending on the focus of instruction. For instance, Keller's (1987) attention, relevance, confidence, and satisfaction model aims to increase motivation and participation in the learning environment; Gustafson and Branch's (2002) instructional system development model considers collaboration among development team members who are introducing a project management component. Wiggins and McTighe's (2005) understanding by design approach suggests a backward design approach while bringing attention to learning outcomes and learning transfer. Willis's (2009) reflective recursive design and development, or R2D2, provides an early example of an agile, flexible, and constructivist ID model. Allen's (2012) successive approximation model takes its inspiration from software design models and guides teachers through a more agile, purposeful, and prototype-based development model. As seen in these ID models, there is no single approach for developing instruction for language programs. Language instructors should consider the needs of students, their teaching methods, learning context, and available resources to select the best ID approach.

The literature is rich with such ID approaches, but it should be noted that there are also two major critiques of ID. First, the purposeful and pragmatic nature of ID practices is criticized, because their rigid approach to ID and development, lack of imagination in the design process, and use of prescribed and inflexible methods result in nonrealistic and inauthentic learning scenarios. Although such critiques may be justifiable for the early ID models of the 1970's that were linear and rigid, most modern ID models provide sound solutions to dominant learning and training issues of the 21st century, such as lack of learner participation, interaction and engagement, retention, multidisciplinarity, the transnational nature of academic disciplines, and technology's transforming role in societies.

The second critique of ID comes from the learning sciences field and from the friction between two fields that lasted for more than 50 years. This critique is so intense that ID is being turned inside out because of the emphasis on 21st century skills. Starting in the 1960's, educational researchers charted divergent paths because of their different views on instruction, the role of technology in the learning process, and use of theory to support teaching strategies. One of these views led the way to the flourishing of the field called *educational technology*, and the other one led to the development of *educational psychology* or *learning sciences* (Gibbons, 2017). Gibbons (2017) argued that neither educational technology nor learning sciences became an independent discipline, since the nature of their content is applied and highly interdisciplinary. Over time, ID merged with educational technology, and in the 21st century it has become popular because of the increase in online learning and teaching practices. Learning sciences, on the other hand, merged alliances with cognitive scientists and information scientists, and it embraced technology, especially the newest developments in data and cognitive sciences as well as computer science (Kirby, Hoadley, & Carr-Chellman, 2005, as cited in Gibbons, 2017). While the whys and hows of this division between two fields are beyond the scope of this chapter, it is an important one to underline because ID (with its emphasis on the design process) and learning sciences (with its emphasis on pedagogy) should be used in conjunction with each other for meaningful learning experiences. For instance, in FL education, traditional approaches are stagnant and disconnected from real-life experiences, but both ID and learning sciences can offer significant improvements to current practices. In recent years, an encouraging new perspective has provided some hope for the future, *design thinking*, which provides a viable solution for designing meaningful and authentic learning opportunities in academia.

In its broadest sense, design thinking is about solving problems while considering users' concerns, needs, and tendencies (Denning, 2013; Huq & Gilbert, 2017). The intellectual leader for design-thinking scholars is considered Stanford University's Design Center, where three main considerations in the design process were proposed: *many eyes* refers to the interdisciplinary nature of the design process with experts in various fields, *customer viewpoint* is about users and the ways they perform certain tasks, and *tangibility* is about creating user experiences around prototypes. All of these processes of design thinking are reminiscent of learner-centered constructivist ID models of the late 20th century, but they go much further than constructivism by shifting from an *information age* focus to a *data age* focus (Gobble, 2014). The realistic and user-oriented nature of design thinking with concrete learning scenarios is a quick, team-based, creative, need-oriented strategy for instructional development. Additionally, in order to solve the problems of those individuals who are at the center of the design process, design thinking brings expertise from a wide range of disciplines.

In the context of FL instruction and professional language learning, design thinking can help identify the problem areas where today's higher education falls short. Currently, it seems like most language course offerings neglect the wide-ranging needs of learners living in the 21st century. Design thinking provides opportunities for scholars to be creative in solving learners' needs and future career-related demands.

3.4. Integrating ID principles and heutagogy into FL learning

Although there is an abundance of research in FL when it comes to the use of technology, instructional, and assessment strategies, the integration of sound ID principles as a whole is a less common practice. A few studies (Ibanez et al., 2011; Wu, Wang, & Chen, 2015) have suggested that the use of Technology-Enhanced Language Learning (TELL) is the best response for integrating ID guidelines into the design of language content. However, TELL only considers how various technologies are integrated into learning and misses the bigger picture. For instance, what learning objectives and goals should guide professional FL learning? What learning theories best address learners' needs? What teaching and learning strategies could be employed to foster meaningful learning? What assessment strategies are suitable and complement learning? All these questions and more can be answered with the application of an ID strategy.

In the professional FL context, adult learning theories and especially *heutagogy*, where learners determine their own learning goals, should accompany an ID model of choice. Heutagogy is a nonlinear form of self-directed learning, which fits the needs of lifelong learners beyond formal education programs (Hase & Kenyon, 2007). Along with an ID model, heutagogy can directly address professional language learning needs because "heutagogy progresses adult learning to become an integrated process related to contexts and situations"

(Rogerson & Rossetto, 2018, p. 413) that can differentiate professional language learning from linguistic-oriented learning. Focusing on contexts and real-life situations, with the assistance of learners who determine their own goals, has true potential to transform FL instruction.

3.5. Formal versus nonformal learning in FL instruction

Higher education institutions with their planned curricula, accredited programs, and academic content and disciplines are the best examples of formal education. Learners who pursue a formal program of study attain a certificate, degree, or diploma. Nonformal education, on the other hand, refers to an organized curriculum outside of formal venues. The purpose is not to gain a credential, but rather a skill or personal enrichment. Nonformal learning is usually short term, practical, personalized, process oriented, participatory, and flexible (Civis Plus, 2017).

In the context of FL learning, nonformal experiences may provide targeted and highly enriching experiences to students. For instance, adult language classes offered in community centers, online webinars, online resources, and assessment sites developed by organizations to target a certain language skill, professional conferences, and other professional development activities are good examples of nonformal learning. With its close ties to lifelong learning, nonformal education can be used within higher education to provide language training to those who need short-term training. When the restrictions of the formal academic curriculum could limit an instructor's ability to respond to learners' needs, in the nonformal setting, the needs of the language learner determine the process. Nonformal learning exists outside of academia, but both formal and nonformal language learning can complement each other by using each other's strengths (Vetter, 2014). While in the European context nonformal education has been recognized as a means of lifelong learning by the Organization for Economic Co-operation and Development (OECD, 1996), regrettably this is not the case in the United States. For instance, the immigration and refugee programs in Europe usually include language-training activities for all age groups so newcomers can be better integrated into society, but in the United States, such programs and activities are not common. In the American system, nonformal education overlaps with the continuing education programs within higher education. Furthermore, nonformal language education is not seen as complementary to formal language instruction. Better engagement with community centers, professional organizations, and nonprofit organizations could help build links between formal and nonformal education.

4. Conclusions

The collegiate FL landscape is in strong need of new perspectives and fresh approaches. In this chapter, after reviewing the status of FL education and FL learning for professional purposes in the United States, a shift in language education toward the development of 21st century skills and the use of technology along with new concepts, models, and approaches relevant to language learning has been suggested. Moreover, use of ID principles that guide the development of language curriculum, in formal or nonformal settings, is recommended. Regardless of the approach used, all ID models require analysis of learner needs, identification of learning goals, and development of implementation, delivery, and assessment plans. In other words, ID is about systematic development of instructional processes from beginning to end. FL in general and professional language learning in specific are in dire need of such a systematic approach to design, development, and delivery of consistent programs.

Transformation in professional language learning starts with a new approach to curriculum development using best practices in the learning design field, where learners and their needs guide the curriculum development process. Learning sciences and concepts such as heutagogy can be used to devise teaching and learning strategies that are in line with learners' desire to select their own goals and offer strategies to reach those goals. Design thinking, as a curriculum development strategy, can identify the major problems and issues existing in FL learning and guide instructors toward a curriculum that better aligns not only with individuals' needs but also societal needs. Nonformal language learning can help reimagine formal language curriculum practices to create better learning processes. Concerning the content of FL courses, instructors can go beyond a curriculum that often privileges linguistic aspects of language and canonical texts and imagine one informed by a practical perspective wherein experiential, authentic, interdisciplinary concepts are incorporated. A better link between formal and nonformal education practices can be established to foster individuals' lifelong learning skills. European countries have established many viable strategies in the last two decades in this regard, but the United States is lagging far behind. Finally, learning technologies present many powerful tools to support instructors and can be used in every stage of language training, whether formal or nonformal, linguistics or professional.

For the success of FL learning, these suggestions and others are worth considering; however, they are also not sufficient. To create a viable solution to the problems of FL education, more research is needed to combine learning design, learning sciences, learning technologies, and other pedagogical approaches in a holistic and coherent fashion. The current problems of language education in the United States and elsewhere cannot be fixed with a single technology or approach. A new framework that takes into account a wide range of perspectives to address the complex needs of the 21st century language learner is required.

5. Future research directions

Although our suggestions present a comprehensive starting point, there are also other ideas to be explored in the future. These ideas could be grouped under two areas: emerging technologies and teachers' roles in language classrooms. First, emerging learning technologies and concepts such as augmented reality, virtual reality, Artificial Intelligence (AI), and adaptive learning present new areas of opportunity and exploration for scholars in the area of language education. For instance, new augmented and virtual reality tools are providing truly immersive experiences that seem to be effective, with considerable implications, such as motivation, learning transfer, and engagement (Barrett et al., 2018; Birt & Cowling, 2017; Quint, Sebastian, & Gorecky, 2015). Advancements in AI technologies present new ways to customize learner preferences, reduce the workload of instructors, and assist with the analysis of large data sets, which results in better personalized instruction (Horizon Report, 2019). According to Johnson (2019), because of AI technologies, "instructors will be able to focus and adapt instruction based on the progress of each learner. This will help make teaching more data-driven and more responsive to individual learner needs" (p. 455). Adaptive learning environments, where needs of the language learners are considered and resources are brought to them depending on individual differences, should be further explored as a means of nonformal learning.

The second area of exploration is about changing instructor roles in professional language learning. Professional language learning may require more customization of instructional content and materials than traditional language teaching, as we see it today. This constant customization of the curriculum and teaching strategies requires flexibility on the instructor's part as well as at the department level. Collegiate language departments should seek interdisciplinary collaborations enabling language teachers to collaborate with experts in various disciplines and create learning opportunities for students that fit their needs. For example, a student majoring in business taking an FL course could create a business plan in the target language, and this plan could turn useful once the student graduates. Another student could use emerging technologies to create podcast episodes in the target language and make such resources available to the wider public. These learning opportunities give students the opportunity to target 21st century skills and lifelong learning. Nevertheless, teacher and curricula flexibility become of central importance so that students can focus on what is relevant to them and their own future. All in all, more research is needed to better understand how teachers can adapt to the new circumstances and how the language curriculum can be customized to fit the needs of the 21st century.

References

AAAS. (2017). *America's languages: investing in language education for the 21st century. Commission on Language Learning.* American Academy of Arts & Sciences. http://www.amacad.org/multimedia/pdfs/publications/researchpapersmonographs/language/Commission-on-Language-Learning_Americas-Languages.pdf

ACTFL. (2011). *The 21st century skills map*. American Council on the Teaching of Foreign Languages.

Al-Ali, S. (2014). Embracing the selfie craze: exploring the possible use of Instagram as a language mLearning tool. *Issues and Trends in Educational Technology, 2*(2). https://doi.org/10.2458/azu_itet_v2i2_ai-ali

Allen, M. (2012). *Leaving ADDIE for SAM: an agile model for developing the best learning experiences*. The American Society for Training and Development.

Altstaedter, L. L. (2016). Developing a Spanish for health professions course: a preliminary mixed-methods study. *Foreign Language Annals, 50*(1), 38-56. https://doi.org/10.1111/flan.12221

Barrett, R., Gandhi, H. A., Naganathan, A., Daniels, D., Zhang, Y., Onwunaka, C., Luehmann, A., & White, A. D. (2018). Social and tactile mixed reality increases student engagement in undergraduate lab activities. *Journal of Chemical Education, 95*(10), 1755-1762. https://doi.org/10.1021/acs.jchemed.8b00212

Birt, J., & Cowling, M. (2017). Toward future "mixed reality" learning spaces for STEAM education. *International Journal of Innovation in Science and Mathematics Education, 25*(4), 1-16.

Blattner, G., Dalola, A., & Lomicka, L. (2016). Twitter in foreign language classes: Initiating learners into contemporary language variation. In V. Wang (Ed.), *Handbook of research on learning outcomes and opportunities in the digital age* (pp. 769-797). IGI Global. https://doi.org/10.4018/978-1-4666-9577-1.ch034

Borau, K., Ullrich, C., Feng, J., & Shen, R. (2009). Microblogging for language learning: using Twitter to train communicative and cultural competence. In M. Spaniol, Q. Li, R. Klamma & R. W. H. Lau (Eds), *Advances in Web Based Learning–ICWL, 2009* (pp. 78-87). Springer. https://doi.org/10.1007/978-3-642-03426-8_10

Chang, Y., Wu, C., & Ku, H. (2004). The introduction of electronic portfolios to teach and assess English as a foreign language in Taiwan. *TechTrends, 49*(1), 30-35. https://doi.org/10.1007/bf02784902

Chen, C. J. (2009). Theoretical bases for using virtual reality in education. *Themes in Science and Technology Education, 2*(1-2), 71-90.

Civis Plus. (2017). *Non formal pathways in language teaching: a booklet for educators active in adult immigrants' language learning*. Erasmus+ Programme of the European Union. https://irp-cdn.multiscreensite.com/0e4f7d89/files/uploaded/Booklet-final.pdf

Correa, M. (2011). Advocating for critical pedagogical approaches to teaching Spanish as a heritage language: some considerations. *Foreign Language Annals, 44*(2), 308-320. https://doi.org/10.1111/j.1944-9720.2011.01132.x

Cox, C. B., & Montgomery, C. (2019). A study of 21st-century skills and engagement in a university Spanish foreign language classroom. *Foreign Language Annals, 52,* 822-849. https://doi.org/10.1111/flan.12426

Crouse, D. (2013). Languages for specific purposes in the 21st century. *The Language Educator, 8,* 32-35.

Cutshall, S. (2012). More than a decade of standards: Integrating "cultures" in your language instruction. *The Language Educator, 7*(3), 32-37.

Damari, R. R., Rivers, W. P., Brecht, R. D., Gardner, P., Pulupa, C., & Robinson, J. (2018). The demand for multilingual human capital in the U.S. labor market. *Foreign Language Annals, 50,* 13-37. https://doi.org/10.1111/flan.12241

Denning, P. J. (2013, December). The profession of IT design thinking. *Communications of the ACM, 56*(12), 29-31.

Eaton, S. E. (2010). *Global trends in language learning in the twenty-first century.* Onate Press.

Eshet, Y. (2004). Digital literacy: a conceptual framework for survival skills in the digital era. *Journal of Educational Multimedia and Hypermedia, 13*(1), 93-106.

Freire, P. (1970). *Pedagogy of the oppressed.* Continuum.

Garrett-Rucks, P. (2013). A discussion-based online approach to fostering deep cultural inquiry in an introductory language course. *Foreign Language Annals, 46*(2), 191-212. https://doi.org/10.1111/flan.12026

Gibbons, A. S. (2017). Points of contact: educational technology and the learning sciences. In A. A. Carr-Chellman & G. Rowland (Eds), *Issues in technology, learning, and instructional design: classic and contemporary dialogues* (pp. 183-193). Routledge.

Gobble, M. M. (2014) Design thinking. *Research-Technology Management, 57*(3), 59-62.

Golonka, E. M., Bowles, A. R., Frank, V. M., Richardson, D. L., & Freynik, S. (2014). Technologies for foreign language learning: a review of technology types and their effectiveness. *Computer Assisted Language Learning, 27*(1), 70-105. https://doi.org/10.1080/09588221.2012.700315

Gustafson, K. L., & Branch, R. M. (2002). *Survey of instructional design models* (ED477517). ERIC. https://files.eric.ed.gov/fulltext/ED477517.pdf

Haley, M. H., Steeley, S. L., & Salahshoor, M. (2013). Connecting twenty-first century skills and world language practices: a case study with teachers of critical need languages. *Theory and Practice in Language Studies, 3*(6), 865-876. https://doi.org/10.4304/tpls.3.6.865-876

Harris, K. (2015). Integrating digital literacy into English language instruction: issue brief. https://lincs.ed.gov/sites/default/files/ELL_Digital_Literacy_508.pdf

Hase, S., & Kenyon, C. (2007). Heutagogy: a child of complexity theory. *Complicity: An International Journal of Complexity and Education, 4*(1), 111-118. https://doi.org/10.29173/cmplct8766

Horizon Report. (2019). *EDUCAUSE horizon report*. Higher education edition. https://library.educause.edu/-/media/files/library/2019/4/2019horizonreport.pdf?la=en&hash=C8E8D444AF372E705FA1BF9D4FF0DD4CC6F0FDD1

Huq, A., & Gilbert, D. (2017). All the world's a stage: transforming entrepreneurship education through design thinking. *Education + Training, 59*(2), 155-170. https://doi.org/10.1108/et-12-2015-0111

Ibanez, M. B., Garcia, J. J., Galan, S., Maroto, D., Morillo, D., & Kloos, C. D. (2011). Design and implementation of a 3D multi-user virtual world for language learning. *Educational Technology & Society, 14*(4), 2-10.

Johnson, L. W. (2019, August). Data driven development and evaluation of Enskill English. *International Journal of Artificial Intelligence in Education, 29*(3), 425-457. https://doi.org/10.1007/s40593-019-00182-2

Keller, J. M. (1987). Development and use of the ARCS Model of instructional design. *Journal of Instructional Development, 10*(3), 2-10. https://doi.org/10.1007/bf02905780

King de Ramírez, C., & Lafford, B. (2018). *Transferable skills for the 21st century. Preparing students for the workplace through world languages for specific purposes*. Sabio Books.

Kirby, J., Hoadley, C. M., & Carr-Chellman, A. A. (2005). Instructional systems design and the learning sciences: a citation analysis. *Educational Technology Research and Development, 53*(1), 37-47. https://doi.org/10.1007/bf02504856

Koper, R., & Tattersall, C. (2004). New directions for lifelong learning using network technologies. *British Journal of Educational Technology, 35*(6), 689-700. https://doi.org/10.1111/j.1467-8535.2004.00427.x

Laurillard, D. (2002). Rethinking teaching for the knowledge society. *EDUCAUSE Review, 37*, 16-27.

Lomicka, G., & Lord, G. (2018). Ten years after the MLA report: what has changed in foreign language departments? *ADFL Bulletin, 44*(2), 116-120. https://doi.org/10.1632/adfl.44.2.116

Looney, D., & Lusin, N. (2018). *Enrollments in languages other than English in United States institutions of higher education, summer 2016 and fall 2016: preliminary report*. Modern Language Association of America. https://www.mla.org/content/download/83540/2197676/2016-Enrollments-Short-Report.pdf

López, L. S. (2015). An analysis of the integration of service learning in undergraduate Spanish for specific purposes programs in higher education in the United States. *Cuadernos de ALDEEU, 28*(1), 155-170.

Lotherington, H., & Jenson, J. (2011). Teaching multimodal and digital literacy in L2 settings: new literacies, new basics, new pedagogies. *Annual Review of Applied Linguistics, 31*, 226-246. https://doi.org/10.1017/s0267190511000110

Martinsen, R. A. (2015). Spanish for you: student-centered and languages for specific purposes methods in lower-division Spanish. *L2 Journal, 7*(4), 42-62. https://doi.org/10.5070/l27418426

Mayer, R. E. (2002). Rote versus meaningful learning. *Theory Into Practice, 41*(4), 226-232. https://doi.org/10.1207/s15430421tip4104_4

McKeeman, L., & Oviedo, B. (2013). Enhancing communicative competence through integrating 21st-century skills and tools. In S. Dhonau (Ed.), *2013 CSCTFL Report* (pp. 39-54). Robert M. Terry.

Mellis, S., Carvalho, L., & Thompson, K. (2013). Applying 21st century constructivist learning theory to stage 4 design projects [Paper session]. *2013 International Conference of the Australian Association for Research in Education (AARE), Deakin, ACT. Australian Association for Research in Education (AARE)*. https://www.aare.edu.au/data/publications/2013/Mellis13.pdf

Meurant, R. C. (2010). The iPad and EFL digital literacy. In S. K. Pal, W. I. Grosky, N. Pissinou, T. K. Shih & D. Slezak (Eds), *Signal processing and multimedia* (pp. 224-234). Springer.

MLA. (2007). Foreign languages and higher education: new structures for a changed world. *Profession, 2007*(12), 234-245. https://doi.org/10.1632/prof.2007.2007.1.234

Morrison, G. R., Ross, S. M., Kalman, H. K., & Kemp, J. E. (2011). *Designing effective instruction*. John Wiley & Sons, Inc.

OECD. (1996). *Recognition of non-formal and informal learning*. http://www.oecd.org/education/skills-beyond-school/recognitionofnon-formalandinformallearning-home.htm

Ollivier, C. (2018). *Towards a socio-interactional approach to foster autonomy in language learners and users*. eLANG Project—Digital literacy for the teaching and learning of language. https://www.ecml.at/Portals/1/5MTP/Ollivier/e-lang%20EN.pdf

Pascual y Cabo, D., & Prada, J. (2018). Redefining Spanish teaching and learning in the United States. *Foreign Language Annals, 51*(3), 533-547. https://doi.org/10.1111/flan.12355

Pufahl, I., & Rhodes, N. C. (2011). Foreign language instruction in US schools: results of a national survey of elementary and secondary schools. *Foreign Language Annals, 44*(2), 258-288. https://doi.org/10.1111/j.1944-9720.2011.01130.x

Quint, F., Sebastian, K, & Gorecky, D. (2015). A mixed-reality learning environment. 2015 International Conference on Virtual and Augmented Reality in Education. *Procedia Computer Science, 75*, 43-48. https://doi.org/10.1016/j.procs.2015.12.199

Reinhardt, J., & Ryu, J. (2014). Using social network-mediated bridging activities to develop socio-pragmatic awareness in elementary Korean. In Information Resources Management Association (Ed.), *Computational linguistics: concepts, methodologies, tools, and applications* (pp. 561-577). IGI Global. https://doi.org/10.4018/978-1-4666-6042-7.ch026

Richards, J. C. (2015). The changing face of language learning: learning beyond the classroom. *RELC Journal, 46*(1), 5-22. https://doi.org/10.1177/0033688214561621

Rogerson, A. M., & Rossetto, L. C. (2018). Accommodating student diversity and different learning backgrounds. *Journal of Intercultural Communication Research, 47*(5), 411-420. https://doi.org/10.1080/17475759.2018.1475293

Ruggiero, D., & Mong, C. J. (2015). The teacher technology integration experience: practice and reflection in the classroom. *Journal of Information Technology Education: Research, 14*, 161-178. https://doi.org/10.28945/2227

Saavedra, A. R., & Opfer, V. D. (2012). Learning 21st-century skills requires 21st-century teaching. *Phi Delta Kappan, 94*(2), 8-13. https://doi.org/10.1177/003172171209400203

Schleicher, A. (2012). *Preparing teachers and developing school leaders for the 21st century: lessons from around the world.* OECD Publishing.

Schmerbeck, N., & Lucht, F. (2017). Creating meaning through multimodality: multiliteracies assessment and photo projects for online portfolios. *Die Unterrichtspraxis/Teaching German, 50*(1), 32-44. https://doi.org/10.1111/tger.12020

Schwienhorst, K. (2002). Why virtual, why environments? Implementing virtual reality concepts in computer-assisted language learning. *Simulation & Gaming, 33*(2), 196-209.

Takeda, I. (2016). Report: project-based learning with 21st century skills for the Japanese language classroom. *Journal of Integrated Creative Studies, 20*, 1-7.

Tishman, S., Jay, E., & Perkins, D. N. (1993). Teaching thinking dispositions: from transmission to enculturation. *Theory Into Practice, 32*(3), 147-153. https://doi.org/10.1080/00405849309543590

Vetter, E. (2014). Combining formal and nonformal foreign language learning: first insights into a German-Spanish experiment at university level. *Studies in Applied Linguistics, 2*, 39.-50. https://www.infona.pl/resource/bwmeta1.element.desklight-59fc0f9f-6ac5-4ff1-bce1-e56f4d6957a2

Ware, P. (2008). Language learners and multimedia: literacy in and after school. *Pedagogies: An International Journal, 3*, 37-51.

Wiggins, G., & McTighe, J. (2005). *Understanding by design*. ASCD Publications.

Willis, J. (2009). *Constructivist instructional design (C-ID). Foundations, models and examples*. Information Age Publishing.

Wu, W.-V., Wang, R.-W., & Chen, N.-C. (2015). Instructional design using an in-house built teaching assistant robot to enhance elementary school English as-a-foreign-language learning. *Interactive Learning Environments, 23*(6), 696-714. https://doi.org/10.1080/10494820.2013.792844

Yamada, E. (2010). Reflection to the development of criticality: an empirical study of beginners' Japanese language courses as a British university. *Intercultural Communication Studies, 19*(2), 253-264.

2. Needs analysis for the design of a professional English curriculum: insights from a French lifelong learning context

Naouel Zoghlami[1]

1. Introduction

For about three decades, Higher Education (HE) institutions across Europe have been facing the challenging task of developing policy measures on lifelong learning, which is acknowledged as one of the major responses to socioeconomic changes related to globalization, rapid technological progress, and demographic transformation in aging societies (EUA, 2008; Holford, Milana, Mohorčič, & Špolar, 2014). This challenge exposes a need to widen education access to an increasingly large range of adults with different professional and personal needs and interests with the aim of enhancing their employability, mobility, and competitiveness. In France, while universities are still struggling to adapt degree programs to adult needs and blur the boundaries between initial and continuing education (Borras & Bosse, 2017)[2], the Conservatoire National des Arts et Métiers (hereafter Cnam) has been successfully tackling these particular issues since the early 1970's (Dubar, 2008). The Cnam is actually a unique HE public institution in that it is exclusively dedicated to lifelong learning and offers a variety of training programs in the economic, technical, and social fields. Adults[3] enrolled in the

---

1. Conservatoire National des Arts et Métiers (Cnam), FoAP (EA 7529), Paris, France; naouel.zoghlamiterrien@lecnam.net; https://orcid.org/0000-0002-0181-6306

2. The authors provide a comprehensive report on the reasons for the low development of lifelong learning in French universities. These mainly include insufficient political and financial support, the difficulty of identifying and classifying adult learners, and the inadequacy of work-study programs.

3. Adult learners in the Cnam are specifically called 'auditeurs' to distinguish them from 'étudiants' (i.e. students) or 'élèves' (i.e. pupils), which generally refer to people enrolled in initial education.

How to cite this chapter: Zoghlami, N. (2020). Needs analysis for the design of a professional English curriculum: insights from a French lifelong learning context. In B. Dupuy and M. Grosbois (Eds), *Language learning and professionalization in higher education: pathways to preparing learners and teachers in/for the 21st century* (pp. 37-70). Research-publishing.net. https://doi.org/10.14705/rpnet.2020.44.1101

Cnam are all professionals pursuing education at all levels of qualifications (undergraduate, graduate, and doctoral levels). They have the opportunity to tailor their training to meet their career aspirations at a pace that suits their personal circumstances – including the possibility to enroll in distance learning and evening or Saturday courses.

Foreign Language (FL) proficiency is a key competence that is significantly promoted in lifelong learning, as it undeniably supports social inclusion and economic growth. In France, the basic effect of the internationalization of business and industry has been the progressive adoption of English as the corporate lingua franca. Research has shown that mastering English at an advanced level is highly valued in the French labor market, and demand for overall expertise in English (including communication and intercultural skills) has been rising continuously and steadily (Chancelade et al., 2016; Taillefer, 2007; Truchot, 2015). Despite the dominant role of English and the existing opportunities to learn it in the French education system – FL[4] learning is compulsory at the primary, secondary, *and* tertiary levels – English proficiency outcomes remain disappointing. The *European Survey on Language Competences* (European Commission, 2012), a large-scale comparison of the English proficiency of pupils finishing formal secondary education (average age=16), revealed that only 14% of French students reach the threshold independent user level or better – that is, B1 or above on the Common European Framework of Reference for languages (CEFR). This actually means that 86% of French students who could potentially pursue HE studies are non-proficient speakers of English. Other studies have corroborated this finding, which (even more unfortunately) seems to have held steady since the Bologna Declaration in 1999 (see for example Bonnet, 2004; Hilton, 2002, 2003; Manoïlov, 2019; Terrier, 2011; Zoghlami, 2015). Most recently, according to the 2018 edition of the *EF English Proficiency Index* – which ranks adult English proficiency in 88 countries and regions all over the world – France placed 35th with a score of 55.49, indicating moderate proficiency[5].

---

4. English is generally taught as the first FL in France.

5. For the sake of comparison, the first place goes to Sweden scoring 70.72 and indicating a very high proficiency in English.

Researchers have tried to explain the low English proficiency of the French. The *ESLC* report (European Commission, 2012) identifies national protection of the French language, the lack of English exposure in everyday life, and the ineffectiveness of teaching approaches in developing communication skills in English as major challenges facing the French education system. In addition, despite revised and increasingly internationalized curricula, no clear language policy has been committed to, let alone a research-based one. Taillefer (2007) described language learning and teaching as being "paradoxical on all levels of the educational system" (p. 137), with no connection between secondary and HE. In particular, English training for non-language majors[6] in universities seems to be sorely lacking institutional structuring. Beyond the shortage of human and material resources as well as the absence of clearly defined learning outcomes and research-grounded teaching practices, English courses are generally poorly integrated into curricula and fall short of meeting the needs of the targeted public, employability needs included (Braud, Millot, Sarré, & Wozniak, 2015; Brudermann, Mattioli, Roussel, & Sarré, 2016; SAES, 2011; Taillefer, 2007). Braud and her colleagues (2015) take this line of argument further and speak of "improvisation" (p. 59) with regard to language programs and pedagogical measures since the teachers who are generally asked to give such courses lack training in what English for Specific Purposes (ESP) involves.

In HE contexts, efforts have been made to address these shortcomings. These efforts, however, are institution specific. In the Cnam, specific measures have been taken to internationalize the curriculum and overcome discrepancies between language (particularly English as an FL – ELF) programs and the labor market while at the same time responding to massification concerns. In this chapter, I report on the findings of a large-scale Needs Analysis (NA) performed to uncover the English communicative needs of Cnam adult learners and thus inform the design of a task-based Professional English (PE) syllabus.

---

6. In the French HE system, ESP courses offered to students specializing in disciplines other than languages are part of what is generally referred to as LANSAD (langues pour spécialistes d'autres disciplines).

Chapter 2

2. Literature review

2.1. Analyzing language needs

Although NA is still often overlooked by teaching professionals and curriculum designers (Chan, 2018; Iizuka, 2019), it is now well established that it is actually central to the design of Learning for Specific Purposes (LSP) programs that can bridge the gap between institutional learning and workplace requirements (Basturkmen, 2010; Brown, 2009, 2016; Huhta, Vogt, Johnson, & Tulkki, 2013; Hutchinson & Waters, 1987). In a lifelong learning context, conducting a sound NA is of paramount importance, as it ensures the development of courses specifically tailored to meet the immediate and future English needs of practicing professionals. Our first concern is then to define what is meant by learner *needs* and the process of NA. It is beyond the scope of this chapter to review the diverse definitions and classifications existing in the literature (see for example the seminal works of Brown, 2016; Hutchinson & Waters, 1987; Richards, 2001). For the purpose of this study, I adopted a straightforward working definition of NA, which does not merely deal with the identification of the language forms to be mastered, but also takes into consideration a range of other factors, including (1) the learners, their actual competencies in English, and their perceptions of their aims for English learning; (2) the reality of the teaching context; and (3) the target workplace situation and the type of work tasks performed in English. Basturkmen (2010) stated that in NA,

> "the language and skills that the learners will use in their target professional or vocational workplace […] are identified and considered in relation to the present state of knowledge of the learners, their perceptions of their needs and the practical possibilities and constraints of the teaching context. The information obtained from this process is used in determining and refining the content and method of the ESP course" (p. 19).

Language needs can be probed from the perspectives of learners, teachers, or professionals from the targeted fields. A number of authors have stressed the subjective nature of NA as being a process dependent on learners' (Richards, 2001, p. 54) as well as teachers' (Hyland, 2009, p. 113) interests, values, and beliefs about what workplace needs can be but also about teaching, learning, and language. For example, Lam, Cheng, and Kong (2014) surveyed resources tailor-made by government bodies and commercial publishers for a special module on learning English through business workplace communication introduced in the senior secondary English language curriculum in Hong Kong. Discrepancies – which could have been avoided if a thorough NA had been conducted – were found regarding the most frequent spoken and written professional genres covered in both settings[7]. This state of affairs is of course neither specific to the teaching of *English* for professional purposes nor limited to this Asian context (Iizuka, 2019; Martin & Adrada-Rafael, 2017; Taillefer, 2014). Long (2015, pp. 147-149) also reported on several studies that identified notable differences between the type of language used in targeted situations and the language modeled for those situations in commercial teaching materials – language that is oversimplified, inauthentic, and presented in unrealistic situations.

Methodological rigor must then be observed to increase NA's reliability and validity. Pertinent guidelines on how to conduct sound NAs – particularly survey use – have been proposed in the literature (Brown, 2016; Huhta et al., 2013; Long, 2005, 2015; Richards, 2001; Serafini, Lake, & Long, 2015). For example, Brown (2016) provided a detailed account of questionnaire design and other qualitative methods of data collection, including interviews, observations, and focus groups. He also discussed ways of analyzing and reporting NA results. In their comprehensive survey of the design, methods, and procedures reported in ESP NAs conducted over the past three decades, Serafini and her colleagues (2015) outlined several methodological inconsistencies, mainly in relation to interactions between the sources and the methods used to collect data and interpret findings. The review enabled the authors to offer a set of practical recommendations – an adaptable methodological checklist (p. 25) – for careful NA practice, emphasizing in particular the importance of methodological triangulation (i.e. employing several sources and methods to study the same

---

7. For example, there was an overemphasis on phone calls and complaint-related genres in the teaching materials, whereas formal meetings and emailing were the top genres in this globalized workplace context (Lam et al., 2014, pp. 72-73).

phenomenon from different perspectives) as well as the contribution of a task-based approach to language NA.

2.2. Motivating the use of a task-based approach to NA

The adequacy of adopting a task-based approach to NA – and thus to LSP courses – is now empirically established (Long, 2005, 2015; Serafini et al., 2015), though it is still not widely implemented, particularly in French HE institutions. Using the *task* as the unit of lesson organization is meaningful, and hence motivating, to professionals. Carrying out a work task (e.g. writing a business report, responding to a customer complaint) has work-related goals that call on adequate language. In addition, the basic tenets of Task-Based Language Teaching (TBLT) are consistent with second language acquisition theory and psycholinguistic research findings (Long, 2015; Nunan, 2004; Robinson, 2011), an essential grounding in theory and research that linguistic NAs have failed to account for. In fact, traditional linguistic approaches rarely go beyond the *text* level, and tend to produce lists of decontextualized units – typically grammatical, lexical, notional-functional, or a combination of these – for learners to master. The task-based NA, however, acknowledges language learning as a complex sociocognitive process with a focus on meaningful units, through the identification of the different types of communication tasks that specific communities of learners need to perform in the real world in the target language (Long, 2005, 2015). Recently, a meta-analysis of TBLT programs and their long-term effect on FL learning demonstrated an overall positive and strong effect (d=0.93) of TBLT as opposed to more traditional pedagogies (Bryfonski & McKay, 2017). The meta-analysis also revealed that stakeholders held positive views regarding such programs.

Although most studies in the LSP literature have investigated *English* needs for *business* purposes, recent task-based NAs have thoroughly examined the needs of learners in other professional contexts. For example, responding to a growing demand for courses of Spanish for specific purposes in American universities, Martin and Adrada-Rafael (2017) conducted a robust multiphase NA to identify the tasks that business professionals have to perform in Spanish, as well as their perceived frequency and difficulty. One of the distinctive features of this study was the numerous sources of information and the genuine interaction of sources and methods. The researchers interviewed both business insiders and outsiders including graduates, professors, researchers, and experts (qualitative phase) to ensure that only tasks really carried out in business settings would be included in the questionnaire administered on a larger scale to students and business professionals (quantitative phase). In the curriculum design phase, the authors proposed regrouping the most frequent tasks identified and classifying them into five more superordinate task categories that constituted the course objectives. The tasks and their corresponding objectives were organized by modality in accordance with the five *C*-goal areas promoted in the ACTFL's World-Readiness Standards (communication, cultures, connections, comparisons, and communities). In a similar vein, Malicka, Gilabert Guerrero, and Norris (2017) relied on in-depth qualitative data obtained from observations in the workplace and semistructured interviews to explore English-use needs in the professional domain of hotel receptionists in Spain. The study made a major contribution as it focused on how NA results can be meaningfully applied to the design of genuinely relevant pedagogical activities, and more specifically, how data about task difficulty can assist in designing tasks that vary in levels of cognitive load, thus providing insights on the importance of task complexity and sequencing in a language curriculum.

In France, the paucity of NAs is striking. A search of the published literature revealed very few studies which investigated real-world workplace language needs, with English being – unsurprisingly – the one FL systematically considered in all these studies (Braud, 2008; Taillefer, 2004, 2007; Wozniak, 2010). For instance, using data obtained from expert and novice guides, Wozniak (2010) assessed the language needs of French mountain guides. A key finding in her study was that oral communication skills represented the most important to improve – rather than knowledge of English related to technical skills. Taillefer's (2004, 2007) projects were institutional as they took place at the University of Toulouse. Already at that time, the author drew attention to the alarming situation of FL training in France. With the objective of encouraging more coherent English training in HE contexts, as is the case in the present study, her large-scale NAs tapped into the professional needs of economics students. The needs were investigated via questionnaires administered to language teachers, economics teachers, undergraduates, and recent graduates. Overall, the researcher highlighted the learners' feeling of being linguistically ill prepared for workplace demands. She noted the mismatch between what is taught at university and what are perceived as professional requirements, in particular with regard to the frequency of FL use, the degree of importance of the four different language skills, and the level of competence necessary in each as expressed in the CEFR scale[8]. As an example, unlike economics graduates, language teachers underestimated target productive and receptive levels of English proficiency, minimizing the importance of written communication in business workplaces (Taillefer, 2007). Accordingly, the researcher provided practical recommendations for language training in the economics sector, which included guidance on raising university and professional stakeholders' awareness of the importance of NA, taking into consideration the specificity of each context, and adopting an interdisciplinary approach to institutional curriculum design by integrating disciplinary and language components.

Only one empirical study – which also took place at the University of Toulouse – explored professional needs within a task-oriented approach (Joulia, 2014). Like Taillefer (2004, 2007), Joulia (2014) underscored the necessity of preparing learners to face the workplace language challenge and advocated for the adoption of a professionalizing approach. To this end, the researcher first probed into the English needs of students in computer science through the observation of programming courses and the use of a questionnaire sent to regional companies hiring programmers, which often recruited the University of Toulouse's computer science undergraduates for internships. The assessment revealed that high-level proficiency in reading comprehension was the most important need. Learners encountered several reading difficulties and applied inappropriate strategies to overcome them (e.g. word-by-word reading). This finding paved

---

8. It is noteworthy to mention here that the actual CEFR levels (A1, A2, B1, B2, C1, C2) were not given in the questionnaires. The researcher argued that when the studies took place between 2002 and 2004, the reference system developed in 2001 was hardly known by most language teachers and not known at all by the general public.

the way for a reading experiment in which the researcher tested the efficiency of online resources in helping learners read and understand authentic technical documentation in English and ultimately enabling them to write lines of code – as they would actually do in their programming sessions and in real work settings. This professionalizing experiment, though not conclusive as far as the role of the chosen resources in assisting reading comprehension is concerned, proved to be highly motivating for learners, as they appreciated the authenticity of the reading content and task.

In light of the above theoretical background highlighting the relevance of the task unit in professionalizing approaches to language teaching, and given that very little attention has been paid to the role of NA in course design in French HE contexts, the present study addressed these issues by exploring the English needs of learners enrolled in the Cnam. The study particularly sought to answer the below research questions.

- What are the typical tasks French adult professionals (specializing in different fields) need to perform in English at work?

- Is there a difference in learners' perception of these tasks across levels of English proficiency (A2, B1, B2) and learning modes (self-directed, blended, face-to-face)?

3. Methodology

3.1. Context

This NA study was carried out at Cnam Paris in the first semester of 2019-2020. The researcher holds an assistant professor position in the languages[9] department, and therefore benefited from direct access to all informants. The study is actually part of a larger action research project undertaken by the

---

9. The Communication en Langues Étrangères department also offers training in languages other than English including French, Arabic, Russian, and Sign Language. English classes, however, have the highest rates of enrollment.

department to internationalize the English curriculum while responding to massification concerns, including the implementation of blended EFL courses on a large scale. It is also worth mentioning that two methodologically distinct EFL training programs are offered. The first one is mainstream in that it involves regular group courses. The second one seeks to promote language learner autonomy via a particular self-directed learning program, which combines autonomous learning guided periodically by an English teacher taking on the role of an adviser during counseling sessions, along with oral practice in groups with a native speaker.

The study is mainly exploratory in nature, as its overall purpose is to expand our understanding of the English-use needs of professionals. It is also action oriented in that it ultimately seeks to inform the design of an English curriculum and illuminate course content. The very particular lifelong learning context of the study guided the multimethod research design adopted, including the combination of both quantitative measures (questionnaires) and qualitative measures (open-ended questions and interviews) used to gather data from EFL adult learners as well as teachers. This methodological triangulation was meant to enhance the overall validity of the NA. Prior to the study, all the respondents were informed about its objective and assured that data would be used exclusively for research and teaching purposes.

3.2. Participants

The present NA involved the collaboration and input of a large number of adult learners enrolled in different non-language programs for the academic year 2019-2020 as well as English teachers from the Cnam languages department. From a total of 564 learners who signed up for either of the EFL programs, 242 (45.5% male and 54.5% female) took part in the study by responding to the learner NA survey (supplementary materials, Appendix 1). The great majority of the respondents (202 out of 242) were French speakers. As for the minority ($n=40$) who reported having a different mother tongue, Arabic and Berber were the most mentioned languages (22 and 12, respectively). The age range varied considerably, as shown in Figure 1, with the group 36-40 years old (20.5%)

slightly outnumbering the other lower age groups. It is also interesting to note that nearly a quarter of our participants (*n*=54) were over age 40.

Figure 1. Age distribution of Cnam adult learners

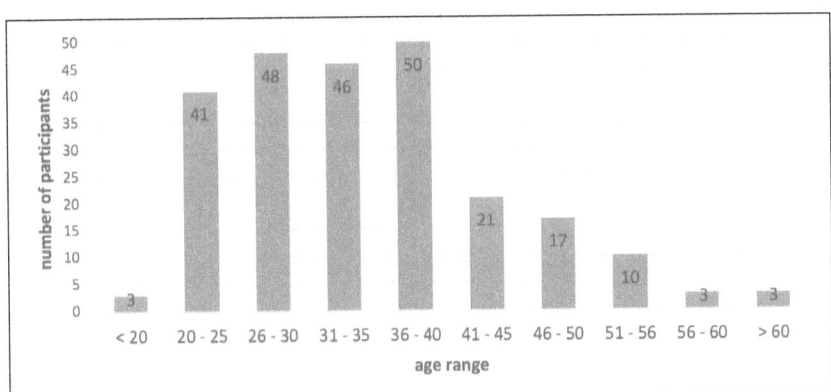

The largest majority of the informants (71%) were employed, while 13% were either undertaking professional retraining or actively looking for a job[10]. As active professionals, our respondents can be considered domain insiders – the most valid data source given their expertise in domain contents and tasks (Long, 2005, 2015). Accordingly, data obtained from the sample is believed to derive from their accurate knowledge of their current or projected language needs rather than a mere perception of these needs.

Regarding the participants' career fields, the answers revealed quite significant diversity. The domain of Information Technology (IT), telecommunications, and interactive digital media had the largest representation (17%), while the fields of accounting and audit (7.4%), management (7%), and business, marketing, and sales (6.6%) were less represented. This finding can probably be explained by the special place held by some of the (prestigious) Cnam institutions[11] –

---

10. About 25% of the surveyed population reported that their return to HE was motivated by their desire to evolve their careers, including being promoted. Nearly 15% indicated personal growth as their main incentive. Another 15% referred to both career evolvement and personal growth, and for 16.4% the pursuit of HE was part of a professional retraining process.

11. Examples include the CNAM Engineering School (EICNAM) and the National Institute for Economic and Accounting Techniques (INTEC), which specializes in accounting, management control, auditing, and finance.

Chapter 2

specializing in engineering, IT and digital media, and accounting and auditing – which seem to attract more lifelong learners than other schools, and in which English training is compulsory for graduation.

Eleven teachers were also included as a valuable source of information about learners' language needs. The English teaching staff of the Cnam language department willingly participated in the study. While the teacher sample had considerable overall teaching experience ($M=16$), their particular experience in the Cnam ranged from 0 to 14 ($M=5$). Two of the instructors were also researchers.

3.3. Data collection instruments

3.3.1. EFL proficiency measure

English proficiency was used as a variable to see if any categorization of needs by FL linguistic level would potentially emerge from the data. In Cnam Paris, learners are placed in different groups according to their level in the targeted language. The placement measure used is the standardized CEFR self-assessment grid. The grid presents the different reference descriptors of receptive and productive proficiency in correspondence to the three broad levels of basic user (A1 and A2), independent user (B1 and B2), and proficient user (C1 and C2). The validity and reliability[12] of the grid are now confirmed (see for example North, 2007, for a discussion of the validity and consistency of the CEFR levels). This type of placement is of particular relevance given the heterogeneity of the learners' professional fields.

3.3.2. Questionnaires

Two questionnaires were developed in order to investigate the perspectives of the different stakeholders involved in our NA: a learners' survey (supplementary materials, Appendix 1) and an EFL teachers' questionnaire (supplementary

---

12. As a member of the Cnam English teaching staff, I actually had the opportunity to observe the consistency of the CEFR self-assessment grid as it yielded accurate learner grouping.

materials, Appendix 2). To design the survey, I reviewed relevant research on language NA (e.g. Brown, 2016; Long, 2005, 2015; Serafini et al., 2015), and conducted informal interviews (a year before the main study) with both learners and teachers to bring out initial data about perceived needs and teaching practices that would inform item construction. Following key guidelines on questionnaire design (Dörnyei, 2003, 2007), the preliminary pool of targeted tasks was piloted with fellow researchers and with a convenience sample from the targeted learner population (N=20), who provided useful feedback on the wording of instructions as well as item readability, redundancy, and relevance. The final version of the survey contained 24 questions spread over five sections, and it took about 15 minutes to complete. In Part 1 (Q1-Q5), the personal profile of the learners is investigated in terms of age range, gender, professional status, major, and reasons for undertaking HE studies at the Cnam. In Part 2 (Q6-Q13), I explore their linguistic profile by looking at their native language, exposure to English, attitudes toward the English language and culture, perceived proficiency in the different language skills, and perceived difficulty of developing these skills. Part 3 (Q14-Q18) investigates the learners' English training. In Part 4 (Q19-Q20), the learners' perceptions of the importance of English for work are explored. Part 5 (Q21-Q24) first taps into the learners' perception of the importance of the target English tasks via a four-point importance scale (1=*not important at all*, 2=*slightly important*, 3=*important*, 4=*very important*). The tasks are organized under five categories pertaining to the five language skills (reading, writing, listening, and oral communication) along with relevant language elements. Perceptions about learner motivation and learning modes were also investigated via a six-point agreement scale (1=*strongly disagree*, 2=*disagree*, 3=*slightly disagree*, 4=*slightly agree*, 5=*agree*, 6=*strongly agree*) in hopes that these would provide further information that would be of benefit in designing blended courses. The survey ends with two open-ended questions meant to elicit qualitative data about perceptions of the most efficient EFL learning activities and English practice outside the classroom. It is noteworthy that I obtained a high reliability index for the final survey (α=.93)[13], suggesting that the items work well together and that the survey should produce consistent answers if used in similar study situations.

---

13. A commonly accepted coefficient of reliability using Cronbach's alpha is .7 or higher.

Chapter 2

The purpose of the teachers' questionnaire was to obtain a more comprehensive picture of the English needs of Cnam adult learners. Its design was then inspired by the learner survey, but it contained mainly open-ended questions. For example, and to obtain accurate and valid data, each teacher was asked to report on the most frequent needs mentioned by learners at a specific level of English proficiency. They were also asked to give their opinions on the most important elements a language course should include, the most successful activities, and the difficulties they and their learners often encounter. The last open-ended question required teachers to reflect on the appropriateness of a task-based course for adult professionals. The questionnaire was also piloted with two experienced English teachers and a researcher who provided comments on its content and layout. About 10 minutes were required to complete the teachers' questionnaire.

3.3.3. Follow-up interviews

The preliminary analysis of the teacher questionnaires yielded interesting responses that were worth further investigation. Unstructured follow-up interviews, lasting about 20 minutes, were conducted with volunteer teachers ($N=3$) to allow them to reflect retrospectively on some of their answers and provide clarifications and additional information. These revolved in particular around the type of language challenges learners encounter as well as their perception of the efficient ingredients for completing a task successfully.

3.4. Procedure and analysis

I administered the questionnaires to teachers and learners concurrently between October and November 2019. The EFL teaching staff was actually already well informed about the NA study and the larger research project in which it fits. As a fellow colleague, the researcher emailed the questionnaire to all the teachers ($N=12$). Emailing was deemed suitable for two main reasons. First, the majority of the teachers expressed their preference for this form of data collection. It also allowed them to contact the researcher if they needed further clarification. Second, the researcher needed to identify the teachers with whom follow-up interviews were to be conducted. Although teacher data was not anonymous, confidentiality was guaranteed to all participants. The teachers emailed back the filled questionnaires. The return rate was highly satisfactory, as only one teacher did not respond. It should be mentioned that the teacher questionnaire was administered in English to guarantee question comprehension, as some of the teachers were English native speakers. However, to further ensure the overall validity of the data obtained, teachers were given the choice of responding in either French or English. A call for voluntary interview participation was also emailed, and three teachers responded positively.

For validity and reliability purposes, the learner NA survey was administered in French a week before the language courses actually started. To ensure a large number of respondents, the survey was generated on Google Forms and distributed via the Cnam Moodle learning platform to which all Cnam learners have access. The survey was withdrawn when I reached a quantitatively acceptable return rate, as mentioned earlier ($N=242$).

Quantitative as well as qualitative analyses were undertaken. The survey quantitative data were analyzed using SPSS (Version 25). In particular, I computed the reliability index of the items (Cronbach's alpha) as well as descriptive statistics including frequency distributions, means, and modes. Pearson chi-square statistics (with a significance value of $p \leq .01$) were performed to account for any differences in response frequencies between learner subgroups corresponding to different learning modes (self-directed learning, blended, face-to-face) and different English proficiency levels (A2, B1, B2). Teachers' perceptions were analyzed both quantitatively and qualitatively. Their answers to the open-ended questions were coded, allowing certain categories to emerge. These related mainly to learners' needs and difficulties, teachers' difficulties, and efficient language activities. A comparison with learners' answers was conducted, and illustrative teacher comments were provided when relevant.

4. Findings

4.1. Learners' English profile

In this section, I draw an English language proficiency profile for Cnam adult learners based on their answers to language biography questions included in Parts 2 and 3 of the survey and covering the following aspects: perceived English proficiency and exposure to English.

Two questions investigated learners' perception of English proficiency. They were first asked to indicate their degree of agreement with a common statement, "the French are bad at English" (Q9). Like other fellow colleagues (e.g. Taillefer, 2007), I have been witnessing this negative self-image[14], and thus sought to investigate the extent of its consistency among the present particular population. Results were quite striking. The mode index showed that the most frequent response (40.2%) was *slightly agree*. However, collapsing the scale into two meaningful categories – *agree* and *disagree* – reveals that the difference between the adult learners who agreed with the statement (59%) and those who disagreed with it (41%) is not as significant as expected. Interestingly, I also obtained quite a similar tendency from language teachers ($N=11$), with seven teachers agreeing (5 of them *slightly*) and four instructors disagreeing. Our learner results differ from those of Taillefer (2007), who asked the same question to French graduates in economics who were using English at work. Nearly 93% of her respondents believed the French were bad at English. In addition, the results of the chi-square test showed that our learners' beliefs about this poor self-image are independent from their own general English level (Q17; $X^2(30, 224)=41.42$, $p=.08$) as well as their perceived proficiency in the different skills (Q12), sketched in Figure 2 below. It is tempting here to speculate that, if the answers I obtained can be considered a reflection of the important personality trait of self-esteem, which is essential to successful (cognitive) learning activity, the French seem to feel less insecure with regard to their English ability than they used to be. However,

---

14. For example, in a previous study on the complex cognitive processes in EFL speech comprehension, we found that 20% of the surveyed French language undergraduates (N=110) rated their English proficiency as poor, compared to only 2% of the surveyed Tunisian counterparts (N=116; Zoghlami, 2015).

caution is due here as our results may be an artifact of the study sample, being confirmed adult professionals who may have gained self-confidence and self-esteem via their work experience. More research is then required in the French context to provide further insights into the issue of self-esteem in FL use.

Figure 2. Cnam learners' perceived English proficiency by skill

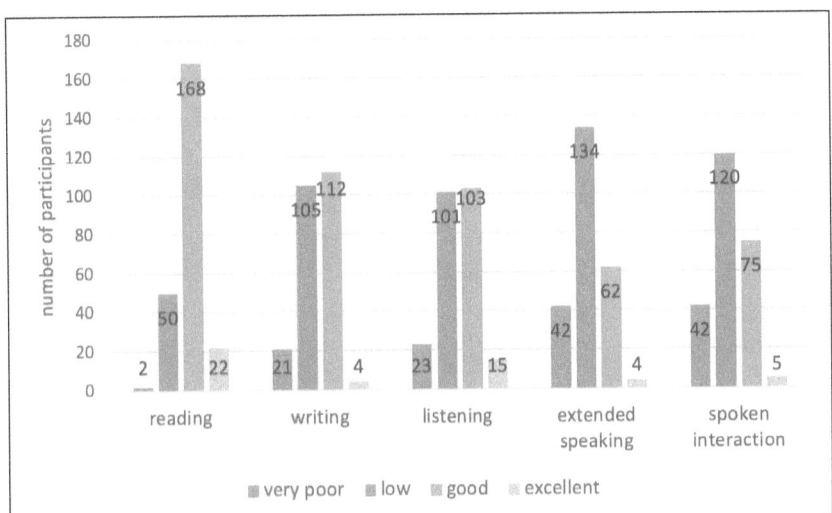

A quick look at the figure reveals quite similar perceptions with regard to the skills of writing and listening in English, with half of the sample believing their level in both skills to be *low* while the other half perceived it as *good*. It is also interesting to note the difference in the learners' perceived proficiency with regard to reading and speaking in English. Most of the respondents considered their reading ability to be good (n=168; 69%), whereas the relative majority believed their speaking ability to be *low* (n=134 extended speaking; n=120 spoken interaction). These results, however, need to be interpreted with caution as the majority of the surveyed learners (62%) are actually at the B1 level of the CEFR.

Learners' English exposure was explored from two angles: previous exposure in academic contexts (Q14) and everyday exposure (Q8). The findings indicate that prior to enrolling in the Cnam, 72% of the respondents pursued English courses at an HE level, while only 18.5% reported having pursued English courses up to the end of (French) high school. Interestingly, only a small number of learners seemed to have benefited from language and study stays (Q7; 6% and 3% respectively), where language contact was probably more regular and intensive. With regard to everyday exposure to English, it appears to be context dependent, as illustrated in Figure 3.

Figure 3. Cnam learners' everyday exposure to English

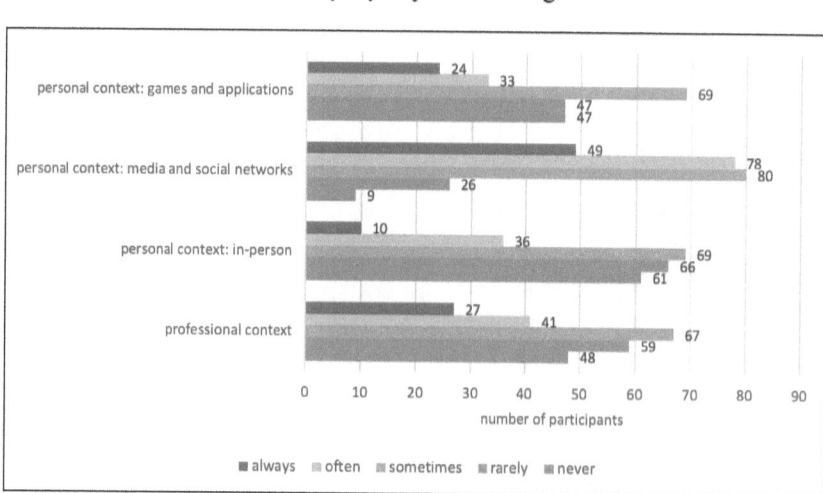

Degree of exposure to English was first examined for three personal contexts. In-person exposure is very limited, as only 46 informants reported regular contact with the language in real in-person communicative situations. However, exposure to English seems to be noticeably more frequent in virtual situations, particularly when using media and social networks (53% *often* or *always*; 33% *sometimes*). Caution should be observed here as the data do not allow speculation on the type of virtual exposure – that is, whether it involved productive or receptive skills. Cnam learners' exposure to English in professional contexts was also relatively limited. In fact, approximately half of the participants were either never ($n=48$) or rarely ($n=59$) exposed to English at work. Sixty-seven informants reported being exposed to English only sometimes while the remaining minority reported frequent English exposure. The lack of contact with English is consistent among the different learners' fields of employment (X^2=112.2, p=.27). This finding is rather unexpected given the continuously growing context of globalization and internationalization of French companies since the 1990's, where FL proficiency – in particular English – is found to bolster employability, mobility, and competitiveness (Chancelade et al., 2016; Truchot, 2015).

4.2. Perceived importance of English

Overall, positive attitudes toward the English language and culture were expressed (Q11; M=3.18), and the majority of the informants viewed English as considerably useful (Q10; M=4.55), which is interesting in light of the results presented above. When asked to indicate the extent to which being able to communicate effectively in English is important (Q19), most of the respondents reported an equally significant relevance of this skill in both professional and personal contexts. In particular, learners perceived work-related English proficiency to be equally important for both *oral* and *written* communication. In fact, frequency results showed that about 86% of the informants perceived oral and written professional communication as *important* or *very important*. Given the learners' reported low speaking proficiency, I would have expected the perceived importance to be more marked for oral communicative proficiency.

Reporting on the importance of English as a career driver (Q20), about 20% of Cnam professionals indicated that their English ability was rather an obstacle for recruitment and professional growth alike. Interestingly, however, it seems that, for the majority of the respondents, being proficient in English was not actually a decisive factor in recruitment or professional growth purposes (42.6% and 47.1%, respectively). This finding aligns with another striking finding emerging from the data, namely the reasons reported for taking the English course at the Cnam (Q18). In fact, a minority of the respondents (12.7%) indicated solely a current and/or a future need for English at work. This result could partly explain the fact that the majority (78%) responded negatively when asked whether they had previously taken PE courses (Q15). Interestingly, among the minority of respondents who seemed to have benefited from such courses, only 5% reported that the course was offered by their company.

Nevertheless, analysis of motivation items (Q22) revealed that our participants seemed to enjoy learning English ($M=4.96$) and were extremely motivated to learn and improve in the language ($M=5.38$), including by undertaking extra language work outside the classroom ($M=4.77$) as confirmed by the numerous examples of activities they provided in answering the last question of the survey.

4.3. English needs: identifying target tasks

Before presenting the results of the target tasks to be performed in English at work and hence perceived as important by our adult learners, I first report on the teachers' thoughts about the relevance of a task-based English course in meeting the needs of such learners (Q12). Interestingly, most of the teachers seem to believe that a task-based course is appropriate for Cnam learners regardless of their level in English. They principally advocate that such an approach is purposeful and motivating:

> "Learners are motivated as it makes sense to them" (Teacher 1).

> "I favour task-based courses ... [they] tend to suit all levels ... popular with students ... [who] appeared to enjoy working on specific tasks that relate to their everyday professional lives" (Teacher 2).

> "[It] makes learning meaningful and gratifying" (Teacher 3).

Some of the teachers ($n=3$), however, argued that the relevance of task-based language courses depends on learners' proficiency and specific needs. For them, learners need to reach a certain level in the language to be able to perform tasks autonomously. In follow-up interviews with these teachers, they clarified that the mentioned specific needs are not work related but rather of a linguistic nature.

The typical work tasks French adults are required to perform in English were investigated quantitatively in Part 5 of the learner survey as well as qualitatively in Section 2 of the teachers' questionnaire. Table 1 displays the quantitative results, mainly the descriptive statistics per item for the whole learner sample (N=242).

Table 1. Descriptive statistics for the perceived importance of English target tasks and language elements (N=242)

Skill	Items	Mode	Mean	SD	Importance in %
Reading	1. Read simple documents (e.g. emails, memos, short letters, job ads)	3	3.04	0.811	77.3
	2. Read long and complex documents (e.g. complex formal emails, reports, contracts, budget plans, instructions)	3	3.19	0.731	83.5
	3. Read newsletters	3	2.89	0.797	71.5
	4. Read articles in specialized magazines	3	3.12	0.739	81.4
	5. Read scientific articles	4	2.95	0.941	68.2
	6. Read the news (whether or not related to your domain)	3	3.16	0.714	83.1
	7. Read for pleasure (short stories, novels, magazines, blogs, social networks)	3	2.88	0.817	70.2
Writing	8. Write your Curriculum Vitae/resume	3	3.05	0.856	76.5
	9. Fill out forms	3	2.83	0.828	69.5
	10. Write formal emails	3	3.26	0.648	90.5
	11. Write informal emails	3	2.92	0.758	72.7
	12. Write reports (e.g. business reports or meeting minutes)	3	3.19	0.747	83.1
	*13. Write memos	3	2.95	0.803	71.9
	*14. Write activity reports	3	3.07	0.851	75.7
	*15. Write complex technical documents (e.g. marketing plan, technical instructions, project proposal)	3	3.05	0.884	75.3
	***16. Write documents specific to my field (e.g. reply to a criticism)**	3	3.17	0.825	82.3
	17. Write abstracts and/or scientific articles	2	2.6	1.006	52.4
	18. Take notes	3	2.97	0.807	75.2
	19. Write on social networks	2	2.31	0.946	40.9

Listening	*20. Listen to presentations	4	3.44	0.63	95
	*21. Attend seminars, conferences/congresses, etc.	4	3.38	0.679	92.1
	22. Listen to debates	3	3.34	0.688	90.9
	23. Follow programs on TV or radio, movies at the cinema, plays, etc.	3	3.18	0.803	81.9
Communication	24. Simulate a job interview	3	3	0.864	72.7
	25. Converse informally and socialize	3	3.21	0.696	88.4
	26. Social and/or professional networking	3	2.77	0.87	64.9
	27. Discuss work-related matters	3	3.27	0.638	92.2
	28. Communicate via telephone	3	3.3	0.671	90.5
	29. Participate in meetings (face-to-face and/or teleconferencing)	3	3.24	0.722	87.2
	30. Make formal oral presentations and respond to audience questions	3	3.23	0.719	85.5
	*31. Request and provide information/clarifications	3	3.3	0.646	91.4
	32. Instruct, explain, and demonstrate (e.g. train foreign clients/colleagues)	3	3.16	0.796	80.1
	33. Argue and negotiate	4	3.17	0.848	79.3
	34. Resolve problems/conflicts	3	3.02	0.869	73.2
	35. Take care of foreign visitors (e.g. welcoming, company visit, various entertainment)	3	2.67	0.887	57
	36. Travel abroad (e.g. organization, bookings, meetings with foreign colleagues, visits)	3	3.05	0.813	78.5
Other language elements	37. Cultural differences in professional contexts	3	2.72	0.904	60.4
	*38. Certifications (e.g. Linguaskill (formerly BULATS), TOEIC, TOEFL)	4	3.08	0.925	73.5
	39. Vocabulary specific to your domain	4	3.31	0.735	88.8
	40. General vocabulary (e.g. everyday English phrases)	4	3.43	0.686	92.2
	*41. Grammar (review and consolidation)	4	3.45	0.63	93.4
	*42. Pronunciation	4	3.43	0.648	92.1

* Tasks for which a significant difference was found in the reported importance frequencies across levels of proficiency (A2, B1, B2) and type of learning mode (self-directed, blended, face-to-face).

In general, Table 1 shows that the most frequent modes correspond to the scale importance ratings *important* (3) and *very important* (4). The relatively high mean scores (i.e. ≥2.75) also indicate that the respondents tended to rate the majority of the tasks as important. Given these figures, I report here only on the sum of the percentages of the *important* and *very important* responses in the rightmost column of the table. For convenience, the items have been translated from French in the table.

According to the overall learner perceptions reported in Table 1, and apart from learners' assigning roughly equal prominence to the examined tasks regardless of the communicative mode – as I actually expected given their answers to Question 19 – the results show that our questionnaire design procedure was highly satisfactory. The initial identification of learner English needs that allowed item construction and which was based on information obtained from learners and teachers seems to have targeted the most frequent tasks encountered by French professionals. Nevertheless, a few striking findings were observed.

The three lowest mean and percentage figures obtained for *writing abstracts and/or scientific articles* (17), *writing on social networks* (19), and *taking care of foreign visitors* (35) indicate that these tasks were perceived by the learners as the least important English tasks. Concerning task 35, only 57% of the respondents perceived it as quite important. The most frequent answer obtained for the writing tasks was *slightly important* (mode=2). The particularity of these tasks can explain the lowest importance scores obtained. In fact, *writing abstracts and/ or scientific articles* may be appealing principally to learners pursuing graduate education and hence have a limited target audience in the Cnam. W*riting on social networks*, on the other hand, is not work related and could be considered not demanding with respect to English proficiency.

Table 1 also shows that of the 36 target tasks, 17 (presented in bold) seemed to be of paramount significance for the majority of Cnam learners, obtaining the highest mean scores with percentages higher than 80%. What can be noticed is that most of these tasks (11 out of 17) pertain to oral communication skills. For example, all four listening skills – Items 20, 21, 22, and 23 – were reported to be important and *very important* by respectively 95%, 92.1%, 90.9%, and 81.9% of the respondents. As for the remaining reportedly essential communicative tasks, these emphasize speaking abilities and relate to situations in which our professionals would need to converse informally and socialize, discuss work matters, communicate by phone, participate in meetings, make presentations, ask for and give information, and instruct, explain, and demonstrate. This result is actually in line with learners' views of the most efficient English learning activities (Q23) as the majority mentioned activities and tasks focusing on speaking practice for the development of oral fluency.

In addition, the analysis of teacher data revealed a similar trend. In fact, when asked to report on the most frequent English needs mentioned by Cnam learners (Q5), all 11 instructors cited developing speaking fluency and listening ability as the major reported needs. The teachers confirmed the necessity to develop oral-aural skills independently of learners' English level in their answers to the question of "which skills and/or language elements should an English course concentrate on" (Q6). Two teacher comments illustrate this finding:

> "'Writing' is not usually a skill they seem interested in developing: they often consider they have already spent a great deal of time writing English (and having been assessed on writing) at school. I mainly focus on speaking/listening activities" (Teacher 1).

> "Ideally, spoken interaction in a face-to-face course, and the other skills via the Learning Management System (so the students can pick and choose depending on their needs, and take their time to work on the content and tasks provided)" (Teacher 4).

Interestingly, apart from language tasks per se, the majority of surveyed learners also reported the high relevance ($M \approx 3.4$) of other language needs – also bolded in Table 1 – including specific vocabulary (88.8%), general vocabulary (92.2%), grammar (93.4%), and pronunciation (92.1%). The high degree of importance given to pronunciation is striking, as most of the learners also agreed with the statement "I prefer having a native English speaker as teacher" (Q22, Item 4), with 32.2% strongly agreeing and 26% agreeing. Only one (non-native) teacher, however, seemed to insist on the role of pronunciation in her answer to Q6, commenting that the English course should concentrate on "spoken English with a strong stress on pronunciation".

Chi-square tests were carried out to answer the second research question – that is, to identify potential differences in the frequencies of the reported task importance and which might depend on the general proficiency level (A2, B1, B2) or the type of learning mode (self-directed learning, blended, face-to-face). The items for which a significant difference ($p \leq .01$) was found are indicated by an asterisk in Table 1. One difference was found between the different level groups for task 31 (*request and provide information/clarifications*), with B1 learners placing more stress on its importance than the other level groups. It is unclear to me why adult B1 learners would perceive this specific task as significant, as the type of tasks investigated here are professional rather than linguistic and proficiency oriented. Given the results on the perceived difficulties reported in the next paragraph, we could hypothesize that they perceived this oral task as more challenging than the others. Interestingly, the comparison revealed more significant differences between groups following different learning modes. These pertain mainly to writing (Items 13, 14, 15, and 16) and listening (Items 20 and 21) tasks, which seem to be less important for learners enrolled in self-directed learning programs. Other differences were found for the perceived importance of *language certifications* ($X^2=30.791$, $p=.000$), *grammar* ($X^2=24.711$, $p=.003$), and *pronunciation* ($X^2=26.02$, $p=.002$), with a noticeably high degree of prominence expressed by learners taking face-to-face group lessons versus a moderate degree of importance for learners enrolled in the blended course.

In addition to identifying the most important target tasks, I sought to explore learners' and teachers' perceptions of the difficulties they might encounter while learning/teaching English. It was deemed that such information might help further classify the tasks as 'easy' or 'difficult'. I first asked learners and teachers to rate the difficulty of skills development in English (Q13 and Q7 in the Learner Survey and Teachers' Questionnaire respectively). Learners reported that speaking skills were the most difficult to develop ($M=2.59$ *spoken extended production*; $M=2.66$ *spoken interaction*). This is interesting considering that oral communication tasks were reported to be of extreme importance for the learners. Listening and writing skills were perceived as *neither difficult nor easy* ($M=3.04$ and $M=3.06$, respectively), whereas reading seemed to be the easiest skill for the learners ($M=3.57$). English teachers' perceptions differed from those of learners only with regard to spoken

Chapter 2

interaction. In fact, six instructors rated this skill as *neither difficult nor easy*, and three as *rather difficult*. Only one of the teachers perceived developing this skill as *very difficult*, adding that "spoken interaction also depends on interpersonal skills". Nevertheless, some caution has to be observed when interpreting these data given the small teacher sample ($N=11$) and the variation in learner English levels. It is surprising to me that FL listening is viewed as only moderately demanding, since research has shown that listening is the most anxiety-provoking and hardest skill to master for language learners regardless of their proficiency (Terrier, 2011; Zoghlami, 2015). It is hard to explain this result, but it might be related to our adults' urgent need to speak English at work, thus minimizing problems posed by other skills.

Other nonlinguistic problems that have to be taken into consideration in task design emerged from teachers' answers to Questions 8 and 9, which asked them to report on recurrent difficulties. Many teachers referred to learners' lack of time to study but more importantly to metacognitive aspects of learning, including learners' frustration and lack of self-confidence, in particular regarding improving speaking abilities. Below are some of their comments for illustration:

> "negative representations they have about themselves as learners (low levels of self-confidence, self-efficacy, and self-esteem) and about learning English in general (including the role of the teacher)" (Teacher 5).

> "I find it hard to get them to talk. Many of them are literally traumatized by their secondary school teachers and are afraid of making mistakes" (Teacher 3).

> "I found that B2 learners could be quite frustrated students. ... [They] sometimes stated that they felt like they had reached a plateau. ... They became irritated that their receptive skills were far greater than their speaking skills and got disheartened when they couldn't express themselves thoroughly" (Teacher 2).

5. Discussion: informing the PE curriculum

In view of improving the existing PE curriculum in the Cnam, I carried out a sound NA to identify the tasks French professionals need to perform in English in the workplace. I believe the methodological design adopted is one of the strengths of the present study. The qualitative method (i.e. informal unstructured interviews) used prior to the administration of the quantitative instrument (i.e. online survey) allowed for the emergence of relevant work-related English-use needs that I, as a domain outsider, might have overlooked. Following methodological recommendations in recent research (e.g. Malicka et al., 2017; Martin & Adrada-Rafael, 2017; Serafini et al., 2015), my aim was to avoid perpetuating the tendency of using a top-down approach to target task identification, an approach based on the researcher-teacher's own intuitions of what students need to learn, and which can be biased by what is offered in commercial resources.

In answer to the first research question, the present study sought to obtain a more comprehensive picture of the target tasks in light of the English profile I drew for the target learner audience as well as the perceived importance of English to them and the difficulties they expressed in the language. All of these elements should be taken into consideration when constructing pedagogical tasks to be integrated in a PE curriculum. As opposed to other French HE contexts (Braud et al., 2015; Brudermann et al., 2016; SAES, 2011; Taillefer, 2007), the similarities in perceptions of English needs and difficulties among the present NA stakeholders (learners and teachers) obviously reflect the effective articulation and interface between the ongoing language measures undertaken in the Cnam and professional life.

The study identified several tasks perceived as significantly important and pertaining to the four language skills. The findings also clearly demonstrate that the learners viewed oral communication tasks as the most important tasks for the workplace, thus confirming previous findings in the French literature – though exploring English needs for specific professional domains (Taillefer, 2007; Wozniak, 2010). The level of importance can be used to decide on the order of appearance of tasks in a curriculum. Accordingly, all the tasks presented in Table 1 could constitute units in a PE course – probably at the exception of the three tasks identified as the least important ones (Items 17, 19, and 35). Training on using English for the essential (bolded) tasks should be introduced first, with priority given to oral communication tasks.

Improving spoken fluency is a major, yet problematic, need. The findings reveal that the learners believed their speaking proficiency to be the lowest, which probably also explains the fact that they found this skill to be the most difficult skill to develop. This result is in line with previous findings on the actual limited French proficiency in speaking English as reviewed in the introduction (Chancelade et al., 2016; European Commission, 2012; Manoïlov, 2019). However, this study hopefully contributes to further explaining this poor level and the oral difficulty expressed. These may be related to the relatively negative self-image of the French as English users. The reported limited exposure to English in daily life, including in professional contexts, is also a key factor. A striking piece of evidence revealed in this study is that still only a minority (approximately one out of five adults) seems to be in frequent contact with English in the French workplace even in the present internationalized economic context. The lack of exposure undoubtedly jeopardizes the acquisition of English (general and specific) vocabulary – also revealed as an important need by the quantitative results. Most importantly, the data seem to indicate that most of the learners wanted to have training on English pronunciation and preferred a native speaker model, as they reported a preference for teachers who are native English speakers. This might mean that Cnam learners merely want an opportunity to be exposed to a native English accent in the classroom. However, it is also possible that they actually target native-like pronunciation when they speak English, which adds further challenges for the development of oral fluency. All of these factors are undeniably connected and need to be accounted for when designing and implementing the identified oral communicative tasks. Some work and awareness raising on the characteristics of spoken English could be injected to improve learners' aural-oral skills, probably during the pre- and post-stages of a task. It is vital, however, that such work be research based. I believe it is critically important to raise EFL teachers' awareness on current psycholinguistic L2 comprehension and production models[15], which highlight the complex processes (cognitive, linguistic, and pragmatic) that make oral L2 communication possible and point to the necessity of automatizing L2 declarative knowledge for L2 aural-oral fluency. Several other studies could be useful for the EFL classroom as they outline the features of English connected speech that are particularly challenging for the French learner (e.g. Hilton, 2003, on the teaching of the spoken form of French-English cognates; Terrier, 2011, on the segmental and suprasegmental features of English speech; Grosbois, 2014, on the role of metalinguistic awareness in reducing the effects of phonetic and phonological nativization).

To answer the second research question, I explored the potential differences in learners' answers with regard to task importance across different levels of English proficiency (A2, B1, B2) and learning modes (self-directed learning, blended, face-to-face). As expected and with the exception of one task, as explained earlier, no significant differences were found across levels of proficiency, a quite reassuring result since the explored tasks investigated in this study were work oriented and required to be performed in English by Cnam adult learners regardless of their real level in the language. In designing the curriculum, I would need however to be mindful of the significant differences that emerged between groups enrolled in methodologically distinct learning modes. This is particularly important in this case as the Cnam language department is currently piloting a blended EFL course in order to deploy it massively in the upcoming years. For example, given the results of this NA on the importance of grammar and language certifications for the blended group, work on these elements could be provided online (via the Moodle English platform being currently tested). Classroom time would then be dedicated to expanding on learners' knowledge of general and specific vocabulary in connection with the productive and receptive professional tasks being practiced – again with a focus on improving English oral communicative abilities. Telecollaboration sessions (pairing French learners with native English speakers) could also be considered in planning the blended course given the associated high level of motivation expressed by this group.

---

15. See Hilton (2014) and Zoghlami (2015) for a review of the production and comprehension models, respectively.

6. Conclusion and directions for future research

The present study attempted to fill the existing gap in the French NA literature by exploring the potential of a professionalizing task-based needs assessment for efficient English training. The findings and the discussion of the teaching-learning implications has shown that NA can certainly provide an accurate profile of a target learner community and reliable guidelines for task-based curricular planning. I also hope that the study has brought to light the necessity of conducting more theoretically driven research in the field of lifelong language learning in HE, another underdeveloped area, at least in France.

This study revealed a few interesting areas for future research. First, a possible weakness of the present NA is that I overlooked the potential cognitive and linguistic difficulties of the tasks themselves (Malicka et al., 2017). Learners' perceived difficulty could have produced more valid data on the complexifying factors and the order in which the pedagogical tasks would appear in the English course. Second, this study further points to the importance of metacognitive aspects – self-esteem and self-confidence – in language learning. It would be interesting to conduct further research to determine the exact nature of these factors as well as the potential teaching techniques that could be applied to raise professional adults' awareness of the impact such factors have on their learning, and ultimately help them overcome their negative self-image.

Every NA is context dependent. Constrained by a heterogeneous grouping for language courses, I have identified real-life tasks that can usually be relevant to adult professionals in different domains. Likewise, every group of learners has specific learning needs. Teachers who would like to investigate their groups' language needs might find it convenient to create and use a shorter version of the learner questionnaire I used for this study. In our particular case, the next step would be to design task-based syllabi per level of proficiency, taking into consideration the task characteristics outlined all through this chapter. To do so, I would further dive into learners' and teachers' reflections about the most efficient English activities. I believe detailed analysis of this qualitative data would undoubtedly enlighten course design – potentially the design of a database of ready-made language teaching units. Finally, great NA effectiveness would be achieved if the informed PE curriculum clearly stipulated the learning outcomes specifying what learners can do in English – another very often neglected dimension in language programs.

7. Supplementary materials

https://research-publishing.box.com/s/xbgrls4zmxoraxhwbn4kl48w3adkz903

References

Basturkmen, H. (2010). *Developing courses in English for specific purposes*. Palgrave Macmillan.

Bonnet, G. (2004). (Ed.). *The assessment of pupils' skills in English in eight European countries*. Ministère de l'Éducation nationale.

Borras, I., & Bosse, N. (2017). Les universités françaises à l'heure de la formation tout au long de la vie : une ultime chance d'ouverture aux adultes? *Formation emploi, 138,* 117-138.

Braud, V. (2008). L'anglais et les magistrats français, résultats d'une enquête de terrain. *ASp, 53-54,* 141-158. https://doi.org/10.4000/asp.3055

Braud, V., Millot, P., Sarré, C., & Wozniak, S. (2015). "You say you want a revolution…" Contribution à la réflexion pour une politique des langues adaptée au secteur LANSAD. *Recherche et pratiques pédagogiques en langues de spécialité - Cahiers de l'APLIUT, 34*(1). https://doi.org/10.4000/apliut.5020

Brown, J. D. (2009). Foreign and second language needs analysis. In M. H. Long & C. J. Doughty (Eds), *The handbook of language teaching* (pp. 269-293). Blackwell.

Brown, J. D. (2016). *Introducing needs analysis and English for specific purposes*. Routledge.

Brudermann, C., Mattioli, M. A., Roussel A. M., & Sarré, C. (2016). Le secteur des langues pour spécialistes d'autres disciplines (Lansad) dans les universités françaises : résultats d'une enquête nationale. *Recherche et pratiques pédagogiques en langues de spécialité - Les Cahiers de l'APLIUT, 35*(3). https://doi.org/10.4000/apliut.5564

Bryfonski, L., & McKay, T. H. (2017). TBLT implementation and evaluation: a meta-analysis. *Language Teaching Research, 23*(5), 603-632. https://doi.org/10.1177/1362168817744389

Chan, C. (2018). Proposing and illustrating a research-informed approach to curriculum development for specific topics in business English. *English for Specific Purposes, 52*, 27-46. https://doi.org/10.1016/j.esp.2018.07.001

Chancelade, C., Janissin, P., Giret, J. F., Guégnard, C., Benoit, P., & Vogt, A. (2016). Analyse des besoins des employeurs français au regard des compétences en langues vivantes étrangères: synthèse d'enquête [Research report]. http://pmb.cereq.fr/doc_num.php?explnum_id=3030

Dörnyei, Z. (2003). *Questionnaires in second language research.* Lawrence Erlbaum Associates.

Dörnyei, Z. (2007). *Research methods in applied linguistics: quantitative, qualitative and mixed methodologies.* Oxford University Press.

Dubar, C. (2008). Les changements possibles du système français de formation continue. *Formation emploi, 101*, 167-182.

EUA. (2008). *European universities' charter on lifelong learning.* European University Association. https://eua.eu/resources/publications/646:european-universities%E2%80%99-charter-on-lifelong-learning.html

European Commission. (2012). *First European survey on languages competences. Final report.* https://op.europa.eu/en/publication-detail/-/publication/42ea89dc-373a-4d4f-aa27-9903852cd2e4/language-en/format-PDF/source-119658026

Grosbois, M. (2014). Mobilité internationale et production orale en anglais L2—réflexion, médiation, dénativisation. *Les Dossiers des Sciences de l'Éducation, 32*, 65-80. https://doi.org/10.4000/dse.679

Hilton, H. (2002). Modèles de l'acquisition lexicale en L2: où en sommes nous? *ASP, 35-36*, 201-217. https://doi.org/10.4000/asp.1668

Hilton, H. (2003). L'accès au lexique mental dans une langue étrangère : le cas des francophones apprenant l'anglais. *CORELA, 1*(2). https://doi.org/10.4000/corela.676

Hilton, H. (2014). Oral fluency and spoken proficiency: considerations for research and testing. In P. Leclercq, A. Edmonds & H. Hilton (Eds), *Measuring L2 proficiency: perspectives from SLA* (pp. 27-53). Multilingual Matters. https://doi.org/10.21832/9781783092291-005

Holford, J., Milana M., & Mohorčič Špolar, V. (2014). Adult and lifelong education: the European Union, its member states and the world. *International Journal of Lifelong Education, 33*(3), 267-274. https://doi.org/10.1080/02601370.2014.911518

Huhta, M., Vogt, K., Johnson, E., & Tulkki, H. (2013). *Needs analysis for language course design: a holistic approach to ESP.* Cambridge University Press.

Hutchinson, T., & Waters, A. (1987). *English for specific purposes: a learning-centred approach*. Cambridge University Press.

Hyland, K. (2009). Specific purposes programs. In M. H. Long & C. J. Doughty (Eds), *The handbook of language teaching* (pp. 201-217). Wiley Blackwell.

Iizuka, T. (2019). Task-based needs analysis: identifying communicative needs for study abroad students in Japan. *System, 80*, 134-142. https://doi.org/10.1016/j.system.2018.11.005

Joulia, D. (2014). Une approche professionnalisante pour des étudiants de DUT Informatique. *Recherche et pratiques pédagogiques en langues de spécialité - Cahiers de l'APLIUT, 33*(1), 91-108. https://doi.org/10.4000/apliut.4190

Lam, P. W. Y., Cheng, W., & Kong, K. C. C. (2014). Learning English through workplace communication: an evaluation of existing resources in Hong Kong. *English for Specific Purposes, 34*(1), 68-78. https://doi.org/10.1016/j.esp.2013.09.004

Long, M. H. (2005). *Second language needs analysis*. Cambridge University Press.

Long, M. H. (2015). *Second language acquisition and task-based language teaching*. Wiley-Blackwell.

Malicka, A., Gilabert Guerrero, R., & Norris, J. M. (2017). From needs analysis to task design: insights from an English for specific purposes context. *Language Teaching Research, 23*(1), 78-106. https://doi.org/10.1177/1362168817714278

Manoïlov, P. (2019). *Les acquis des élèves en langues vivantes étrangères*. Cnesco.

Martin, A., & Adrada-Rafael, S. (2017). Business Spanish in the real world: a task-based needs analysis. *L2 Journal, 9*(1), 39-61. https://doi.org/10.5070/L29131409

North, B. (2007). The CEFR common reference levels: validated reference points and local strategies. *Policy Forum on the Common European Framework of Reference for Languages (CEFR) and the development of language policies: challenges and responsibilities*. https://rm.coe.int/16805c3896

Nunan, D. (2004). *Task-based language teaching*. Cambridge University Press.

Richards, J. C. (2001). *Curriculum development in language teaching*. Cambridge University Press.

Robinson, P. (2011). *Second language task complexity: researching the cognition hypothesis of language learning and performance*. John Benjamins.

SAES. (2011). *Évolution et enjeux des formations et de la recherche dans le secteur LANSAD*. Commission Formation de la SAES. http://saesfrance.org/arc/pdf/ASP-LANSAD-Didactique_de_l_anglais_DEFdoc.pdf

Serafini, E. J., Lake, J. B., & Long, M. H. (2015). Needs analysis for specialized learner populations: essential methodological improvements. *English for Specific Purposes, 40,* 11-26. https://doi.org/10.1016/j.esp.2015.05.002

Taillefer, G. (2004). Une analyse critériée des besoins linguistiques dans l'enseignement universitaire des Sciences économiques. *ASp, 43-44,* 107-124. https://doi.org/10.4000/asp.1095

Taillefer, G. (2007). The professional language needs of economics graduates: assessment and perspectives in the French context. *English for Specific Purposes, 26*(2), 135-155. https://doi.org/10.1016/j.esp.2006.06.003

Taillefer, G. (2014). Éditorial. *Les dossiers des sciences de l'éducation, 32,* 7-15. http://journals.openedition.org/dse/640

Terrier, L. (2011). *Méthodologie linguistique pour l'évaluation des restitutions et analyse expérimentales des processus de didactisation du son. Recommendations pour un apprentissage raisonné de la compréhension de l'anglais oral par les étudiants francophones du secteur LA.* Doctoral dissertation. Université Paul SabatierToulouse 3, Toulouse.

Truchot, C. (2015). *Quelles langues parle-t-on dans les entreprises en France? Les langues au travail dans les entreprises internationales.* Éditions Privat.

Wozniak, S. (2010). Language needs analysis from a perspective of international professional mobility: the case of French mountain guides. *English for Specific Purposes, 29*(4), 243-252. https://doi.org/10.1016/j.esp.2010.06.001

Zoghlami, N. (2015). *Foreign language listening: bottom-up and top-down processes—issues for EFL teaching and research.* Doctoral dissertation. Université Paris 8, Paris, France.

3. Questioning the notion of 'professionalisation': LANSOD contexts and the specific case of a musicology undergraduate programme

Aude Labetoulle[1]

1. Introduction

Most university degrees in France include languages as part of the curriculum. LANguages for Students of Other Disciplines (LANSOD) courses refer to language courses destined to students whose major is not languages, but another discipline such as musicology or chemistry. It is estimated about 90% of students enrolled in French higher education attend LANSOD classes (Causa & Derivry-Plard, 2013). At the same time, it is agreed that French universities should 'professionalise' students – that is, prepare them for their future professional lives. LANSOD courses should be no exception and should be included in this process, yet French universities appear to struggle with the design of language courses that are relevant to the future professional needs of learners.

This chapter aims at questioning the notion of professionalisation in the specific context of LANSOD university courses in France. To do so, I will first investigate how 'professionalisation' is commonly defined and how it is implemented in French universities, especially in LANSOD courses. The second part of this article will deal with the particular case of a LANSOD undergraduate course at the University of Lille; the point is to illustrate how complex it can be to design

---

1. Conservatoire National des Arts et Métiers (Cnam), FoAP (EA 7529), Paris, France; aude.labetoulle@lecnam.net; https://orcid.org/0000-0001-7822-1557

How to cite this chapter: Labetoulle, A. (2020). Questioning the notion of 'professionalisation': LANSOD contexts and the specific case of a musicology undergraduate programme. In B. Dupuy and M. Grosbois (Eds), *Language learning and professionalization in higher education: pathways to preparing learners and teachers in/for the 21st century* (pp. 71-98). Research-publishing.net. https://doi.org/10.14705/rpnet.2020.44.1102

a curriculum relevant to learners' future professional needs and to provide practitioners with tools that could prove useful in similar contexts for the design of professionalising LANSOD courses.

2. Context overview: professionalisation, French universities, and language courses

2.1. 'Professionalisation' and French universities

2.1.1. Definitions and rationale behind 'professionalisation'

The 'professionalisation' of objectives, courses, and students is now a key mission of French higher education (Bourdon, Giret, & Goudard, 2012; Stavrou, 2011; Van der Yeught, 2014). Yet it is only quite recently that the idea has started to take hold that French universities should be involved in training qualified staff for the private sector (Leroux, 2014). Until the 1960's, apart from a few faculties that provided students with vocational training, such as medicine and law (Gayraud, Simon-Zarca, & Soldano, 2011), the "sole idea of professionalisation [...] within general curriculum subjects met great hostility from part of the university world" (Renaut, 1995; as cited in Leroux, 2014, p. 95). Any interest in the active life (*vita activa*) over contemplative life (*vita contemplativa*) was mostly perceived as an obstacle to true disinterested knowledge and research (Van der Yeught, 2014). Besides, universities long put off professionalisation to the benefit of great schools (*grandes écoles*), which are separate from the public university system; they are aimed at educating the nation's administrative and technical elite (Leroux, 2014) and are characterised by competitive recruitment and technical and professionalised knowledge.

Yet European integration policies and the rising problem of graduate unemployment in the past four decades in France has spurred a continuous movement towards the professionalisation of university courses (Leroux, 2014). The Maastricht treaty and Amsterdam treaty (1993 and 1997), the Lisbon strategy (2002), and the Bologna declaration (1999) were key in setting professional integration as a high-priority goal for Europe. In France more specifically, the creation of the University Technical Institutes (1966), the Faure law (1968), the Attali report (1998), the *Plan réussite en licence* (a national programme to support undergraduate education, 2007), and the Aghion report (2010) all contributed to putting the professionalisation of students on the agenda of French universities (Bourdon et al., 2012; Gachassin, Labbé, & Mias, 2013; Gayraud et al., 2011; Stavrou, 2011). In recent years, the number of vocational[2] undergraduate and postgraduate programmes has dramatically increased (Gayraud et al., 2011), and there is a clear trend towards giving vocational emphasis to all university courses (Leroux, 2014). This is made evident in university contracts, the description of degree courses, and the fact that university funding is now calculated in part on the employment rate of graduates (Leroux, 2014).

It is striking to note that the definitions of the key term 'professionalisation' in European and French directives either differ from one text to another or are rather vague (Doray, Tremblay, & Groleau, 2015; Stavrou, 2011). In its most general meaning, 'professionalising' university courses refers to a process whose aim is to "provide the productive system with a flow of highly skilled workers" (Leroux, 2014, p. 89). The main underlying argument is that the professionalisation of higher education would ease graduates' integration into working life, thereby stimulating economic growth (Doray et al., 2015). To that end, there needs to be a proper fit between university education and the labour market, socio-economic demands, and job opportunities (Doray et al., 2015; Stavrou, 2011); it is the professional field that tends to dictate what should and should not be taught, and how (Stavrou, 2011). As such, 'professionalisation' is very much linked to 'employability', a notion that started to be in the spotlight in the 1990's (Forrier & Sels, 2003). 'Employability' refers to

> "the capacity to build, entertain and develop useful skills, adapted to the local market, while ensuring productivity, flexibility and mobility. Important elements of employability should be acquired during

---

2. In this article, the terms 'occupational', 'vocational', and 'professional' are used interchangeably. For a discussion on these various terms, see for example Wedekind (2018).

studies: a recognised qualification (degree), knowledge (general and professional), suitable business behaviours and adaptation capacities" (Leroux, 2014, pp. 96-97).

This broad interpretation of 'employability' reveals competing understandings as to what professionalising university courses should consist of. Should there be a strict match between a particular job and a particular course? Or should there be a focus on the acquisition of more general knowledge, skills, and existential competence that can be transferable from one distinct professional field to another (Doray et al., 2015; Stavrou, 2011)? These various interpretations then impact the design of courses differently.

2.1.2. *Implementations of 'professionalisation' in French universities*

Together with Chirache and Vincens (1992), Leroux (2014) stressed that "all higher education courses have a vocational element, to a greater or lesser extent, in that they have a vocational purpose. This is still the situation because such courses generally lead to employment for most of the students" (p. 94). However, there is considerable variation in the degree of professionalisation of courses, so that together with Doray et al. (2015) and Gayraud et al. (2011), we argue that professionalisation can be viewed on a continuum. At one end of the continuum, courses lay emphasis on clearly defined professional purposes in preparation for jobs that require students to obtain specific university diplomas that then guarantee access to specific professions, such as in the medical field (Doray et al., 2015). At the other end of the continuum, degree courses purposefully lead to a wide range of professions (Gayraud et al., 2011); this is often the case for undergraduate studies that cover several fields without targeting specific jobs, such as most bachelor's degrees in history and biology (Gayraud et al., 2011). There are many possible scenarios in between, including degree courses that depend on strict accreditation processes and frames of reference, but students in such programmes do not automatically get a position after graduation, and they benefit from a larger pool of job opportunities, as is the case with university engineering schools.

Apart from increasing the number of vocational courses, there are many other ways for universities to professionalise academic courses (Annoot et al., 2019; Doray et al., 2015; Gachassin et al., 2013; Gayraud et al., 2011; Stavrou, 2011). Curricula can be specifically designed to facilitate employment. Practical training can be set up in the form of internships, job placements, and practical courses. Professionals can intervene in the design of the course, during one-off interventions and in university-business forums. Teachers might decide to favour active learning grounded on the notion of 'competence', understood as either a specific or a transversal skill relevant to the job market, and propose individualised activities relevant to each learner's professional objectives.

The second way to foster the employability of university students is to provide them with relevant information concerning the job market. For example, the BAIP (Career Support Centre) oversees the advertisement of internships and jobs in universities; the mission of the OFIVE (Student Affairs Office) is to produce data on academic success and on the job integration of former graduates. Last but not least, selective admission and the promotion of work experience through VAEs (Validation Of Acquired Experience leading to a certification) are other means to increase graduate employability.

2.2. 'Professionalisation' and language courses in French universities

2.2.1. The emergence of LANSOD professionalising courses

The fact that languages have progressively gained importance in curricula can be in part related to the professionalisation of courses in universities. Indeed, computer literacy, good analytical skills, and modern languages have started to be considered necessary transversal skills (Gayraud et al., 2011), and structural university reforms such as the *Plan réussite en licence* (plan to foster academic success in undergraduate programmes) have highlighted the importance of providing students with multidisciplinary skills that could be useful in all professions (Leroux, 2014).

This accounts for why, from the 1970's onwards, languages have started to appear systematically in higher education curricula. Language courses tended to be optional initially, before becoming more widely spread and compulsory (Van der Yeught, 2014). Progressively, the LANSOD sector took shape. The term LANSAD (LANgues pour Spécialistes d'Autres Disciplines) and its equivalent in English – LANSOD – were coined in 1993 and in 2016, respectively (Mémet, 2001; Van der Yeught, 2016). As was mentioned previously, the great majority of students enrolled in higher education in France are taught foreign languages in LANSOD courses; in other words, languages now seem well-established in curricula, especially English, which is the most studied foreign language by far (Braud, Millot, Sarre, & Wozniak, 2015).

LANSOD courses, just like degree courses more generally, can also be viewed on a continuum, from general and transversal courses to highly professionalising and specialised courses. A distinction that is commonly made is based on the weight given to disciplinary and/or professional content, as opposed to the L2 (Figure 1).

Figure 1. Continuum of programmes that integrate content and language (adapted from Thompson & McKinley, 2018)

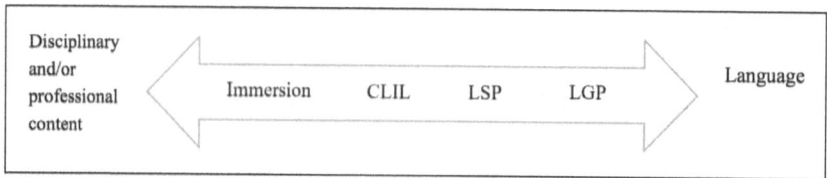

In immersion programmes, learners benefit from an important amount of subject instruction in a sheltered classroom environment via the L2; the assumption is that the L2 will be acquired via exposure to comprehensible input (Thompson & McKinley, 2018). In content and language integrated learning, students generally receive both content and language classes, and the content class is primarily carried out in the L2 by content-trained instructors (Thompson & McKinley, 2018). Languages for Specific Purposes (LSP) are more focussed on language learning but give great importance to the discipline/profession of the learners, while languages for general purposes focus on the language without making specific reference to a discipline/profession. The most common types of courses in LANSOD contexts are LSP classes and general language classes; therefore, they will remain the focus from here on.

Many researchers advocate a strong integration of disciplinary and professional components in LANSOD courses (Brudermann, Mattioli, Roussel, & Sarré, 2016; Sarré, Millot, Wozniak, & Braud, 2017; Sarré & Whyte, 2016; Wozniak & Millot, 2016). For example, Hardy (2013a) argued that "it is [...] part of [the] mission [of LANSOD teachers] to help their learners acquire the keys to the language-culture of a specific professional environment"[3] (para. 1). For Van der Yeught (2014), all LANSOD students "should be taught to communicate in foreign languages in the professional perspective which they chose, that is that they should study the language for specific purposes related to their disciplinary training" (para. 52). LSPs are particularly relevant because they aim at "making learners operational in oral and written communication situations in particular professional contexts"[4] (Hardy, 2013b, para. 1). Moreover, several studies have indicated that specialised language courses trigger learner motivation (e.g. Toffoli & Speranza, 2016; Wozniak & Millot, 2016). Sarré (personal communication, December 13, 2018) has advocated a gradual integration of specialised and professionalising content over the course of the LANSOD training programme (Figure 2 below). He differentiated general and specific purposes, as well as academic, professional, and occupational purposes.

To professionalise LANSOD courses, we may integrate content specific to a certain discipline (e.g. history, mathematics, or musicology), or a profession (e.g. archivist, statistician, or songwriter). Content can focus on terminology (Resche, 1996), phonetics (Péchou & Stenton, 2001), genre analysis (Swales, 2004), relevant intercultural knowledge (Narcy-Combes, 2003), case studies

---

3. Translated from the French: "Faire acquérir à leurs apprenants les clés de la langue-culture d'un milieu professionnel fait donc partie de leur mission".

4. Translated from the French: "L'enseignement d'une langue de spécialité vise à rendre l'apprenant opérationnel dans des situations de communication, orales ou écrites, dans un contexte professionnel particulier".

Chapter 3

(Van der Yeught, 2017), or activities based on professional experiences (such as professional reports). We can also rely on teaching and learning methodologies that aim at fostering general transferable skills and knowledge, to mention the distinction that was made earlier. Learner autonomy, defined as "the educational objective of progressively enabling students to manage their learning activities responsibly" (La Borderie, 1998, p. 14)[5], and critical thinking have often become explicit objectives of LANSOD courses (Iglesias-Philippot, 2013; Macré, 2014; Toffoli & Speranza, 2016). In general, methodologies tend to favour active pedagogies (e.g. project-based or task-oriented; Whyte, 2013). The course can be tailored to individual needs (Deyrich, 2004), while group work can be used to favour the development of interpersonal skills.

Figure 2. What content for LANSOD courses? Progressive specialisation of content (adapted from Sarré, slide 16)

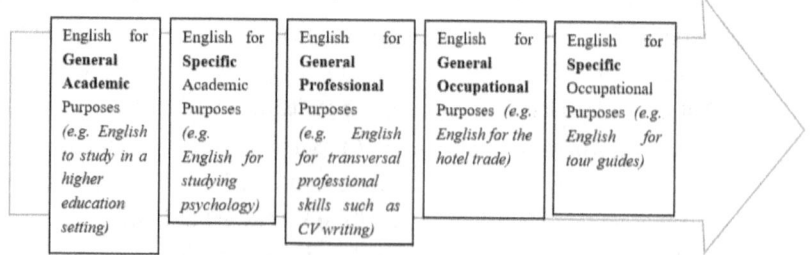

2.2.2. The slow and problematic integration of 'professionalisation' in LANSOD courses

Despite the importance the LANSOD sector has gained over the years, its emergence did not automatically constitute a decisive contribution to the professionalisation of learners. If language teaching and learning has become more communication oriented, this change has not necessarily been accompanied by the professionalisation of objectives, content, and methods (Van der Yeught,

---

5. Translated from the French: "objectif éducatif qui consiste à rendre progressivement les élèves capables de gérer, de manière responsable, leurs activités d'apprentissage".

2014). Quite often, what is expected of a LANSOD course is still not explicit. The mission of LANSOD teachers is often presented as 'foreign languages: two hours per week' in the descriptions of courses, and they often have to find out the objectives, content, and teaching methods of the course on their own (Van der Yeught, 2014).

The assessment of whether and how disciplinary and professional content and methods should be integrated into the L2 course can be influenced by many factors (Brudermann et al., 2012). Based on a literature review, we identified several recurring solid obstacles to the professionalisation of LANSOD courses. First of all, few resources have been allocated to LANSOD courses, which tend to have a secondary status compared to disciplinary subjects in the curriculum (Van der Yeught, 2014). In undergraduate education especially, language classes involving several dozens of students of highly heterogeneous language proficiency levels in large amphitheatres are not rare, and lecture rooms often lack proper teaching equipment (such as projectors). Measures implemented these past 15 years to remedy these deficiencies have done little to improve the quality of learning and teaching (Fave-Bonnet, 2012).

Teaching and researching in the LANSOD sector are also poorly regarded. There are few permanent teaching positions, so many LANSOD courses are taught by temporary teachers who lack the means to properly structure courses in the long term, and when permanent teaching positions are available, 90% of candidates do not fit the profile (Van der Yeught, 2014). Although there is teacher training to teach languages in primary and secondary education, teachers are poorly trained in SLA (Whyte, 2016), and there is virtually no training for higher education, let alone for teaching LSP (Van der Yeught, 2014). Moreover, collaboration between language teachers and disciplinary teachers is not always possible or easy. In addition, there is little research investment in characterising LSP (e.g. English for the police, English for journalism) compared to the needs in the field. Researchers teaching in LANSOD courses are rare, and where they exist, their research is often not related to LANSOD issues. There are few doctoral theses investigating the field (Van der Yeught, 2014), and many areas have been left unexplored.

Chapter 3

What is more, assessing the professional language needs of the learners in order to design a relevant syllabus is particularly challenging for several reasons. First, heterogeneous groups – in terms of language proficiency, disciplinary background, and professional objectives – tend to be the norm. For example, it is not uncommon for LANSOD courses to gather students from various disciplines together – such as Master's students in music and philosophy – which makes it quite challenging for teachers to adapt the syllabus to everyone's professional language needs. Second, teachers and programme supervisors often lack the time to conduct proper needs analyses with the aim of identifying the language that students will use in their target professional or vocational workplace or in their study areas in order to design relevant LANSOD courses (Basturkmen, 2010). Last but not least, some LANSOD courses are highly dependent on certification exams – such as the TOEIC for engineering students – however irrelevant that exam might be regarding their future professional needs (Van der Yeught, 2014).

In other words, the notion of 'professionalisation' applied to the LANSOD sector is problematic because it proves difficult to define and implement. The aim of the case study that follows is to exemplify the challenges that can be met, as well as to provide tools to help practitioners overcome some of these challenges.

3. Case study: professionalising a LANSOD course

3.1. Methodology of the study

An action-research project was conducted over the course of four semesters between 2015 and 2018 at the University of Lille (France), with all undergraduate students in Year 1 and Year 3 studying musicology, as well as with dance students during the first semester. There were between 25 and more than 60 students in each group (two groups in Year 1 and one group in Year 3). The aim was to design a relevant English LANSOD course adapted to their needs. The project went through several steps.

The needs analysis aimed at identifying the problems in the existing course in order to design a new course. The methodology was based on recent reviews of language needs analyses and procedures of data collection (Serafini, Lake, & Long, 2015). An exploratory approach was favoured with the use of open-ended questionnaires (Q; see supplementary materials) and interviews (I). Data were obtained from five groups of participants: two language supervisors (Q+I), two content supervisors in charge of the undergraduate programmes (Q+I), four English teachers (Q+I), 43 current students of musicology (Q), and six former students of the undergraduate programme (Q)[6].

The new course was evaluated at the end of each of the four semesters with questionnaires submitted to all the learners and the teachers (supplementary materials), and interviews were conducted with the teachers at the end of the fourth semester. In total, 347 student questionnaires and 12 teacher questionnaires were collected and analysed, and three interviews were conducted for the evaluation of the course.

For both the needs analysis and the evaluation procedure, Microsoft Excel (Version 14.0.7177.5000) and Alber's Sonal (Version 2.0.77) were used to filter and analyse the quantitative and qualitative data.

3.2. The difficulties met in identifying professional needs in English for the new LANSOD course

The needs analysis was focussed on answering the following questions: What are the problems in the existing course? How much importance is given to professionalisation in this training context? How can it be defined based on the learners' needs and the job market? What could be a relevant syllabus?

At the University of Lille, though 'professionalisation' was a key word at the political and institutional levels, it seemed to have a limited impact on the field,

---

[6]. The needs analysis for dance students was not as in-depth as that of music students, as they were to leave the group after one semester. The data presented here is mostly focussed on music students and the class taught after they left the group.

Chapter 3

and we met many obstacles when trying to define the relevant objectives of a professionalising English LANSOD course.

First of all, there were obstacles to the research process. There was no official student follow-up at the undergraduate level. The BAIP and the OFIVE only gathered information on the former students' study success rates, not on the jobs they took after studying. We could not get official access to the former students' email addresses via the administrative or IT departments for confidentiality reasons, which considerably restricted the number of people who could be reached.

The students in the English LANSOD classroom came from four distinct undergraduate programmes, which displayed various degrees of professionalisation (Figure 3).

Figure 3. The LANSOD classroom, which brings together students from four training programmes

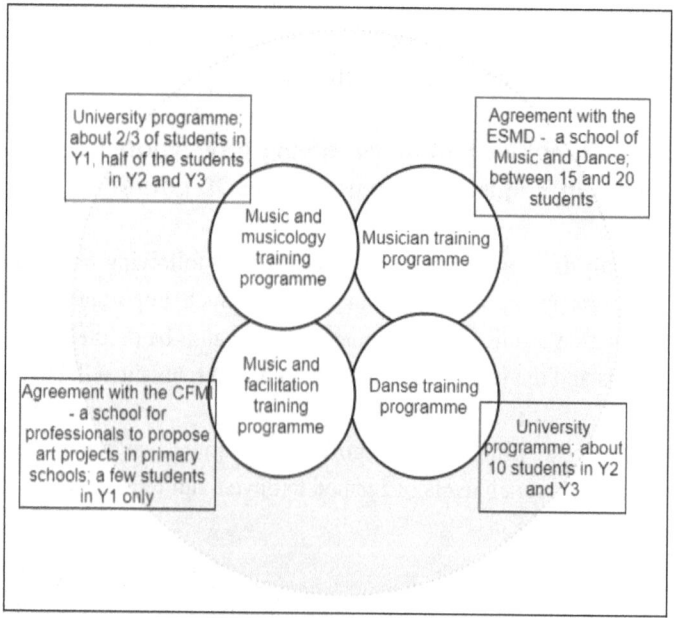

We looked at the official descriptions of the four programmes to identify the official status given to professionalisation in each. The music and musicology and the dance undergraduate programmes (*parcours musique et musicology* and *parcours études en danse*) did not lay a particular emphasis on professionalisation. Their objectives were to train students on subjects such as music analysis and aesthetics in the music programme and practical and theoretical knowledge of choreographic culture in the dance programme. Most students were encouraged to pursue further studies with Master's degrees. The musician training programme (*parcours de formation du musicien*) came across as much more professionalising as it was reserved for students who wanted to become professional musicians and music teachers in music schools, and classes took place both at the conservatory of music and at the university. Being a musician and a facilitator (*musicien intervenant*) consists in accompanying primary teachers in their artistic projects. The description of the programme was the most explicit when it came to professional objectives, defining the professional missions of the *musiciens intervenants*.

A further obstacle to the clear definition of the learners' professional needs in English was that the composition of the LANSOD group was about to change. Although dance students were mixed with music students when the needs analysis was carried out, they were meant to be put in separate groups one semester after the new course started. This made designing the new course quite challenging, as the course designer had to design the course when it included, then excluded, the dance students.

Moreover, there was no overall consensus as to what the objectives of the LANSOD course should be and how much importance should be given to professionalisation. When the teachers, the students, and the supervisors were asked what the purposes of the undergraduate LANSOD classes should be, the answers were quite diverse, ranging from a curt 'provide students with grades', to elaborate descriptions. However, 'professional objectives' and 'professionalisation' were not frequently mentioned, except by disciplinary supervisors, the LANSOD supervisor of the arts department, and a few students. Besides, there were several other considerations to take into account, which downplayed the importance of specialisation and professionalisation, such as students being encouraged by the university to take a certification exam, the *Certificat en Langues de l'Enseignement Supérieur* (CLES), which focusses on general English for the lower levels.

When asked what their career plans were, music students gave quite varied answers, as can be seen in Table 1 below. Although teaching was a common objective, it could take on many forms: teaching several subjects in primary school, teaching music in middle school, in a music school, at the conservatory of music, teaching private lessons, and others. In these different contexts, the students' professional needs in English were not the same. These data confirmed the statements of former students, who in 2015-2016 were music teachers in secondary school (3/6) or in primary school (1/6), a cultural mediator (1/6) and a composer and sound designer (1/6). All of the former students stressed the importance of English, but to varying degrees and according to their professional field: the needs of a music teacher in a middle school in France were indeed very different from the needs of an instrumentalist working abroad.

Table 1. Career plans of undergraduate students of musicology at the University of Lille in 2015-2016

Occupations		Number of answers
Teacher	Unspecified	2
	Music teacher in middle or high school	3
	Instrumentalist and music teacher	3
	Primary school teacher	2
	Music teacher	2
	Teacher in a conservatory of music	1
Research		3.5[7]
"Musicien intervenant"		2
Communications manager, cultural mediator		1
Instrumentalist		1.5
Music therapist		2

---

7. When students specified two professional objectives, their answer was counted as 0.5 + 0.5 so as to give equal weight to all the students' answers.

Instrument maker	1
Other profession related to music	2.5
Other profession not related to music	2
Sound engineer	0.5
No answer	6
An idea but not specified	4
No idea	4
Total	43

Learners had heterogenous English proficiency levels; language teachers and learners assessed their levels to range from A1/A2 to C2 on the Common European Framework of Reference for languages (CEFR). As stated before, the sizes of the groups varied greatly, ranging from 25 to more than 60 students.

As regards teachers, they had little training in LANSOD teaching. As described in Labetoulle (2017, p. 39), of the two teachers with tenure, two contract teachers, and four teaching assistants, five had little or no prior experience of teaching at university level. Their majors included English for Specific Purposes (ESP), literature, translation, and French, in France or abroad. They were generally interested in music, but very few (1/8) were familiar with the domain of musicology and dance, let alone ESP in this area. In addition, there was a high teacher turnover rate. Seven of the eight English teachers had not previously taught this class, and only two eventually continued teaching the following year.

The teachers could also not rely on published literature to define the content of the course, as there are very few studies conducted in the characterisation of ESP in the humanities, let alone in musicology. Of the 32 needs analyses studied by Serafini et al. (2015) between 1984 and 2014, only two relate to social sciences (Sešek, 2007, on teaching, and Gilabert, 2005, on journalism). Likewise, of the 508 articles, editorials, and reports published in the French journal *Asp*, which deals with ESP, less than ten were related to the humanities (such as Baud, 2003, on cinema and Gould, 2001, on art). To my knowledge, there have been only two studies on ESP related to musicology. A blended LANSOD course was set up at the Fryderyk Chopin University of Music (Warsaw) for future instrumentalists, and its content is described in a research article by Lesiak-

Bielawska (2014). As part of my Master's degree research project, I tentatively offered a characterisation of 'music English' based on 15 research articles in musicology; however, this study was very limited in that only the authors' stances and engagements were studied, and the results were never published. Overall then, a teacher wanting to set up a relevant professionalising LANSOD course had very little to start with.

Offering a coherent, 'professionalising' course thus appeared quite a challenge. Overall, this particular context appeared quite similar to the generic context that was described in the context overview, as I faced many constraints that were identified earlier (large groups with heterogeneous language proficiency levels and professional objectives, high teacher turnover rate, teachers with little training and experience in LANSOD courses, little research on the ESP of the particular domain, etc.). Let us now turn to how these obstacles were faced in designing a professionalising LANSOD course.

3.3. The definition, integration, and evaluation of 'professionalisation' in the new LANSOD course

3.3.1. The identification and integration of professionalising components in the LANSOD course

Taking the various contextual elements into consideration and following the advice of researchers such as Sarré (personal communication, December 13, 2018), it was decided to specialise and professionalise content gradually, starting with more disciplinary components in Year 1 and working toward more professional content in Year 3. Thanks to the data gathered in the questionnaires and interviews with the learners, former students, and content supervisors, communication situations[8] and language activities that require English in professional settings were identified. The most frequently mentioned were a desire to:

---

8. These are defined here as "a unified set of components [consisting of] the same general topic, and involving the same participants, generally using the same language variety, maintaining the same tone or key and the same rules for interaction, in the same setting" (Saville-Troike, 2008, p. 23).

- get by abroad;
- talk about one's instrument and instrument practice;
- have satisfactory pronunciation when working on songs;
- understand lyrics of songs;
- give music classes in English;
- be convincing in a recruitment interview;
- write a résumé and cover letter;
- understand a foreign conductor;
- communicate in an orchestra;
- comment on a piece;
- read specialised articles;
- use specialised software;
- welcome companies, artists, and the audience.

Based on how frequently some communication situations were mentioned and the feasibility of transforming them into language learning objectives, the syllabus was organised around tasks. In Year 1, one semester was organised around the topic of music festivals. In groups, learners had to present a plan for a music festival to sponsors and write its programme. During the second semester, learners were invited to read, listen to, talk, and write about four topics linked to music, which also enabled them to study transversal themes requiring the expression of habits, emotions, and preference: "your routine when it comes to music", "why I am a musician", "music and feelings", and "the best musician ever". In Year 3, the main theme of Semester 1 was one's instrument; learners had to write an ad to sell their instrument, improvise when asked about their instrument and their practice, and read part of a score in English. In the second semester, more importance was given to professional topics with an introduction to CV and cover letter writing as well as job interviews. In addition, learners could decide between doing an oral analysis of a music piece or participating in a debate unrelated to their specialist domains.

Considering the diversity of the students' professional objectives and language proficiency levels highlighted in the needs analysis, the syllabus was meant to be diversified and flexible. Thus, the language activities included listening, reading, writing, spoken interaction, and spoken production. Both individual and collective work was proposed. If many activities were strongly focussed on disciplinary and professionalising components, general topics were also studied, such as transhumanism, the news, and studying abroad. For the same reason, and because objectives deemed relevant by the learners and adapted to their needs were more likely to trigger motivation (Ellis, 2005; Narcy-Combes, 2005, p. 169), it was also decided to adapt the LANSOD course to individual needs as much as possible. Thus, a 'personal projects' activity was introduced, which relied on the principles of project-based learning (Bell, 2010). Learners individually chose which language activity they wanted to work on, whether it was linked to their discipline or future profession, devised a plan to work on that language activity, submitted their work to the teacher for feedback during the semester, and presented their work to the class at the end of the semester. This project enabled students to individualise the degree of professionalisation of the course according to their specific needs. Evaluations were also personalised to some extent, as learners could regularly choose which task they would be assessed on (e.g. oral analysis of a music piece or participation in a debate on transhumanism in Year 3).

In terms of more transferable skills, the LANSOD course laid emphasis on learner autonomy. Therefore, teaching methods and activities were selected with this goal in mind. Each semester, some time was spent exploring methods and tools for learning languages more autonomously (online dictionaries, language apps, news websites, etc.). One key aim of the personal project was also to develop learner autonomy, as the learners had to work on a project on their own over the course of a semester.

The course was a blended course, alternating face-to-face classes and online modules. This format encourages learners to be autonomous as "particularly when learning in a BL [blended learning] environment, students have to know when to take action and when they can hand over responsibility [...] and they] have to be able to handle different degrees of responsibility over the process and the content of learning" (Neumeier, 2005, p. 175).

3.3.2. Results from the evaluation of the course

Before presenting the results of the evaluation of the course, some important limitations to this action-research project should be mentioned. Quite importantly, it was not possible to verify how relevant the new LANSOD course was as regards the professionalisation of students in the long term, since it is very difficult to keep track of students once they have left the university. Moreover, the author of this chapter was also the person who conducted the needs analysis, analysed the data, designed and evaluated the course, and was one of the teachers of the course.

However, the longitudinal evaluative procedure yielded much data in support of the idea that the course was relevant according to the various participants in the study. Indeed, overall, students and teachers were satisfied with this course compared to what had been set up before; it was given an average rating of 3.8 out of 5 on a Likert scale, as opposed to 2.3 previously. The disciplinary supervisors validated the syllabi, and the learners judged the course to be generally relevant to their needs, with an average of 3.9 out of 5. Students also declared having progressed more; 68% of them felt they had progressed, as opposed to 40% previously.

As regards specialising and professionalising components in the syllabus more specifically, the learners reported being quite satisfied. These elements were mentioned positively in 99 learner questionnaires (out of 347 questionnaires); 14 students would have wanted the course to be even more specialised and professional, and 11 students would have liked to talk more about topics not related to music. Some of them remarked:

> "The content corresponded to what I expected, to my future professional needs"[9].

> "The course was in line with my needs as a musicology student"[10].

---

9. Translated from the French: "Contenu adapté à mes attentes, à mon futur professionnel".

10. Translated from the French: "Le cours était en phase avec mes besoins en tant qu'étudiante en musicologie".

"Being able to work on our discipline was a very good exercise, I would really like to be able to continue this"[11].

"I would have liked to go further on the musical themes"[12].

"The LANSOD English course was too specialised: I would like to work on a wider variety of subjects than always music. Maybe on current events, or topics from everyday life"[13].

The training was frequently described by learners as 'complete', 'diversified', or 'varied' (80 occurrences in all questionnaires). The learners were very satisfied with the language activities (4.1/5 on average). The efforts made to meet the needs of each individual were acknowledged (45 occurrences). Personal projects were frequently deemed the most useful learning activity of the course (89 occurrences, or 31% of responses to the question). The learners argued that this component of the course allowed them to progress because they could choose what to work on according to their weaknesses and desires, it triggered pleasure and commitment, and it allowed for greater learning autonomy. To finish, 75% of respondents considered they were more autonomous when learning English than before.

4. Discussion

The case study confirmed the observations made in the context overview: 'professionalisation' was a challenging concept to define, and there were considerable obstacles when trying to set up a more professionalising LANSOD course. Yet, the results of the new LANSOD course tend to indicate that we managed to design a relevant professionalising LANSOD course, and therefore,

---

11. Translated from the French: "Pouvoir travailler sur notre discipline était un très bon exercice, j'aimerais vraiment pouvoir continuer cela".

12. Translated from the French: "J'aurais voulu aller plus loin sur les thèmes musicaux".

13. Translated from the French: "Trop de spécialité dans la formation d'anglais LANSAD : j'aimerais travailler sur des sujets plus variés que toujours la musique. Peut-être sur l'actualité, ou des sujets de la vie quotidienne".

that many challenges can be overcome. An obstacle that is quite difficult to surmount, however, is the lack of proper training for LANSOD teachers, on which we wish to elaborate now.

Zourou and Torresin (2019) have shed light on "the absence of appropriate training during university studies and initial […] education" (p. 41) of LANSOD teachers in Europe, and therefore call for "more sustainable and more professional LSP training opportunities" (p. 27). In this regard, we argue that practitioners should be presented with practical tools to conduct needs analysis and design professionalising training courses. The case study provided an example of a possible method to define the concept of 'professionalisation' and design a syllabus in a LANSOD setting. The method yielded satisfying results, and we argue that each step was instrumental in the overall success of the course. The needs analysis aimed at addressing key questions focussed on defining the notion of 'professionalisation' and its impact on the content and methodology of the L2 course. Many participants took part in the study, which strengthened its reliability, and the design of the course relied on current Second Language Acquisition (SLA) and ESP research. The questionnaires and the interviews helped me gain an insider's view of what 'professionalisation' could mean in that context. Communication situations and language activities that require English in professional settings were identified, which then underpinned the language tasks around which the syllabi were centred. The evaluation of the course based on another set of questionnaires and interviews was key in the general process, helping me measure how relevant the definition and the implementation of 'professionalisation' ultimately were.

From a practical point of view, however, there are limits to this method: it was complex and time-consuming. There were different sets of questionnaires and interviews, different tools were needed for analysing quantitative and qualitative data, and the results are not directly transferable, as the way of defining professionalisation and setting up a LANSOD professionalising course should be adapted to each context. The researcher who conducted this study was also trained in ESP and SLA and was very familiar with needs analysis and course design. That is why an ongoing project consists in testing some of the tools and methods used in this study in other LANSOD contexts to make them more user-friendly and transferable. As far as LSP training is concerned, a recent collaborative European project called CATAPULT aims to "offer training and tools to language teachers teaching [LSP] in adult and higher education, and to therefore make sure they are equipped with the necessary professional skills to train LSP learners in the digital era" (CATAPULT, 2020, para 1). As of May 2020, the consortium had published the results of a situational survey, developed a common competence framework, and set up a massive open online course.

To conclude, the case study highlights that LANSOD classes can have an important role to play in professionalising learners. This point is regularly made by the French ESP community and LSP communities more generally, who reflect on the objectives of LANSOD courses (Sarré & Whyte, 2016; Van der Yeught, 2014) and characterise specialising and professionalising components to introduce them in LANSOD courses. Together with the practitioners and researchers in the field, we argue that the notion of professionalisation should be debated on a more systematic scale and on a broader stage, and practitioners should be encouraged to thoroughly define 'professionalisation' as regards each specific context. This is all the more important at a time when university language education is being reshaped in France, as in April 2020 a ministerial decision imposed that all undergraduate students must take an English certification exam in order to get their diploma[14]. This decision was widely criticised by language experts, who fear that French universities will turn to private certification companies and that language courses will become more standardised (SAES, 2020).

5. Conclusion

The aim of this chapter was to question the notion of 'professionalisation' in the specific context of LANSOD university courses in France. It appeared as a problematic concept and a recent, polymorphous development. Indeed, although

---

14. Arrêté du 3 avril 2020 relatif à la certification en langue anglaise, 2020: https://www.legifrance.gouv.fr/eli/arrete/2020/4/3/ESRS1922076A/jo/texte

'professionalisation' is now a key mission of French universities, its definition is not always clear, and it is integrated and implemented in varying ways and to varying degrees. Supervisors and teachers of LANSOD courses are still struggling to define appropriate objectives and content linked to the language that the students will use in their target professional workplace, so courses are not always relevant in that respect.

The case study conducted at the University of Lille demonstrated how complex the training environment could be. It accounted for why providing learners with relevant LANSOD professionalising courses can indeed be quite challenging. In this particular context, it was argued that professionalising the language course meant specialising content progressively by focussing initially more on disciplinary components, then on professional components, based on communication situations and language activities identified in a needs analysis. The other keywords for the design of the new course were flexibility and diversity in terms of content and teaching and learning methodologies so as to adapt the course to the diversity of the learners' various future professional needs, and autonomy, understood as a transversal competence.

The case study showed that LANSOD courses can be relevant for professionalising learners. Therefore, I have argued that the notion of 'professionalisation' should be debated on a more systematic scale and on a broader stage, whether it applies to the LANSOD courses or to LANSOD teacher training, especially at a time when undergraduate language education is being reshaped in France. To facilitate the design of professionalising LANSOD courses, I believe LANSOD teachers should be presented with ready-to-use tools. The case study provided an example of a procedure for setting up a professionalising LANSOD course, which could be replicated in similar contexts once the tools and methods are tested in other LANSOD contexts to ensure they are user-friendly and less time-consuming.

6. Supplementary materials

https://research-publishing.box.com/s/w8f5hru6fb8kspbi3mchubakjhsewysf

References

Annoot, E., Bobineau, C., Daverne-Bailly, C., Dubois, E., Piot, T., & Vari, J. (2019). *Politiques, pratiques et dispositifs d'aide à la réussite pour les étudiants des premiers cycles à l'université : bilan et perspectives* [Report]. CNESCO.

Basturkmen, H. (2010). *Developing courses in English for specific purposes*. Springer.

Baud, D. (2003). Analyse de genre : la critique de cinéma dans la presse quotidienne britannique. *ASp, la revue du GERAS*, 39-40, 37-45. https://doi.org/10.4000/asp.1282

Bell, S. (2010). Project-based learning for the 21st century: skills for the future. *The Clearing House: A Journal of Educational Strategies, Issues and Ideas, 83*(2), 39-43, https://doi.org/10.1080/00098650903505415

Bourdon, J., Giret, J.-F., & Goudard, M. (2012). Peut-on classer les universités à l'aune de leur performance d'insertion ? *Formation Emploi. Revue Française de Sciences Sociales, 117*, 89-110.

Braud, V., Millot, P., Sarré, C., & Wozniak, S. (2015). « You say you want a revolution... » Contribution à la réflexion pour une politique des langues adaptée au secteur LANSAD. *Recherche et Pratiques Pédagogiques En Langues de Spécialité. Cahiers de l'Apliut, 34*(1), 46-66. https://doi.org/10.4000/apliut.5020

Brudermann, C., Demaison, C., & Benderdouche, F. (2012). Le CECRL : un outil pour construire une politique des langues ? Retour d'expérience sur l'évaluation et la certification à l'UPMC (2009/2011). *Recherche et pratiques pédagogiques en langues de spécialité – Cahiers de l'APLIUT, 31*(3), 31-41. https://doi.org/10.4000/apliut.3033

Brudermann, C., Mattioli, M.-A., Roussel, A.-M., & Sarré, C. (2016). Le secteur des langues pour spécialistes d'autres disciplines dans les universités françaises : résultats d'une enquête nationale menée par la SAES. *Recherche et Pratiques Pédagogiques En Langues de Spécialité. Cahiers de l'Apliut, 35*(spécial 1). https://doi.org/10.4000/apliut.5564

CATAPULT. (2020). *What's CATAPULT?* http://catapult-project.eu/

Causa, M., & Derivry-Plard, M. (2013). Un paradoxe de l'enseignement des langues dans le supérieur : diversification des cours pour les étudiants et absence de formation appropriée pour les enseignants. In M. Derivry-Plard, P. Faure & C. Brudermann (Eds), *Apprendre les langues à l'université au 21e siècle*. Riveneuve Éditions.

Chirache, S., & Vincens, J. (1992). *Rapport de la commission professionnalisation des enseignements supérieurs*. HCEE.

Deyrich, M.-C. (2004). Exploration didactique de la langue du milieu professionnel à l'université : quel apport pour la définition de tâches d'enseignement-apprentissage? *ASp. La Revue Du GERAS, 43-44*, 125-134. https://doi.org/10.4000/asp.1106

Doray, P., Tremblay, E., & Groleau, A. (2015). Quelle professionnalisation dans les universités québécoises ? *Formation Emploi. Revue Française de Sciences Sociales, 129*, 47-64.

Ellis, R. (2005). Principles of instructed language learning. *System, 33*(2), 209-224. https://doi.org/10.1016/j.system.2004.12.006

Fave-Bonnet, M.-F. (2012). Postface : des étudiants en quête d'avenir. *Formation Emploi. Revue Française de Sciences Sociales, 117*, 111-115.

Forrier, A., & Sels, L. (2003). The concept employability: Aa complex mosaic. *International Journal of Human Resources Development and Management, 3*(1), 102-124. https://doi.org/10.1504/ijhrdm.2003.002414

Gachassin, B., Labbé, S., & Mias, C. (2013). Les étudiants face à la professionnalisation à l'université. Exemple en sciences de l'éducation. *Recherche & formation, 73*(2), 37-56. https://doi.org/10.4000/rechercheformation.2087

Gayraud, L., Simon-Zarca, G., & Soldano, C. (2011). Université : les défis de la professionnalisation. *Notes, Emploi, Formation (Céreq), 46*, 36.

Gilabert, R. (2005). Evaluating the use of multiple sources and methods in needs analysis: a case study of journalists in the Autonomous Community of Catalonia (Spain). In M. H. Long (Ed.), *Second language needs analysis* (pp. 182-199). Cambridge University Press. https://doi.org/10.1017/cbo9780511667299.007

Gould, C. (2001). L'Art Internet ou la médiation esthétisée : contribution à la réflexion sur l'anglais dans les filières artistiques. *ASp, la revue du GERAS*, 31-33. https://doi.org/10.4000/asp.1884

Hardy, M. (2013a). Editorial. *Recherche et Pratiques Pédagogiques En Langues de Spécialité : Cahiers de l'APLIUT, 32*(1). http://journals.openedition.org/apliut/3535

Hardy, M. (2013b). Editorial. *Recherche et Pratiques Pédagogiques En Langues de Spécialité : Cahiers de l'APLIUT, 32*(2). https://journals.openedition.org/apliut/3754

Iglesias-Philippot, Y. (2013). L'éthique dans l'enseignement-apprentissage des langues de spécialité : le cas de l'espagnol en Économie. *Recherche et Pratiques Pédagogiques En Langues de Spécialité. Cahiers de l'Apliut, 32*(2), 82-103. https://doi.org/10.4000/apliut.3782

La Borderie, R. (1998). *Lexique de l'éducation*. Nathan.

Labetoulle, A. (2017). Dynamic and complex system approach to needs analysis, course development and evaluation of LANSOD courses in a French musicology undergraduate programme. In C. Sarré & S. Whyte (Eds), *New developments in ESP teaching and learning research* (pp. 31-50). Research-publishing.net. https://doi.org/10.14705/rpnet.2017.cssw2017.744

Leroux, J.-Y. (2014). The professionalisation of degree courses in France. *Higher Education Management and Policy, 24*(3), 87-105. https://doi.org/10.1787/hemp-24-5jz8tqsdn4s1

Lesiak-Bielawska, E. (2014). English for instrumentalists: designing and evaluating an ESP course. *English for Specific Purposes World, 15*(43), 1-32.

Macré, N. (2014). Les apprenants LANSAD de niveau A2/B1 en première année d'anglais en autonomie accompagnée médiatisée : quels besoins? *Recherche et Pratiques Pédagogiques En Langues de Spécialité. Cahiers de l'Apliut, 33*(2), 118-142. https://doi.org/10.4000/apliut.5053

Mémet, M. (2001). Bref historique de l'enseignement et de la recherche en anglais de spécialité en France : de l'anglais pour non-spécialistes à l'anglistique du secteur LANSAD. In M. Mémet & M. Perrin (Eds), *L'anglais de spécialité en France, mélanges en l'honneur de Michel Perrin* (pp. 309-319). GERAS.

Narcy-Combes, M.-F. (2003). La communication interculturelle en anglais des affaires : transfert ou conflit d'interprétation? Analyse d'une pratique d'enseignement en LEA. *ASp. La Revue Du GERAS, 39-40*, 119-129. https://doi.org/10.4000/asp.1341

Narcy-Combes, J.-P. (2005). *Didactique des langues et TIC : vers une recherche-action responsable*. Ophrys.

Neumeier, P. (2005). A closer look at blended learning—parameters for designing a blended learning environment for language teaching and learning. *ReCALL, 17*(2), 163-178. https://doi.org/10.1017/s0958344005000224

Péchou, A., & Stenton, A. (2001). Encadrer la médiation : le cas de la prononciation. *ASp. La Revue Du GERAS, 31-33*, 153-162. https://doi.org/10.4000/apliut.3470

Renaut, A. (1995). *Les révolutions de l'université : essai sur la modernisation de la culture*. Calmann-Lévy.

Resche, C. (1996). La terminologie comparée au service de l'enseignement en langue de spécialité en 3e cycle DEA Monnaie-Finance-Banque. *ASp. La Revue Du GERAS, 11-14*, 195-205. https://doi.org/10.4000/asp.3501

SAES. (2020, April 9). Société des anglicistes de l'enseignement supérieur. *Communiqué de la SAES, 9 avril 2020*. http://saesfrance.org/wp-content/uploads/2020/04/Communiqu%C3%A9-de-la-SAES-9-avril-2020.pdf

Sarré, C., Millot, P., Wozniak, S., & Braud, V. (2017, May 8). « Non, Brian n'est pas dans la cuisine, il est au boulot » : quelle formation linguistique pour les étudiants non-linguistes ? *The Conversation.* www.theconversation.com/non-brian-nest-pas-dans-la-cuisine-il-est-au-boulot-quelle-formation-linguistique-pour-les-etudiants-non-linguistes-75671

Sarré, C., & Whyte, S. (2016). Research in ESP teaching and learning in French higher education: developing the construct of ESP didactics. *ASp. La Revue Du GERAS, 69,* 139-164. https://doi.org/10.4000/asp.4834

Saville-Troike, M. (2008). *The ethnography of communication: an introduction* (vol. 14). John Wiley & Sons.

Serafini, E. J., Lake, J. B., & Long, M. H. (2015). Needs analysis for specialized learner populations: essential methodological improvements. *English for Specific Purposes, 40,* 11-26. https://doi.org/10.1016/j.esp.2015.05.002

Sešek, U. (2007). English for teachers of EFL–toward a holistic description. *English for Specific Purposes, 26*(4), 411-427. https://doi.org/10.1016/j.esp.2006.11.001

Stavrou, S. (2011). La « professionnalisation » comme catégorie de réforme à l'université en France. De l'expertise aux effets curriculaires. *Cahiers de La Recherche Sur l'éducation et Les Savoirs, Hors-série n° 3,* 93-109.

Swales, J. M. (2004). *Research genres: explorations and applications.* Cambridge University Press.

Thompson, G., & McKinley, J. (2018). Integration of content and language learning. In J. I. Liontas, M. DelliCarpini, & S. Abrar-ul-Hassan (Eds), *The TESOL encyclopedia of English language teaching* (pp. 1-13). Wiley. https://doi.org/10.1002/9781118784235

Toffoli, D., & Speranza, L. (2016). L'autonomie comme facteur déterminant dans la réussite d'un enseignement Lansad en sciences historiques. *Recherche et Pratiques Pédagogiques En Langues de Spécialité. Cahiers de l'Apliut, 35*(Spécial 1). https://doi.org/10.4000/apliut.5505

Van der Yeught, M. (2014). Développer les langues de spécialité dans le secteur LANSAD – scénarios possibles et parcours recommandé pour contribuer à la professionnalisation des formations. *Recherche et pratiques pédagogiques en langues de spécialité. Cahiers de l'Apliut, 33*(1), 12-32. https://doi.org/10.4000/apliut.4153

Van der Yeught, M. (2016, August 23). *Developing English for specific purposes (ESP) in Europe: mainstream approaches and complementary advances* [Sub-plenary lecture]. ESSE Conference, Galway, Ireland.

Van der Yeught, M. (2017). L'étude de cas en anglais financier et ses fondements théoriques. *Les Langues Modernes, Association Des Professeurs de Langues Vivantes*. https://hal.archives-ouvertes.fr/hal-01632980/document

Wedekind, V. (2018). Vocational versus occupational qualifications: is there a difference, and does it make a difference? [transcription of the Chairperson's Lecture]. https://doi.org/10.13140/RG.2.2.16681.70241

Whyte, S. (2013). Teaching ESP: a task-based framework for French graduate courses. *ASp. La Revue Du GERAS*, *63*, 5-30. https://doi.org/10.4000/asp.3280

Whyte, S. (2016). Who are the specialists? Teaching and learning specialized language in French educational contexts. *Recherche et Pratiques Pédagogiques En Langues de Spécialité. Cahiers de l'Apliut*, *35*(Spécial 1). https://doi.org/10.4000/apliut.5487

Wozniak, S., & Millot, P. (2016). La langue de spécialité en dispute. Quel objet de connaissance pour le secteur Lansad ? *Recherche et Pratiques Pédagogiques En Langues de Spécialité. Cahiers de l'Apliut*, *35*(spécial 1). https://doi.org/10.4000/apliut.5496

Zourou, K., & Torresin, G. (2019). *CATAPULT - Situational Survey: LSP teachers' needs for skills and training*. CATAPULT consortium. http://catapult-project.eu/wp-content/uploads/2019/05/O1_Full_Report_Final_CATAPULT.pdf

4. Graduate student teacher voices: perception of and apprenticeship in multiliteracies-oriented teaching

Tara Hashemi[1]

1. Introduction

As Lord, Liskin-Gasparro, and Lacorte (2013) put it, "it is to everyone's benefit that our graduate students become well-prepared, competent language teachers. The graduate students benefit, of course, but so do the students in the language courses and the department as a whole" (p. 107). Approximately 77.5% of Graduate Student Teachers (GSTs) assigned to Foreign Language (FL) departments support language learners at the important stages of beginner and intermediate development (Allen, 2011). However, relatively little effort is made by FL departments to ensure that GSTs receive appropriate professional development, and yet "good teaching doesn't happen by accident" (White, Martin, Hodge, & Stimson, 2008, p. 18). In 2007, the Modern Language Association (MLA) recommended to "provide substantive training in language teaching and in the use of new technologies" (MLA, 2007, p. 7) and "enhance and reward graduate student training" (p. 8) so GSTs would be better prepared to help FL students reach "translingual and transcultural competence" (p. 3). The report, however, did not provide guidelines on the content or form that this professionalization should take in order to achieve its goals (as discussed by Allen & Dupuy, 2010; Allen & Negueruela-Azarola, 2010). While it was suggested that literacy-based approaches might be particularly appropriate to achieve the report's recommendations, less attention was given to the nature

---

1. California State University, Fresno, California, United States; tarahashemi@csufresno.edu

How to cite this chapter: Hashemi, T. (2020). Graduate student teacher voices: perception of and apprenticeship in multiliteracies-oriented teaching. In B. Dupuy and M. Grosbois (Eds), *Language learning and professionalization in higher education: pathways to preparing learners and teachers in for the 21st century* (pp. 99-134). Research-publishing.net. https://doi.org/10.14705/rpnet.2020.44.1103

of professional development opportunities that should be offered to GSTs in order for them to be better able to instantiate such approaches in their classrooms.

Given the frontline position held by GSTs when curricular reform efforts are being undertaken (Gómez Soler & Tecedor, 2018) and in a context in which little is known about the changes that need to be introduced in GSTs' professional development to facilitate the implementation of literacy-based teaching at the basic level, the purpose of the current study aimed at examining GSTs' perceptions of the use of such approaches as well as the professional development opportunities they have received in order to teach in ways that align with such approaches. The current study's results show that although it is clear that GSTs in programs informed by a literacy-based framework receive what they perceive as adequate professional development, they still would like more opportunities to improve their teaching skills.

2. Literature review

2.1. Overview of GSTs' professional development in FL programs

In an effort to move away from the 'fragmented' and 'unfocused' (Freeman, 1989) approach to GSTs' professional development, scholars have for many years advocated that FL departments provide graduate students with several opportunities to enhance their professional development. Very often due to time and budget restrictions, the most typical opportunities adopted by FL departments remain as of today a preservice workshop or orientation, a one-semester long methodology course, occasional observations conducted by a GST's supervisor or an experienced GST, and occasional meetings that most often focus on housekeeping issues. With over a decade apart, Di Donato (1983) and Azevedo (1999) provided several guidelines meant to prepare preservice GSTs in about a week-long orientation context. Di Donato (1983) explained that during this time, GSTs should be exposed to a 'shock' language session and experience first-hand what it is like to be a basic language student. He further suggested that orientation should also provide an opportunity for GSTs to partake into collaborative sample lesson planning, get familiarized with university and departmental policies, be introduced to former first-year GSTs, get acquainted with available material (labs, textbooks), and participate in other interventions. Azevedo (1999) also argued that a preservice workshop is the least preparation that should be offered to GSTs. He added that orientation could also serve as a time to perform a teaching demo and to get to meet not only the GSTs' direct supervisor but also higher hierarchy faculty members.

Ryan-Scheutz and Rustia (1999) however underscored that while a preservice workshop might theoretically seem beneficial to GSTs, it would be unrealistic to expect them to be competent and well prepared to teach after only a week of orientation. That is why in-service professional development is also crucial to GSTs' training in teaching. Allen and Negueruela-Azarola (2010) showed that in-service professional development often takes the shape of a three-credit methods course for new GSTs concurrent to their first teaching assignment and usually focuses on lower-level language instruction. It thus represents for many GSTs the core of their training as FL instructors, hence the numerous scholarly articles that analyze its efficacy, constraints, and need for improvements. In an empirical study aiming at finding out how the FL methods course had evolved since the 1940's, Warford (2003) concluded that it had shifted from "a prescriptive approach focusing on an essential core of pedagogical knowledge to a way of seeing FL teaching that puts teacher beliefs and decisions making at the core of the curriculum" (p. 29). Yet, the author highlighted the fact that, as recommended by the contemporary literature, it might be time to "articulate a course sequence beyond the one-semester methods course" (Warford, 2003, p. 33) that defines one out of three main criticisms against the method course that I will discuss later in this chapter.

Most studies in considering GST training reform have called for fundamental change in the training structure (e.g. Arens, 2010) or have made concrete pedagogical suggestions for educating future FL professors (Blyth, 2011; Enkin, 2015).

2.2. The issue of the current professional development structure

As can be seen from the above-mentioned approaches to GST professional development, FL departments are still primarily in a 'teacher training paradigm' addressing short-term teaching-centered themes and not so much in a 'professional development' dynamic that reflects long-term needs of graduate students (Allen & Dupuy, 2010). In very few cases will GSTs ever have to select course materials, collaborate on the development of a curriculum or a syllabus, or even have the occasion to partake in an informed discussion about their performance with experts in language pedagogy (a fundamental part of GSTs' training according to Brandl, 2000).

Given the current makeup of GST training, one is left to wonder whether the goals of professional development set by the ad hoc MLA committee in 2007, namely that it should "provide substantive training in language teaching and in the use of new technologies" (MLA, 2007, p. 7) and "enhance and reward graduate student training" (p. 8) in order to create "educated speakers who have deep translingual and transcultural competence" (p. 3), can be achieved. The lack of guidelines on content or form to be able to reach these goals (as discussed by Allen & Dupuy, 2010; Allen & Negueruela-Azarola, 2010) might be part of the problem.

As Lord et al. (2013) pointed out, "a preservice orientation, a teaching methods course, and ongoing professional development opportunities and workshops" are elements that "share the primary function of ensuring that instructors have the knowledge and skills needed to carry out their duties" (p. 107). In reality, the literature shows that GSTs may not uniformly receive training based on these proven methods, or even tailored to their specific needs as instructors from varied disciplinary backgrounds. In this respect, the specter of disciplinary turf wars looms large over the topic of appropriate and effective teacher training.

Though the methods course is the only guaranteed opportunity during which substantive training in language teaching is provided to GSTs in most universities, many scholars have highlighted its flaws (Allen & Dupuy, 2010; Allen & Negueruela-Azarola, 2010; Allen, Paesani, & Dupuy, 2011; Angus,

2016; Freeman, 1989; Grosse, 1993). Indeed, it appears that most methods classes today may continue to rely on an inadequate and outdated model of transmission of knowledge (Johnson, 2009) that compresses large amounts of theory into a single-semester course. Freeman (1993) referred to this as the frontloading model, where GSTs are provided with maximum knowledge to be used in their immediate professional development to meet the short-term needs of the department in which they teach rather than an investment in their long-term professional development. Furthermore, this approach has also been proven to be problematic by studies that focus on GSTs' perspectives over their training in language teaching. Novice GSTs are sometimes unwilling and maybe even unable to translate the instructed theory from the methods course to their classroom (Allen, 2011; Brandl, 2000; Rankin & Becker, 2006). Wilbur (2007) argued that this might be due to the fact that most activities in the methods course often fail to illustrate a connection between theory and practice. What might also influence the theory/practice gap for GSTs is the standardized approach of the methods course, which fails to acknowledge the various backgrounds of graduate students. Indeed, as Allen and Negueruela-Azarola (2010) argued, the "one-size-fits-all professional development model does not reflect the reality of graduate students as diverse individuals with varied cultural and educational backgrounds and unique needs" (p. 388).

Finally, and probably most importantly, because the methods course mostly focuses on training GSTs to teach in lower-division FL classes without introducing them to strategies for teaching upper-division literature or content classes, it further promotes the long-standing 'two-tiered' system that divides language and literature faculty and results in a precarious situation for SLA-focused faculty and graduate students operating in these departments, and even arrogance on the part of literature faculty when considering the importance of teaching, as "teaching language is consistently viewed as a less sophisticated, hence less difficult, task than teaching literature" (Kramsch, 1993, p. 7). Along the same line, Bernhardt (2001) added that:

> "[i]t is indeed within 'the methods course' that the (future) profession is socialized into the 'lang-lit split'. [...] If the only teacher preparation

available is language teacher preparation, a clear message is sent that language gets taught, but the corollary collocation for literature remains awkward. A further part of the message communicated within the structure of the traditional methods course is that language and literature are clearly separable units. As long as this message is sent from the outset of the graduate student socialization process, the 'lang-lit split' will remain entrenched in graduate departments" (p. 199).

2.3. GSTs' perceptions of their professional development

While the professionalization of GSTs may still have some limitations, studies examining their experiences working in FL programs are relatively few. Gonglewski and Penningroth (1998), Brandl (2000), and Angus (2016) examined GSTs' perceptions of professional development opportunities available to them and found that overall GSTs desire more opportunities for collaboration in publication, conference presentations, and course development. They however do not usually take the initiative to request any of these opportunities, primarily because of their lack of confidence in themselves as future scholars. Interestingly, some GSTs seem to favor their roles as 'researcher' or 'student' over their professionalization as teachers, which Angus (2016) explained to be "unsurprising given the two-tiered system that exists in some FL departments [(MLA, 2007)]" (p. 834).

Among all possible forms of professional development opportunities, GSTs appear to value informal discussions with peers and their supervisor, end-of-course student evaluations, and small-group student interviews most. Angus (2016) also reported that collaborating in teaching courses, reading current research about language teaching, and assembling a teaching portfolio were selected by GSTs as making the greatest contributions to their success in their current roles.

Zannirato and Sánchez-Serrano (2009) and Gómez Soler and Tecedor (2018) examined differences in perceptions of training effectiveness between GSTs and different departmental stakeholders, including Language Program Directors (LPDs). They found substantial differences of opinion between GSTs and faculty in charge of the training regarding the different professionalization opportunities. For LPDs, GST training must include lesson planning sessions, lectures targeting in-classroom and out-of-classroom time management, and SLA theory and practice. On the other hand, GSTs expressed a preference for 'how-to' workshops (how to lesson plan, prepare exams, motivate students, grade, teach grammar), interaction with senior GSTs on 'what students have responded well to in the past' or on 'good or bad experiences of activities that work or don't work', and classroom visits (i.e. by all new teachers to other new experienced teachers). While most GSTs agreed on the usefulness of some sort of formal training in FL teaching, to the question "I feel the department should do more to train me in foreign language teaching", only 23% GSTs responded that they agreed. Zannirato and Sánchez-Serrano (2009) explained that more work needed to be done to understand this contradiction but that the respondents' inflated levels of self-confidence in their teaching might be reduced with more training to reveal their basic needs and gaps in knowledge of teaching preparation. Similar observations as the ones reported above were made by Mills and Allen (2007) and Mills (2011), who found that GSTs were not confident in their ability to teach literature even though they had reported satisfaction with the amount of professional development they had received in general. The authors argued that "since [Teaching Assistants (TAs)] essentially never teach such content courses, the limited amount of professional development that they do receive has tended to focus on instructional approaches that are appropriate in the first four semesters – that is, for beginning- and intermediate-level courses" (Mills & Allen, 2007, p. 231), which explains the findings.

Furthermore, it seems that all parties suffer from "problems of discord and disenfranchisement at the departmental level and on some classroom-specific or administrative issues" (Gómez Soler & Tecedor, 2018, p. 48), which often stem from curricular bifurcation with differences in objectives between lower-level classes that are more focused on language and advanced-level classes focused on literature.

In sum, even with the dearth of studies examining the experiences of GSTs working in FL programs, previous research seems to point toward a disconnect between the professional development opportunities available to GSTs and their actual use of these resources. GSTs' lack of perceived importance of what is offered by language programs and the discrepancy that exists between what they need and what they would like to receive as professional development might explain why this training is based on immediate teaching needs rather than long-term professionalization goals.

2.4. The literacy-based framework

The MLA (2007) report called for a replacement of "the two-tiered language-literature structure with a broader and more coherent curriculum in which language, culture, and literature are taught as a continuous whole", arguing that it would "reinvigorate language departments as valuable academic units central to the humanities and to the missions of institutions of higher learning" (p. 3). Drawing on the concept of multiliteracies (New London Group, 1996), several scholars (e.g. Allen & Paesani, 2010; Kern, 2000; Paesani, Allen, & Dupuy, 2015; Swaffar & Arens, 2005) foregrounded the notion of these newly redefined literacies as a possible way forward to unifying the undergraduate FL curriculum, as they could "envelop communication in the textual" (Paesani et al., 2015, p. 9) throughout the four-year FL curricular sequence. Such an approach has been articulated in a variety of ways in the literature and all rely on the same critical set of notions and assumptions, namely,

> "(1) a view of language as a socioculturally situated semiotic system (Halliday, 1978), and of language learning as a process of gaining access to meaning-making resources; (2) a curriculum that is 'text'-based including written and multimodal texts; and (3) a pedagogy that emphasizes 'what texts do and how texts mean rather than what they mean'" (Bazerman & Prior, 2004, p. 3, cited in Kumagai, López-Sánchez, & Wu, 2015, p. 3).

In other words, such a curriculum merges language and content while focusing on contextualized language use through meaningful interaction with authentic literary and non-literary texts. As put by Kern (2000), this purpose-sensitive and dynamic view of literacy "entails at least a tacit awareness of the relationships between textual conventions and their contexts of use, and ideally, the ability to reflect critically on these relationships" all while "drawing on a wide range of cognitive abilities, on knowledge of written and spoken language, on knowledge of genres, and on cultural knowledge" (p. 16). Paesani et al. (2015) add that a literacy-based framework "unifies, rather than separates, the study of language and the study of literary-cultural content" (p. 22), including "an understanding of the relationships among various oral, written, and visual forms and how these forms contribute to textual meaning; the ability to construct meaning through the process of creating and transforming knowledge; and a recognition of the dynamic nature of language and the socially and culturally embedded resources used in literacy-based practices" (p. 21).

In the multiliteracies framework, "meaning design" reflects the view of "discovering" in learning "because it is a dynamic process of discovering form-meaning connections through the acts of interpreting and creating written, oral, visual, audiovisual, and digital texts" (Paesani et al., 2015, p. 23). To be able to 'meaning design', the New London Group (1996) evokes four different components/stages to be implemented in a lesson plan: situated practice, overt instruction, critical framing, and transformed practice. In the situated practice stage, learners use their real lived experiences to deduce meaning from a text by looking at what is 'available' to them (culturally, linguistically, socially). In overt instruction, learners refer to the metalanguage (Kern, 2000) of the text and understand it enough to be able to reuse it in the 'transformed practice' stage of the lesson. Critical framing relies on the learner's understanding of the text from a sociocultural perspective. Finally, 'transformed practice' sees learners using acquired knowledge of the text to elaborate a new text of their own, by adapting or adding to it for example. These pedagogical stages may occur in any order but must occur not only concurrently but also in a related way.

It cannot be expected that GSTs will understand and apply the complex notions on which the multiliteracies framework and multiliteracies pedagogy are built without proper professional development. In fact, Allen and Paesani (2010) explained that "given the predominance of CLT (Communicative Language Teaching) in introductory-level textbooks and pedagogical materials, graduate [TAs] and part-time instructors teaching in introductory programs are by necessity trained in CLT, and thus may have limited or no knowledge of alternative frameworks, such as the multiliteracies approach, or how to apply them in the classroom" (p. 125).

In two longitudinal case studies, Allen (2011) and Allen and Dupuy (2012) analyzed the conceptual development of novice GSTs. Allen (2011) explained that the most valuable opportunities where her participants developed concepts about the literacy-based framework were two pedagogy seminars as well as ongoing dialogic mediation with their LPD. Allen (2011) concluded her study by suggesting that "expanding formal pedagogy instruction for FL graduate students beyond the methods course and focusing on one framing construct relevant to language and literary-cultural teaching" (p. 101) while maximizing extant forms of professional development such as the methods course and classroom observations would contribute to "articulate alternative means of supporting conceptual growth" (p. 101). In fact, Allen and Dupuy (2012) demonstrated how GSTs' participation in an advanced pedagogy seminar several semesters after they had taken a methods course contributed to their conceptual understandings of literacy, its application in classroom instruction, and its role as a framework to structure the undergraduate FL curriculum (p. 186). As mentioned in the above-cited studies, a literacy-based framework would support the replacement of a two-tiered language-literature structure and as such, with relevant professional development opportunities, would bolster GSTs' confidence in their ability to teach across the four-year language curriculum.

3. Methodology

3.1. Research questions

In a context where current common professionalization options might not entirely succeed in providing GSTs with adequate knowledge and experience to implement the MLA (2007) report recommendations and more specifically teach within a literacy-based approach, this study sought answers to the following Research Questions (RQ):

> RQ1: How do GSTs understand a literacy-based approach to teaching, and how do they respond to being taught about it?

> RQ2: How are GSTs teaching in a literacy-based curriculum professionalized?

> RQ3: What are GSTs' perceptions of their professional development as it relates to the literacy-based framework?

3.2. Participants and context of the study

After approval was received from the Institutional Review Board, a questionnaire was distributed by email in the fall of 2018 to GSTs teaching in literacy-based FL programs in three different U.S. public institutions and four different language programs. Study participants were recruited from language programs that had recently undergone curricular changes guided by the multiliteracies framework so that they would align with the recommendations of the MLA (2007) report. These programs were specifically selected based on the published research done by the LPDs regarding the programs they are or were directing. Data about each LPD was also collected in order to better understand their academic rank and background, as it would reflect on the type of professional development they might favor (Table 1 below).

Twenty-four GSTs teaching and studying in four different language programs (in French, German, and Spanish) at three different public universities agreed to participate. Sixteen were domestic students and eight were international, and their teaching experience ranged from less than a year to three years. Three were pursuing a Master's degree, and the remaining 21 were enrolled in a doctoral program. For additional demographic data, see supplementary materials, Appendix 1.

Table 1. LPDs in charge of participants' programs

Language Program	Gender	Rank	PhD in	Language in charge of	Years as LPD	University
1	Female	Associate Professor	German Studies	German	5 to 10 years	Western R1 Public
2	Female	Assistant Professor	Linguistics	Spanish	1 to 5 years	Midwestern R1 Public
3	Female	Associate Professor	French/Education	French	5 to 10 years	Midwestern R1 Public
4	Female	Professor	Applied Linguistics	French	over 10 years	Western R1 Public

3.3. Data collection and analysis

Data were collected by means of a questionnaire that included both closed and open-ended questions. Participants took on average 28 minutes to complete the questionnaire. It focused on three main topic areas: the participant's biographical information (eight questions), the participant's personal conception of multiliteracies-oriented language teaching (nine questions), and the participant's nature and perceived quality of professional development opportunities (five questions). For every question, participants had to choose among a predesigned list of options and were always offered the possibility of adding their own choices.

Quantitative results were analyzed using Excel. To supplement and elaborate on the quantitative data, qualitative data were collected through the open-ended questions of the questionnaire. I used an inductive approach to code the qualitative data and looked for recurring themes related to multiliteracies teaching and professional development.

4. Findings

Findings for each research question are reported in turn.

4.1. RQ1: How do GSTs understand a literacy-based approach to teaching and how do they respond to being taught about it?

To answer this first research question, I focused on responses related to multiliteracies-oriented teaching, definitions of a multiliteracies approach, and text use. When asked if they believed their teaching was anchored in a multiliteracies perspective, a majority of the study participants reported that it was. The remaining participants replied that they were not sure because of the use of certain methods that they judged contrary to multiliteracies-oriented teaching (Figure 1).

Figure 1. Multiliteracies-oriented teaching

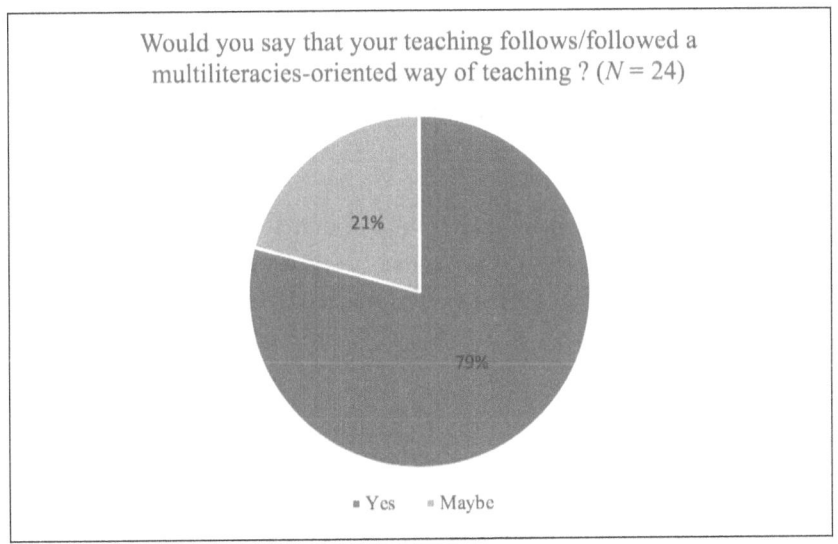

Emily, a fourth-year PhD student in Hispanic and Lusophone literatures, cultures, and linguistics and a GST in advanced-level Spanish, explained that because of the nature of the class she was teaching (a 'writing intensive' class), she had to focus on explicit grammar lessons "to support stronger writing skills" which to her brings a certain nuance to multiliteracies-oriented teaching. Just like Emily, Kimmy, a PhD student in French literature and a GST in French, indicated that she was not comfortable saying that her teaching was multiliteracies-oriented because of the way she introduced grammar in her classroom (she used "overt grammar instruction", which would not be considered consistent with a multiliteracies-oriented way of teaching). However, her use of authentic texts "whenever possible" and the pre, during, and post scaffolding activities she used were more multiliteracies oriented, which told her that her teaching was a "mix of communicative multiliteracies and overt instruction". By communicative instruction, it is assumed that Kimmy meant instruction that fell within CLT. Other reasons for arguing that their teaching might not follow a multiliteracies orientation included the lack of 'transformed practice' activities in which students get to apply what they have learned in new ways because "the classes are too short" (Anna) or because of the heavy focus on a certain kind of text rather than another ("my class has a heavy literature focus", Kristen).

Kate, who used to teach a Global Simulation (GS) class in French, also answered that

> "in the beginning (pre-GS) [the class] did not follow an ML approach, as I was not as sensitive to that approach at the time. In the development of the GS, principles of ML were incorporated by using the [four curricular components] as a guide to plan different ways of getting students to engage with texts".

GSTs who replied that their teaching was indeed multiliteracies-oriented justified it by either explaining that it was because of the nature of the materials they used or the kinds of activities carried out by students. Peter, for example, mentioned, "I use authentic materials and different media", and Gerdine added, "I use a variety of texts such as music videos, music, poems, statistics and books from Germany to teach the students". One could however argue that using authentic materials/sources could also be part of a communicative language teaching-oriented classroom; what one does with texts is more indicative of one's orientation to teaching than the types of texts used. Other participants focused on the types of activities they conducted with students to show that their teaching was multiliteracies-oriented:

> "With these texts I guide students through pre, during, and post text reflection, focusing first on global meaning before drawing their attention to detail, and finally using an expansion activity to have them recycle pieces of the text in their own work" (Kimmy).

> "I scaffold my lessons around the processes of experiencing, analyzing, practicing, transforming, and reflecting" (Cassy).

While most GSTs replied that their teaching was multiliteracies-oriented, it was important to know what that implied for them. Participants were asked, "How would you define a multiliteracies-oriented approach to language teaching"? The definitions provided by the study participants were divided into two main groups: definitions with an emphasis on the nature of material used (such as Laura's: "Using a wide variety of literature and other types of written/spoken media to assist in teaching language") and definitions with an emphasis on the types of activities that would be included in a multiliteracies-oriented approach (such as Daphne's: "Integrating all the skills, not trying to teach them in isolation, and way of teaching"; supplementary materials, Appendix 2).

In order to find out how participants engaged in multiliteracies-oriented teaching, GSTs were asked to say more about their use of texts in the classroom. All GSTs but two reported that they used texts to introduce something new (a new topic, a new grammatical point, new vocabulary). Over half reported using texts as "models to teach many skills that students can then reproduce" (Helen). Two GSTs from Program 2 reported relying on their textbooks to find texts once a week to teach culture: "we have an online textbook and each chapter has a short excerpt that is called the 'lectura'. Thursdays in class we go over strategies and then answer questions on it" (Renee). Sandra explained that most texts from lectura are aimed at "practicing reading" and "doing activities based on the content of the text".

4.2. RQ2: How are GSTs teaching in a literacy-based curriculum professionalized?

GSTs were asked to report the kind of professional development opportunities in which they had participated (Table 2).

Table 2. GSTs' participation in professional development opportunities

Professional development opportunity	Count (N=24)
Preservice orientation	24
Methods course	22
In-service meetings	18
In-class visit by my language program director	22
Other	5

The data show that all participants reported having taken a methods course, including two GSTs who reported having taken their methods course at their previous institution while completing a master's degree. All GSTs reported that they had participated in a preservice orientation. A total of six participants indicated that they did not have any in-service meetings. They were all from different institutions (three [33.3%] from Language Program 1, including two former GSTs, one [11%] from Language Program 2, and one [33.3%] From Language Program 3). Most participants (91%) had classroom visitations from their language program director or a graduate student coordinator at least once a semester. Other professional opportunities reported by four (16%) GSTs included co-teaching sessions, workshops and conferences, and classroom material sharing.

The GSTs were also asked to provide a brief description of the professional development opportunities in which they had participated. An analysis of their descriptions revealed very little variation between their experiences across the four language programs included in this study. Consequently, all participants' answers were combined while still providing details about the content of each professional development opportunity.

4.2.1. The preservice orientation

All participants reported that they had participated in a week-long preservice orientation before the start of the fall semester when they were incoming GSTs. It was conducted by the LPD and included presentations from the FL department's administrators as well. GSTs described it as the time when they were introduced to the language program's culture, the syllabus with which they would be working, and the teaching method adopted in the level they would be teaching. The preservice orientation was also the time GSTs got familiarized with the adopted textbook and its online platform. Finally, GSTs reported that their preservice orientation included teaching demonstrations by senior GSTs or language professors from other language programs.

4.2.2. The methods course

In all four language programs included in this study, the methods course consisted of a three-credit course offered in the fall semester. Although usually taught by an LPD, it was not always taught by the LPD of the language program in which a GST taught, and the course appears to have been taught by different professors every year, which led to variation in the GSTs' experiences since each professor might follow a different approach to teaching this course. Overall, the data show that the methods course introduced a myriad of different teaching approaches. Some GSTs reported that it was very general, and others reported it had a strong focus on communicative language teaching or on literacy-based teaching. Students from Language Programs 1 and 4 also had as part of their methods class hour-long sessions, usually led by a senior graduate student from their language programs. One student wrote, "there was a departmental breakout session that at the time did not align with the content of the methods course whatsoever" (Daphne).

4.2.3. In-service meetings

The GSTs' experience with the in-service meetings varied as the frequency and content of the meetings differed greatly. GSTs from Language Program 1 reported meeting every week or every other week; GSTs from Language Program 2 every other month; GSTs from Language Program 3 and 4 every month. Meetings were conducted by the LPD and the GSTs' course coordinator when applicable (Language Program 3). The in-service meetings served as time to discuss "course-specific issues (tests, projects, students), but also teaching in general" (Kristen). GSTs reported that it is during in-service meetings that they usually bring up questions they might be facing in their teaching: "In-service orientation gave me the opportunity to discuss any concern and issues that you could have in our classrooms" (Elodie).

4.2.4. Classroom visitations

The frequency of classroom visitations varied as well. While GSTs in Language Programs 1 and 2 reported being observed teaching once per semester, those in Language Programs 2 and 4 reported being observed once in the fall semester "during our 5th week of the semester" (Sandra). GSTs from Program 3 were visited by the LPD in the fall and by the head GST in the spring, whereas the GSTs in other programs were visited by the LPD. All class visits were done by at least the LPD or the head GST, and in the context of Language Program 1, the LPD was accompanied by other GSTs. All visits appeared to be followed by a post-observation meeting where the GSTs received feedback on their teaching: The "director came to watch class and then discussed positive and negative aspects of my teaching in a one-on-one meeting" (Laura) and the impact of the lesson on students: "We discussed how the overall class went" (Callie).

4.2.5. Ranking of professional development opportunities

The GSTs were asked to rank the above-cited professional development opportunities from most useful to least useful for their understanding of what is involved with a multiliteracies approach. Many students from Language Program 1 reported that all the above-cited professional development opportunities were seen as somewhat helpful, but the methods class was the professional development opportunity that garnered the most uneven support. Laura indicated, "I have found all four to be helpful", and Helen wrote, "I don't find any of these very much more beneficial than the others". Gerdine volunteered, "I don't consider any of these to have been unhelpful". It is however worth noticing that four out of nine GSTs ranked the preservice orientation as least helpful, with some feeling "really overwhelmed by all the new information" (Carol), an opinion echoed by Cassy, who wrote, "Preservice orientation just went too fast. There was a lot of good information, but not enough time to process it". Others indicated that the content of the preorientation did not align with the approach adopted in the language program. For example, Daphne volunteered, "The preservice orientation was fine, but at that time was conducted by the predecessor of the current LPD, who did not work from a multiliteracies perspective". Two GSTs, Laura and Gerdine, who had never taught before, however ranked the preservice orientation as the most helpful professional development opportunity they received. Laura wrote, "The preservice orientation was most helpful, as it provided a basis for teaching that I didn't previously possess", and Gerdine reported, "I had not taught in a classroom before I started with the MA program. The preservice orientation was therefore most helpful to help me find my feet and to know what is expected of me".

Finally, any forms of direct feedback from the LPD, whether it was after in-class visits or in-service meetings, were thought of as being very useful to GSTs. For example, Cassy wrote, "I found the direct feedback from my LPD the most valuable". Callie shared, "Getting personal feedback in the midst of the semester was the most helpful because I could implement it quickly". Direct and personalized feedback from the LPD was also given high marks by Anna, who reported that she believed that "in class visit has [sic] more benefits that [sic] the methods course. The advisor can provide accurate feedback of [sic] your class". Ralph wrote that he often did best "with concrete examples of what I am doing well and what I need to work on". Similarly, another GST shared that "getting personal feedback in the midst of the semester was the most helpful because I could implement it quickly" (Callie).

While LPDs' feedback was considered very useful, GSTs were divided when it came to the usefulness of the methods course. Renee, a GST in Language Program 2, confessed that "the methods course I'm enrolled in seems to be a bit repetitive and too much course load for teachers who are currently learning by doing". Laura, another GST from Language Program 1, admitted that she "ranked the methods course as the least useful because it feels difficult to apply the things, we are learning in the methods course in such a low-level, fast-paced Spanish course". The difficulty of putting theoretical knowledge into practice was a common thread in the participants' answers across the language programs. As Laureen, one of the participants from Language Program 2, shared, "it's not always easy to transfer what you learn, even the practical parts, to your teaching practice without further guidance and feedback". Gerdine, from Language Program 2, also felt that the focus on one single method was unfortunate and would have liked to learn about other teaching approaches as well. Meanwhile, Shery from Language Program 3 shared that "the methods course was helpful since [...] we use the multiliteracies methods, it was a new approach for me". Similarly, Celia from Program 4 reported that the methods course allowed her to "understand (her) craft", and Elodie from the same program explained that it allowed her "to gain a deeper understanding of the expectations at a college-level".

The results show that most of my participants participated in a preservice orientation, a methods course, and in-service meetings, and some had in-class visits. I provided a description of what these professional development opportunities look like and had study participants rank them in terms of usefulness. The data show that the preservice orientation was the least useful one, as it tends to be too overwhelming and fast-paced. It was however reported to be useful by some GSTs who appreciated being given the basic tools for their teaching as well as clear expectations regarding their jobs. Direct feedback from the LPD was definitely appreciated by GSTs in this study. Finally, rankings of the methods course diverged: some GSTs reported that it was too much course load and provided information that was too difficult to apply. Others enjoyed having a dedicated opportunity to learn about the literacy-based framework.

4.3. RQ3: What are the GSTs' perceptions of their professional development as it relates to the literacy-based framework?

To answer my last question, I asked my participants about the appropriateness of their pre- and in-service professional development opportunities. Although preservice orientation was not ranked as the most useful professional development opportunity in any of the programs included in this study, results show that a majority of GSTs believed that they had received appropriate professional development prior to starting teaching (Figure 2).

Figure 2. GSTs' perceptions of appropriateness of professional development opportunities before service

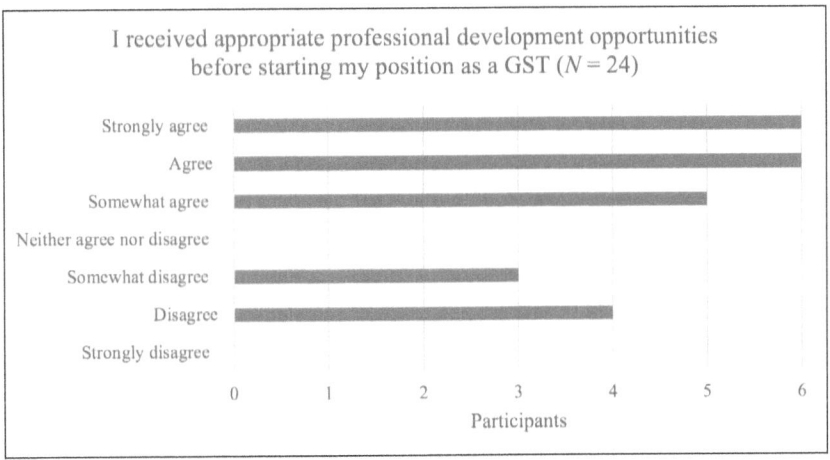

As Laureen explained, "I think we got all the information we needed and could have digested before actually starting in and trying it ourselves". Her most useful experience was to see examples of lessons, including one based on the multiliteracies framework, and then working in collaboration with other GSTs to lesson plan. Coming from the same program, Ralph shared, "the university has given me very good opportunities to prepare myself for my position as a TA. This included weeks of preparation on an individual level, as well as ongoing instruction about teaching throughout my first semester". Shery appreciated interacting with more experienced GSTs during her orientation and explained that her institution's orientation is complete and very well organized. Many GSTs also shared that the experience they received at their previous institution along with the preservice orientation made them confident to teach as a GST.

While most GSTs agreed that they received appropriate professional development opportunities before starting their position as a GST, many nuanced their justifications. Cassy, for example, shared that the preservice orientation provided her with too much information to process in too little time. She also explained that she would have benefited from having the methods course before she started teaching, but also felt it was useful "to be trying out the things (she) was learning right away". Just like Cassy, Emily (who had no teaching experience when she started as a GST in Spanish) believed that a single week of orientation was insufficient to prepare her. Kimmy, who disagreed that she received appropriate training prior to taking on her role as a French GST, argued that "throwing people into a teaching role with no more than two days of training, with NO [sic] classroom management advice, is not enough. Pedagogical theory in general is not enough. We need linguistic training on theories of acquisition as well".

4.3.1. Teaching beyond the lower level

In this study, 19 participants (79.17%) reported that they were teaching lower-level classes (first to fourth semester), and five (20.83%) were teaching advanced-level classes. The vast majority believed that the professional development opportunities they had received had taught them to teach both lower-level and upper-level FL classes (Figure 3 below).

A significant number of GSTs explained that their knowledge of the multiliteracies framework made them confident that it would be 'transferable' to any level. Shery underscored that "the multiliteracies framework are [sic] the foundation of our teaching. From there, we are prepared to teach any level". Cassy also shared that although she had yet to teach upper-level courses, she felt confident that her "knowledge of scaffolding lessons around texts and content" had prepared her to teach "more culturally-focused courses". Gerdine also reported that "the focus on scaffolding a lesson as to support students to understand the work is applicable at both beginner and advanced levels". However, many GSTs had more nuanced answers, mainly because of the curricular divide between lower- and upper-level classes. Elodie wrote,

> "I agree that these professional development opportunities were enough for me as an experienced language teacher, but I am not sure it was enough for novice teachers. In addition, the fact the lower-level and upper-level are separated in terms of focus (language versus literature), I am not sure novice teachers are fully prepared to do both".

Figure 3. GSTs' perceptions on capacity to teach lower- and upper-level classes

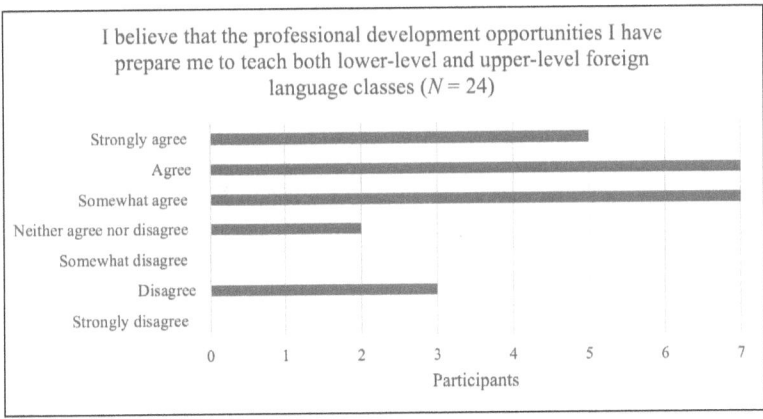

Emily also shared that given the differences in-between levels in terms of teaching approaches, she was not sure that she was provided with the best tools to teach at all levels. She noted, "There is a certain inconsistency across our course levels about different methodologies, which made our professional development opportunities either too broad or too specific to each class".

Finally, some GSTs believed that because of their lack of training in teaching upper-level classes and the curricular divide between lower- and upper-level classes, they were not only not prepared to teach upper-level classes but also did

Chapter 4

not feel ready to be on the job market. Ashlee shared that she would like more professional development opportunities in teaching upper-level classes to better understand the differences between the different levels and more particularly the teaching of literature versus language. Danielle, a former GST in German, argued that the lack of experience in teaching upper-level classes but also in designing her "own syllabi for any level" were things that "would have prepared (her) even better for the academic job market".

4.3.2. The need for more professional development opportunities

As I previously indicated, a majority of GSTs reported that they had received appropriate training prior to starting teaching and believed that the professional development they had received prepared them to teach both lower- and upper-level classes. Nonetheless, it also appears that the vast majority of the GSTs in this study would have liked more professional development opportunities to improve their multiliteracies-oriented teaching skills (Figure 4).

Figure 4. GSTs' perceptions of quantity of professional development

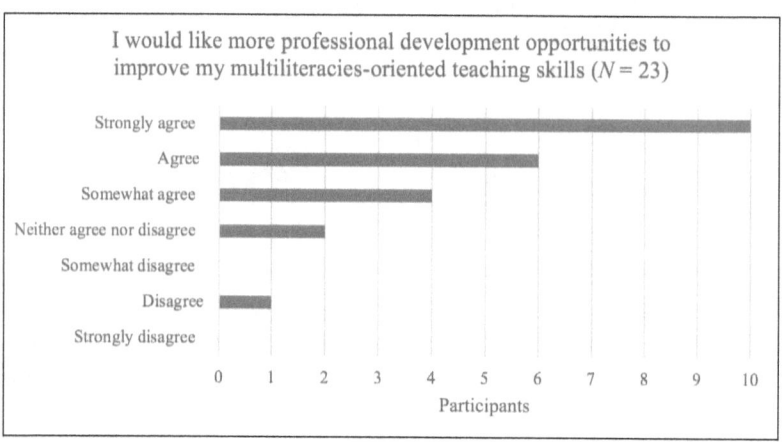

As Gerdine put it, "I agree that we received professional development opportunities, but [teaching with a multiliteracies framework] was still a very daunting process to go through". Many GSTs expressed their need for

more demonstration of multiliteracies-oriented lessons from which they could model their teaching as well as more professional development opportunities to guide them into finding and creating materials for the classroom. Elodie, for example, shared her struggles with the approach used by textbooks and their lack of alignment with the multiliteracies framework: "I think CLT is still too present in most of the textbook and departmental expectations, and more professional development would help to shift this CLT tendency". Making proper or appropriate use of their teaching material was a challenge many GSTs also reported. Several GSTs shared that they were not sure what was important and what was not when using texts. Kristen wondered, "Is all grammar meaningful? Sometimes I feel it's only on a grammatical level (like adjective endings in German). How do I deal with these structures"? Cynthia, a former GST in French, also worried about "the authenticity of the contexts" she was bringing in the classroom. As a nonnative speaker of French, she shared that she "feared that my contexts were too stereotypical and not reflective of actual French culture and language".

In addition to making proper use of their teaching material, a vast majority of GSTs shared their concerns about "covering everything" in a short amount of class time: "it is difficult to go beyond the superficial cultural components with such little time to work with" (Sandra). Just like Sandra, Laureen shared her struggles with the lack of time she had when teaching from a multiliteracies perspective:

> "it's definitely time consuming. These texts are very rich. There is a lot of information, and much of it is new to me. Our in-class discussions can go kind of long, which can be great, but it's always taking time away from something else. I wish I had more time to really learn a lot about the text we are treating".

Time management was not only an issue in the classroom but also in the GSTs' professional development. Many shared that although rewarding at times, using the multiliteracies framework is "time consuming and ask[s] for a lot of reflection while doing it" (Elodie). Kate also shared that because she was "teaching a full-time section, taking three grad-level classes, plus preparing for [the] Master's exam, prelim exams, dissertation proposal, and/or the dissertation itself', she found it very difficult to spend more time on developing multiliteracies lessons. As a result, some GSTs shared that although they would like more professional development opportunities, it just did not seem very realistic given their already very busy schedules.

5. Discussion and implications

This study was purposefully focused on a specific sample of GSTs. All study participants belonged to language programs that had recently undergone curricular changes and had implemented a multiliteracies framework at the basic level. In this context, it was important to find out if adequate measures had been taken to adapt the GSTs' professional development in such a way that they could implement a multiliteracies approach in their classrooms.

I started by asking the participants whether they believed their teaching was multiliteracies oriented and how they would define it. While 79% of respondents said they believed their teaching was informed by the multiliteracies framework, 21% said it was not. Emily and Kristen argued that because of the nature of the classes they were teaching ("writing intensive" for Emily and with a "literature focus" for Kristen), they believed their teaching might not be totally informed by the framework. It is worth mentioning that intensive writing and literature-focused classes are not incompatible with a multiliteracies framework. In fact, through a multiliteracies perspective, "writing is an act of meaning design that includes linguistic, cognitive, and sociocultural dimensions" and is a modality closely intertwined with reading (Paesani et al., 2015, pp. 179-180). As such, the nature of the classes taught cannot serve as a pretext for not being able to implement a multiliteracies teaching approach.

On the other hand, Kimmy and Anna also felt uncomfortable saying that their teaching was multiliteracies oriented because of a focus on explicit grammar for Kimmy and a lack of transformed practice activities for Anna. Their strong reliance on the textbook in use might help explain this. Indeed, "the approach taken by many textbooks suggest that mechanical practice of structural patterns is effective for acquisition of grammar and vocabulary" (Paesani et al., 2015, p. 87), which goes against the implementation of meaningful grammar and vocabulary instruction grounded in textual instruction as well as transformed practice activities. Although textbook use may vary between institutions, curricula, programs, and instructors, textbooks maintain their "enduring centrality in classrooms around the world" (Gray, 2013, p. 2) and remain "the bedrock of syllabus design and lesson planning" (Kramsch, 1988, p. 63). Far from only having an impact on learners, the content of language textbooks impacts the work of LPDs and the professional development of the GSTs they oversee when implementing a literacy-based curriculum. LPDs often find themselves adapting and supplementing textbooks or even choosing to replace the commercial textbook altogether with an open education resource that they find easier to use in a literacy-based classroom (see Hashemi, forthcoming). While textbooks might present an obstacle to teaching using a multiliteracies framework at the basic level, I thought it would also be important to clarify what our participants' definitions of this concept was. I soon realized that although all the definitions included at least one of the words 'text', 'authentic text', 'material', 'source/input', 'different modes of meaning', 'variety of literature', and 'cultural and linguistic components', a number of definitions revealed confusion among some study participants.

This is the case of the definitions provided by Emily and Kimmy. To the question, Emily replied, "an approach that considers anything to be a 'text'". Although not incorrect, this definition lacks important consideration of the purpose for using texts. Kimmy on the other hand defined the multiliteracies approach as "using authentic texts (with potential slight modifications to be appropriate for levels) to demonstrate grammar and communicate culture". Kimmy's definition rightfully includes the notions of authentic texts, grammar, and culture. It does however seem that the sole purpose of the text is to illustrate a grammatical point she might have introduced in a prior lesson or to illustrate a cultural point to her students. As previously mentioned in this study, the multiliteracies pedagogy assumes "an understanding of the relationships among various oral, written, and visual forms and how these forms contribute to textual meaning; the ability to construct meaning through the process of creating and transforming knowledge; and a recognition of the dynamic nature of language and the socially and culturally embedded resources used in literacy-based practices" (Paesani et al., 2015, p. 21).

As such, rather than giving her students an opportunity to create meaning from the texts she incorporated in her instruction, Kimmy instead remained at a shallow level of analysis and failed to engage her students in finding the ways in which a text's goals are achieved or the context in which the text was produced for example. The selected definitions included in supplementary materials, Appendix 2 show that a fair number of participants are able to offer a definition that I believe is correct although each chose to emphasize different aspects based on what they believed to be important. At this point of the study, I could already tell that my participants had received recent, and even extensive, training in multiliteracy-oriented teaching and were thus able to word the important aspects of a complicated concept. It is important, however, to proceed with caution here, as the ability to correctly define a concept does not mean that it is appropriately implemented (see Grossman, Smagorinsky, & Valencia, 1999). Overall, GSTs' reported knowledge about and use of literacy-based approaches to teaching show that there seems to be an understanding of what this approach implies in terms of the nature of the material used and the goals of using such material in the classroom. In fact, because of GSTs' awareness of the importance of authentic texts to situate learning in social and historical contexts, many of them seemed to be increasingly frustrated when having to use made-up texts from the textbook (see for example Andersen, Lund, & Risager, 2006; Brown, 2010; Etienne & Sax, 2009; Gilmore, 2007). Instead, they would have preferred to bring texts that were truly reflective of language use in the target language and to which students could relate.

Results related to the GSTs' professionalization showed that although this study's participants did follow a rather traditional professional development path with a preservice orientation week, a one-semester methods class, and in-service meetings including occasional visits from the LPD or a course coordinator, it was also clear that efforts had been made to provide them with useful preparation. While a few GSTs shared that their methods course was useful, the data show that the professional development of the GSTs in this study was still by and large frontloaded (Freeman, 1993) and continued to focus on providing them with information and strategies for their immediate rather than their long-term professional development teaching needs. Ongoing reflection and practice with understanding the relationship between SLA, content, and pedagogy to articulate better and more cohesive curricular design and cultivate self-reflective (and collaborative) practices would probably benefit GSTs the most in the long term.

This study's participants shared on various occasions that direct personalized feedback and teaching demonstrations showing examples of a multiliteracies-oriented lesson were elements that proved to be the most useful to them, which is similar to Zannirato and Sánchez-Serrano's (2009) findings indicating that GSTs favor 'how-to' professional development. In several comments made by my participants who wished they had more professional development opportunities, a 'how-to' pattern emerged: how to create material for the class, how to work with a CLT textbook, how to teach grammar, how to not be too stereotypical, and how to 'cover everything' in short classes. Paradoxically, a majority of my participants also reported that they were satisfied with the professional development opportunities they had gotten prior to setting foot in the classroom. A few reported that although it had been an overwhelming process, they were confident that the knowledge they had acquired would allow them to teach all levels across the curriculum. It was however noted that with multiliteracies programs being focused on the basic level and with some programs in this study still in the current state of bifurcated curricula, where lower-level classes are focused on language and advanced-level classes are focused on literature, GSTs might not be fully prepared to teach at the advanced level.

A number of practical implications for LPDs and other collegiate FL entities in charge of GSTs' professional development relate to my findings. First, this chapter shows that all GSTs participating in this study received professional development opportunities beyond the methods course. As mentioned by Allen and Dupuy (2012), formal instruction on the theoretical construct of literacy or a series of face-to-face or online workshops (since "not all TAs initially consider formal training […] beneficial to them", Brandl, 2000, p. 366) are essential in order to provide GSTs with continual grounding in classroom practices. GSTs in this study expressed difficulty in practically applying the notions of the multiliteracies approach to teaching, especially in a 50-minute class format, thus proving a need for more opportunities to apply their conceptual understanding. A way to meet GSTs' needs in that aspect would be for LPDs to teach a basic-level FL class once a year and have GSTs visit each other's classes a couple of times a month. Visits could be followed by online peer discussions about what GSTs thought about the lesson and the students' response to it and thus engagement in ongoing lesson study.

Furthermore, this study's participants shared that they favored personal and targeted feedback from their LPDs on their teaching. This is not a surprising finding, since a 'one-size-fits all' approach to professional development is inadequate (Allen & Negueruela-Azarola, 2010; McKibbin, 2001). As such, it is important to provide GSTs with continual mentorship (Angus, 2016) that they can use not just in their current teaching assignments but beyond their career as graduate students. While I am aware of the long list of tasks LPDs have to attend to, I would like to suggest that they encourage senior and more experienced GSTs to take these mentorship roles, which could prove to be a valued and valuable experience when they are on the job market and beyond. For example, they could visit their peers' classes and provide them with feedback. In order to conduct low-anxiety observations, the LPD might want to reorient the observation to be not so much on the GSTs' performances but more so on their students' responses to the different parts of the lesson. As such, these observations would be purely formative instead of being evaluative/punitive. The LPD could also implement or encourage some action-reflection assignments, modeling Grosbois and Sarré (2017), in which GSTs would implement and teach a lesson that was collaboratively prepared with other GSTs and the LPD and then post a reflection on a shared platform regarding that same lesson.

Finally, this study showed that most GSTs believed that their professional development prepared them to teach both lower and advanced levels. While this is an encouraging result, it must be interpreted carefully. It shows that GSTs believed that the multiliteracies framework can be applied across the curriculum; however, it does reveal the participants' perspectives on how this could be done. Some GSTs expressed that they were aware of the curricular divide in most FL programs. It would be beneficial to GSTs to be taught how to apply a multiliteracies approach to writing courses taught at the upper level, for example, even when teaching in a bifurcated department.

Some important limitations apply to this study's findings. First, for the data analysis, it would have been preferable to establish an interrater reliability coefficient when coding the open-ended responses. Second, as is often the case with long questionnaires, participants may have responded with brief answers, preventing me from getting the full picture. Follow-up interviews would have allowed me to contextualize some of the collected answers, especially when there was variation in answers among GSTs from the same language program. Focus groups would also have been beneficial when discussing the notions of multiliteracies-based teaching and the types of texts the participants would like to favor in their classrooms. Finally, being able to observe my participants' teaching over a given period of time would have further informed this study about the teaching practices used (or not) to implement a multiliteracies-based framework.

6. Future research and conclusion

Professional development is understood as a complex relationship between a wide range of factors, including reflective and critical stances taken by the instructor. Future research should control for GSTs' academic disciplines and years of experience, as well as other factors such as university, language taught, and other local factors.

This study of GSTs' professionalization and perceptions of professionalization in a context of multiliteracies-oriented teaching revealed that although some clear efforts are being made by the LPDs to provide them with a large variety of tools to teach in optimal conditions, GSTs could benefit from more opportunities that would provide them with direct and personalized feedback on their teaching as well as more demonstrations of concrete lessons applying the concepts of this framework. Some recommendations have been made in order to better meet GSTs' needs and move away from professional development "directed much more toward the needs of institutions than toward preparing graduate students to be self-reliant and knowledgeable practitioners" (Guthrie, 2001, p. 43).

Therefore, it is hoped that LPDs or other stakeholders in applied linguistics will implement more conceptually driven, reflection-focused, and classroom-based professional development opportunities in order to cater to GSTs' needs.

7.   Supplementary materials

https://research-publishing.box.com/s/lvqm0q96v7t86a586j2pj9p406zgoxnp

References

Allen, H. W. (2011). Embracing literacy-based teaching: a longitudinal study of the conceptual development of novice foreign language teachers. In K. E. Johnson & P. R. Golombek (Eds), *Sociocultural research on second language teacher education: exploring the complexities of professional development* (pp. 86-101). Routledge.

Allen, H. W., & Dupuy, B. (2010). Evolving notions of literacy-based foreign language teaching: a case study of graduate student instructors. In H. W. Allen & H. Maxim (Eds), *Educating the future foreign language professoriate for the 21st century* (pp. 171-191). Heinle Cengage.

Allen, H. W., & Dupuy, B. (2012). Evolving notions of literacy-based foreign language teaching: a case study of graduate student instructors. In H. W. Allen & H. Maxim (Eds), *Educating the future foreign language professoriate for the 21st century* (pp. 171-191). Heinle Cengage.

Allen, H. W., & Negueruela-Azarola, E. (2010). The professional development of future professors of foreign languages: looking back, looking forward. *Modern Language Journal, 94*(3), 377-395. https://doi.org/10.1111/j.1540-4781.2010.01056.x

Allen, H. W., & Paesani, K. (2010). Exploring the feasibility of a pedagogy of multiliteracies in introductory foreign language courses. *L2 Journal, 2*(1), 119-142. https://doi.org/10.5070/l22l9064

Allen, H. W., Paesani, K., & Dupuy, B. (2011, November 19). The methods course revisited: from a skills-based to multiliteracies approach. *ACTFL 2011 Annual Convention, Denver, CO*.

Andersen, H., Lund, K., & Risager, K. (2006). *Culture in language learning*. Aarhus University Press.

Angus, K. (2016). Saying vs. doing: a contradiction in the professional development of foreign language teaching assistants. *Foreign Language Annals, 49*(4), 819-835. https://doi.org/10.1111/flan.12239

Arens, K. (2010). Training graduate students to teach culture: a case study. *ADFL Bulletin, 23*, 35-41. https://doi.org/10.1632/adfl.23.1.35

Azevedo, M. M. (1999). Professional development of teaching assistants: training versus education. *ADFL Bulletin, 22*(1), 24-28. https://doi.org/10.1632/adfl.22.1.24

Bazerman, C., & Prior, P. A. (2004). *What writing does and how it does it: an introduction to analyzing texts and textual practices*. Lawrence Erlbaul Associates. https://doi.org/10.4324/9781410609526

Bernhardt, E. (2001). Research into the teaching of literature in a second language: what it says and how to communicate it to graduate students. In V. M. Scott & H. Tucker (Eds), *SLA and the literature classroom: fostering dialogues* (pp. 195-210). Heinle.

Blyth, C. (2011). From the director. *COERLL Newsletter: Textbooks for an Open World, Fall 2011* (p. 3). https://repositories.lib.utexas.edu/bitstream/handle/2152/15275/COERLL-Newsletter-Fall2011.pdf?sequence=2&isAllowed=y

Brandl, K. K. (2000). Foreign language TAs' perceptions of training components: do we know how they like to be trained? *The Modern Language Journal, 84*(3), 355-371. https://doi.org/10.1111/0026-7902.00074

Brown, D. (2010). What aspects of vocabulary knowledge do textbooks give attention to? *Language Teaching Research, 15*(1), 83-97. https://doi.org/10.1177/1362168810383345

Di Donato, R. (1983). TA training and supervision: a checklist for an effective program. *ADFL Bulletin, 15*(1), 34-36. https://doi.org/10.1632/adfl.15.1.34

Enkin, E. (2015). Supporting the professional development of foreign language graduate students: a focus on course development and program direction. *Foreign Language Annals, 48*(2), 304-320. https://doi.org/10.1111/flan.12131

Etienne, C., & Sax, K. (2009). Stylistic variation in French: bridging the gap between research and textbooks. *The Modern Language Journal, 93*(4), 584-606. https://doi.org/10.1111/j.1540-4781.2009.00931.x

Freeman, D. (1989). Teacher training, development, and decision making: a model of teaching and related strategies for language teacher education. *TESOL Quarterly, 23*(1), 27-45. https://doi.org/10.2307/3587506

Freeman, D. (1993). Renaming experience/reconstructing practice:developing new understandings of teaching. *Teaching and Teacher Education 9*(5/6), 485-497. https://doi.org/10.1016/0742-051x(93)90032-c

Gilmore, A. (2007). Authentic materials and authenticity in foreign language learning. *Language teaching, 40*(2), 97-118. https://doi.org/10.1017/s0261444807004144

Gómez Soler, I. G., & Tecedor, M. (2018). Foreign language teaching assistant training: a contrastive analysis of trainers and trainees' perspectives. *Hispania, 101*(1), 38-54. https://doi.org/10.1353/hpn.2018.0083

Gonglewski, M., & Penningroth, A. (1998). German graduate student professional development: report on a survey of perceptions (1994–95). *Die Unterrichtspraxis, 31*(1), 70-77. https://doi.org/10.2307/3531448

Gray, J. (2013). (Ed.). *Critical perspectives on language teaching materials*. Palgrave Macmillan.

Grosbois, M. M., & Sarré, C. G. (2017). Learning to teach for next-generation education: a careful blend of action and reflection. In *Preparing foreign language teachers for next-generation education* (pp. 153–174). IGI Global. https://doi.org/10.4018/978-1-5225-0483-2.ch009

Grosse, C. U. (1993). The foreign language methods course. *Modern Language Journal, 77*(3), 303-312. https://doi.org/10.1111/j.1540-4781.1993.tb01976.x

Grossman, P. L., Smagorinsky, P., & Valencia, S. (1999). Appropriating tools for teaching English: a theoretical framework for research on learning to teach. *American Journal of Education, 108*(1), 1-29. https://doi.org/10.1086/444230

Guthrie, E. (2001). The language program director and the curriculum: setting the stage for effective programs. *ADFL Bulletin, 32*(3), 41-47. https://doi.org/10.1632/adfl.32.3.41

Halliday, M. A. K. (1978). *Language as social semiotic: the social interpretation of language and meaning*. Hodder Arnold.

Hashemi, T. (forthcoming). Multiliteracies-oriented basic foreign language programs: language program directors' insights on instructional materials, assessments and the professionalization of graduate student teachers.

Johnson, K. E. (2009). *Second language teacher education: a sociocultural perspective*. Routledge.

Kern, R. (2000). *Literacy and language teaching*. Oxford University Press.

Kramsch, C. (1988). The cultural discourse of foreign language textbooks. In A. J. Singerman (Ed.), *Toward an integration of language and culture* (pp. 63-88). Northeast Conference on the Teaching of Foreign.

Kramsch, C. (1993). *Context and culture in language teaching*. Oxford University Press.

Kumagai, Y., López-Sánchez, A., & Wu, S. (2015). (Eds). *Multiliteracies in world language education*. Routledge.

Lord, G., Liskin-Gasparro, J. E., & Lacorte, M. (2013). *Language program direction: theory and practice*. Pearson Higher Ed.

McKibbin, M. (2001). One size does not fit all: reflections on alternative routes to teacher preparation in California. *Teacher Education Quarterly, 28*, 133-149.

Mills, N. (2011). Teaching assistants' self-efficacy in teaching literature: sources, personal assessments, and consequences. *Modern Language Journal, 95*(1), 61-80. https://doi.org/10.1111/j.1540-4781.2010.01145.x

Mills, N., & Allen, H. W. (2007). Teacher self-efficacy of graduate teaching assistants of French. In H. J. Siskin (Ed.), *Thought to action: exploring beliefs and outcomes in the foreign language program* (pp. 213-234). Heinle & Heinle.

MLA. (2007). Foreign languages and higher education: new structures for a changed world. *Profession, 2007*(12), 234-245. https://doi.org/10.1632/prof.2007.2007.1.234

New London Group. (1996). A pedagogy of multiliteracies: designing social futures. *Harvard Educational Review, 66*(1), 60-93. https://doi.org/10.17763/haer.66.1.17370n67v22j160u

Paesani, K. A., Allen, H. W., Dupuy, B. (2015). *A multiliteracies framework for collegiate foreign language teaching*. Pearson Prentice Hall.

Rankin, J., & Becker, F. (2006). Does reading the research make a difference? A case study of teacher growth in FL German. *Modern Language Journal, 90*(3), 353-372. https://doi.org/10.1111/j.1540-4781.2006.00429.x

Ryan-Scheutz, C. M., & Rustia, T. (1999). The status of TA training and professional development programs for teachers of Italian at North American colleges and universities: a quantitative overview. *Italica, 76*(4), 454-468. https://doi.org/10.2307/480251

Swaffar, J., & Arens, K. (2005). *Remapping the foreign language curriculum.* Modern Language Association.

Warford, M. K. (2003). The FL methods course: where it's been; where it's headed. *Northeast Conference, 52*, 29-35.

White, R., Martin, M., Hodge, R., & Stimson, M. (2008). *Management in English language teaching.* Cambridge University Press.

Wilbur, M. L. (2007). How foreign language teachers get taught: methods of teaching the methods course. *Foreign Language Annals, 40*(1), 79-101. https://doi.org/10.1111/j.1944-9720.2007.tb02855.x

Zannirato, A., & Sánchez-Serrano, L.(2009). Using evaluation to design FL teacher training in a literature program. In J. M. Norris, J. M. Davis, C. Sinicrope & Y. Watanabe (Eds), *Toward useful program evaluation in college FL education* (pp. 97-116). NFLRC.

Part II
(Multimodal) communication and professionalization

5. Digital storytelling for developing students' agency through the process of design: a case study

Elyse Petit[1]

1. Introduction

Today's use of technology and media in daily life has altered the dominant role the written word has played in communication over centuries. Currently, educational settings take into consideration the combination of different modes of representation that exist in an array of everyday texts. "Developing knowledge about linguistic, visual and digital meaning-making systems" (Unsworth, 2001, p. 10) has become a key learning objective. In the digital era, students develop literacy by understanding the organization and display of information through multiple modes of communication and the ways these different modes cooperate in the creation of meanings (Jewitt, 2009; Kress, 2009; Lemke, 1998; Unsworth, 2001). As a result, teaching through and about media is crucial in foreign language classrooms to promote transcultural and translingual competencies (Lebrun, Lacelle, & Boutin, 2012). Yet foreign language educators must learn how the *relationships* (Kern, 2006) or *orchestration* (Kress & van Leeuwen, 1996; Nelson, 2006) *within* and *across* semiotic modes (Kress, 2003), including language, facilitate the ways learners create meaning. Developing activities that teach students the tools of multimodal texts and how to reapply these resources in a personal way forces teachers to reflect upon ways their teaching practices facilitate language learning (Anderson, Chung, & Macleroy, 2018; Jiang, 2017; Ollivier, 2018).

---

1. Vanderbilt University, Nashville, Tennessee, United States; elyse.b.petit@vanderbilt.edu

How to cite this chapter: Petit, E. (2020). Digital storytelling for developing students' agency through the process of design: a case study. In B. Dupuy and M. Grosbois (Eds), *Language learning and professionalization in higher education: pathways to preparing learners and teachers in/for the 21st century* (pp. 137-166). Research-publishing.net. https://doi.org/10.14705/rpnet.2020.44.1104

Conducted in an intermediate French-language curriculum grounded in the pedagogy of multiliteracies (New London Group, 1996), and Cope and Kalantzis's (2015) framework of learning by design, this study investigates Digital Storytelling (DS) (Lambert, 2002) within a social synesthetic semiosis (Nelson, 2006; Oskoz & Elola, 2016; Yang, 2012) with particular attention to the transformation and transduction processes (Bezemer & Jewitt, 2009; Kress, 2003). In other words, I explore how DS supports students' selection and orchestration of semiotics to construct layers of meaning and foster language development.

Findings from two case studies of fourth-semester French learners highlight participants' ability to circumvent challenges and convey their stories in multiple modes, including the target language. The study underscores to foreign language teachers the potential of media projects anchored in the multiliteracies framework to enhance students' media literacy skills as they critically reflect on the use of media from the perspective of both consumers and producers.

2. Background

2.1. Multiliteracies

These past decades, within the field of literacy studies, numerous educators and scholars (Cope & Kalantzis, 2009, 2015; Gee, 2008; Kern, 2000, 2015; Kress, 2003; New London Group, 1996) have stressed the changes occurring as a result of new social practices and discussed what it means to be literate in today's world. The concept of being literate has shifted from knowing how to read and write printed text to gaining the ability to read and produce varied texts across a set of social and cultural contexts through multiple digital devices. Today's texts are produced, distributed, and consumed through visual, aural, sensorial, spatial, and gestural modes which, when combined, communicate particular meanings, achieve specific purposes, and reach certain audiences. Thus, language – in its linguistic dimension – can no longer be considered the sole mode of conveying messages. Foreign language educators should no longer privilege the linguistic mode at the expense of other modes. Instead, they should address these new literacies and new ways of creating meanings to help students navigate through and negotiate with multimodal texts and their meanings to become multiliterate.

According to Lebrun et al. (2012), the teaching of new literacies and multiliteracies is central in foreign language classrooms, and a few studies have demonstrated the significance of its implementation. Most instructors teach using multimodal texts rather than teaching how to read and write them. Because instructors lack knowledge of what makes a text multimodal, they privilege the linguistic mode over other semiotic resources. Thus, scholars promote the integration of teaching new literacies into language curricula and stress the importance of incorporating innovative pedagogical frameworks into teachers' professional development (Anderson et al., 2018; Ollivier, 2018; Oskoz & Elola, 2016).

Although the implementation of these frameworks is challenging and time-consuming, they allow teachers to reflect on their teaching practices. The concept of design (Cope & Kalantzis, 2009, 2015; Kern, 2015) in the multiliteracies framework proposes developing a classroom application as an active process of transformation from the known to the new. Through acts of designing and redesigning, students build knowledge. Design elements included in text, image, sound, gesture, space, and sense allow students to move back and forth among the modes of representation and foster meaning-making. Such multimodal design provides interconnection across and between other modes, and learning emerges from mode switching. Students become more sensitive to the semiotics used in texts and their meaning potential. They gain the ability to make intentional choices while producing their own multimodal texts through a variety of means in the target language (Jiang, 2017).

Furthermore, the learning by design approach applies to both learners and teachers. The former take control of their apprenticeship to become designers of their knowledge through action-taking, collaboration, and active participation in and outside formal learning (Anderson et al., 2018). The latter plan and organize teaching sequences around multimodal texts, identify learning strategies, and reflect on assessment and learning outcomes.

Moreover, instructors should experiment with innovative and collaborative approaches to fulfilling foreign language learners' needs and fostering learning competencies as a whole rather than in isolation (Anderson et al., 2018). Across scholarships, there emerge various implementations of experiential learning in foreign language education. These curricula have provided L2 learning and teaching approaches that fostered multiliteracies, such as the use of social media (Reinhardt & Zander, 2011), gaming (Reinhardt, Warner, & Lange, 2014), social reading (Blyth, 2014), and global simulation (Michelson & Dupuy, 2014).

2.2. DS and language learning

DS is a textual narrative embedded with other modes of communication (Alismail, 2015; Robin, 2006). It consists of "short, two to three-minute mini-films usually based on still photos brought into a multimedia format, with a textual narrative read with the narrator's voice" (Lundby, 2008, p. 366). The multimodal dimension of a DS empowers digital storytellers who engage with multiple modes of representation that have an "exponentially more complex impact" on themselves and their audience (Lambert, 2013).

Many studies have examined the integration of digital stories in educational settings, but few studies have explored DS in Foreign Language (FL/L2) learning contexts. Studies have shown that DS, through formal and informal learning, have a beneficial impact on students' cognition and language learning, as well as on their technology, media, and social competencies (Anderson et al., 2018; Burgess, 2006; Podkalicka & Campbell, 2010; Vinogradova, Linville, & Bickel, 2011). In developing their digital stories, students learn how to collect information, using technology, or search in the 'real' world (e.g. taking pictures, composing music or recording sounds, and interviewing members of a community). Through their production, students combine various modes (soundtrack, voiceovers, and images) and genres (interviews, documentaries, and moving and still images). They develop coherent narratives in which they can express their emotions and values. In addition, they gain the ability to compose stories using technology and to collect and arrange textual, visual, and audio elements, as well as to perform orally (Anderson et al., 2018; Burgess, 2006; Jiang, 2017; Vinogradova et al., 2011).

Furthermore, the implementation of DS in FL/L2 classrooms involves using all language modalities: writing, reading, listening, and speaking. As they develop the composition of their story, language learners must make selective linguistic choices in terms of genre conventions, morpho-syntactic features (e.g. tenses, vocabulary, grammar), language register, and discourse appropriateness. As producers of digital stories, students need to learn how to write narratives following genre conventions and often with a limited number of words. According to Paulus (1999), the use of a multiple-draft approach is best for practicing writing in FL/L2 classrooms. Digital stories also support students' improvement in their speaking skills (Kim, 2014; Nelson, 2006). To perform the task of speaking, students have to practice pronunciation and work on their intonation. Studies on the use of online recording programs and self-assessment demonstrate significant improvement in speaking accuracy and communicative performance (Jiang, 2017; Lynch, 2007; Volle, 2005). In addition, the multimodal dimension of DS places students beyond the single act of learning how to read, write, and speak in an FL. It engages learners in viewing and showing, communicating through sounds and visuals, and combining resources to create meanings. In the same way that they make written or spoken choices, they must make choices around design elements including color, font, layouts, background, and transition effects. They have to envision their project, anticipate the audience's reaction, and manage the challenges presented by the creation of multimodal texts (Anderson et al., 2018; Castañeda, 2013; Jiang, 2017; Kern, 2006; Miller, 2009; Van Gils, 2005). DS allows students to learn how language "as one important dimension of semiosis among others" (Nelson & Kern, 2012, p. 61) is anchored in sociocultural contexts and interconnected with other modes of representation to produce meanings. It goes beyond the sole learning of lexico-grammatical features (e.g. syntactic structures, grammar rules, vocabulary lists).

3. Methodology

3.1. Course context and description

The study was conducted in two sections of a fourth-semester French course in which I implemented critical media literacy frameworks combined with Cope and Kalantzis's (2015) knowledge processes to foster language learning and emergent literacies. Throughout the semester, students explored topics through authentic texts culturally embedded in French society. For instance, students designed political cartoons addressing global issues after reflecting upon the controversial French magazine *Charlie Hebdo* and the role of cartoonists in the world. They also made promotional posters to advertise the National Museum of Immigration in Paris. They created informative posters to promote web safety among youth and their families. Finally, they produced their digital story. These projects occurred throughout the semester and allowed students to explore multiple media representations and various linguistic and semiotic forms of multimodal texts. Students engaged with these texts from the perspective of consumers and language learners and produced media artifacts drawing upon the concepts of ethics, audience, and ideology of the target culture.

Inspired by the Story Center's movement and mission to "create spaces for listening to and sharing stories" and to provide "skills and tools that support self-expression, creative practice and community building" (https://www.storycenter.org/about), I used the Center Story's steps into the curriculum to help students to develop their final project. Although tied to specific codes and conventions, DS offers creative writing and production, allowing students to apply and reflect on what they have learned during a course. Before creating their digital story, students explored one particular digital story that I carefully selected on the Story Center's website and discussed the relationships of the semiotics chosen by the author. Then, as homework, students chose two different digital stories and reflected on what they watched and the semiotic element(s) that captured their attention and could potentially be used in their project. I evaluated students' work at every step of the process, including French to respond to language obstacles and learners' needs. I gave feedback on the written scripts and the pronunciation, intonation, and language flow of the voiceover. Before the final submission, students were able to verify and evaluate their projects according to a rubric used to assess the final version of the project.

3.2. Research questions

This article seeks to answer the following research question: in what ways does DS contribute to a student's understanding of how the selection and orchestration of semiotics constructs layers of meaning and impacts multiliteracy skills and language development?

3.3. Participants

I focused on two case studies of students who identified themselves as L2 French learners and were enrolled in an intermediate French class, the final course of the basic language sequence at the university. Criteria for selecting these students included their commitment to the class, their motivation in learning the target language and culture, and their high level of participation in class. By selecting these two case studies, I intended to present a contrastive sample of how students in the class had chosen to develop their digital story with specific semiotics in mind. These examples aim to illustrate possible learning strategies that students, consciously or unconsciously, implemented to achieve their projects.

Born in Mexico, Maïze (pseudonym) arrived in the United States with her family when she was seven years old. At the time of the study, she was 19 years old, a sophomore majoring in psychology and minoring in French. In a postsemester interview, Maïze tied her interest in French to her belief that learning a language expands creativity and cultural knowledge. As a native speaker of Spanish, she enjoyed comparing the differences of the languages. Raised within American culture with Hispanic traditions, she was often able to grasp the similarities between the French and the Mexican cultures and see how they differed from American culture.

Chapter 5

Maïze's DS is entitled "Choses Oubliées [Forgotten Things]" and is intended to raise "a global controversy" that she described as follows. "Likes, hearts, followers and subscribers. Every day, these things fill up our thoughts; they intoxicate our beliefs and influence us to behave in a way that the rest of society expects and wants us to behave".

Fanny (pseudonym) is a 20-year-old American white woman who grew up in Houston, Texas. Her mother was American, and her father immigrated from England to the United States when he was 18 years old. Fanny was an only child who was born with a missing arm. Her parents raised her according to the belief that having one arm is incidental and should not be used as an excuse for not doing what others can. Fanny demonstrated a strong personality, always speaking for herself and standing up for her opinions. At the time of the study, Fanny was a freshman majoring in geology and physics in the College of Sciences. Before undertaking the French course, Fanny spent her last high school semester in France at a private bilingual international school, in Paris. Although disabled, Fanny was not registered at the university's Disability Resource Center and did not ask for any accommodations.

Fanny's DS is entitled "Ma vie". In her initial proposal, the tentative title of her story was "The One Arm Wonder", which she described as follows. "In 199[…], on August […], I was born without my right arm. Being born this way has given me the beautiful opportunity to see life th[r]ough a unique perspective that has made me who I am today. I have learned valuable lessons that I wish to share with the world with the goal of teaching about perspective and the power of the individual".

For this study, I refer to data collected from these two stories as ways to best exemplify how DS impacts meaning-making, multiliteracies, and language development. In comparing and contrasting these two stories, disparities emerged in how the students selected and orchestrated the semiotic resources at their disposal. For instance, whereas Fanny, who felt that her technological skills were limited, presented her project as a PowerPoint slideshow, Maïze created a complex project that incorporated photos, videos, music, transitions, and effects.

Another difference between Fanny and Maïze lies in their choices of resources to tell their story. Fanny decided to tell her story by relying primarily on linguistic resources. In contrast, Maïze developed her project around the use of visuals and aesthetics, avoiding the overuse of linguistic features.

Furthermore, even though these case studies were selected as examples of students' processes of design, gaps exist in the data collection as a result of what participants gave access to in their consent forms. While Maïze agreed to provide a postsemester interview, Fanny did not. In addition, although consent forms were collected by a third party and given to me after the official release of final grades, participants were fully aware of the research agenda and knew that their work could be shown in an academic context. Thus, conflicts of interest may appear in a study where participants complete a classroom project that calls for personal statements.

Finally, in terms of audience, the students did not display their artifacts on a participative website. The tasks did not bring students beyond the educational boundaries and therefore, although fostering digital literacies, did not "involve real-world processes of language use" (Ollivier, 2018, p. 36).

The following analysis should be considered alongside these limitations.

3.4. Data collection

The data were collected from diverse sources: the DS steps described below and the students' final artifacts. In addition, Maïze's two postsemester interviews were analyzed.

Students developed their projects following six steps and used L1 except for Steps 4 and 5. Feedback was given for Steps 1, 3, 4, and 5.
1. Propose a story.
2. Complete a prequestionnaire to reflect on the design process.
3. Develop a storyboard.
4. Draft a narration.

5. Record a voiceover.

6. After submission, complete a postquestionnaire to reflect on learning outcomes.

3.5. Postsemester interviews

Maïze consented to give a postsemester interview in English. Her first interview was exceptionally long (44:39 min), and she agreed to give a second interview. The two interviews, conducted in person and recorded, took place in a university library study room. The first interview happened during the spring semester following the course, and the second occurred during the summer. The first interview was semistructured with direct questions about the critical media literacy framework and the creation of media artifacts. Less directive, the second interview focused on the artifact itself and the decisions made by the participant while designing it.

3.6. Data analysis

The study followed Nelson (2006) and Bezemer and Jewitt's (2009) analytical focus. The analysis identifies the modes of communication (e.g. verbal, visual, aural, gestural, spatial) and investigates the decisions made by the participants to construct meanings.

The qualitative data analysis of participants' artifacts involved two phases.

3.6.1. Phase 1: analytic memos and initial coding

Based on grounded theory (Bryant & Charmaz, 2007), the analysis of data started with written analytic memos followed by open coding. First, I recorded and reported the general patterns, categories, and subcategories of the data. Then, I used in vivo coding for participants' pre and postquestionnaires and Maïze's semistructured interviews. Interviews were transcribed in written form, and data were analyzed for new insights about the process of creation based on the participants' goals. Finally, I compared storyboards, written drafts, and the final project version to investigate any significant differences.

3.6.2. Phase 2: multimodal arrangement

Scrutinizing the final artifacts and the arrangement of modes helped me to better understand participants' process of design while developing their digital stories. First, I quantitatively tabulated and coded the diverse modes of communication – textual, oral, aural, and visual – based on the purposes for using these modes. Then, I explored whether a specific mode was predominant or if the participants used modes evenly. Finally, I analyzed the disparities that emerged between and within the modes of representation.

4. Findings

The following section discusses how the two participants decided to select and use particular semiotics over others to convey meanings. Participants showed autonomy and personal learning strategies.

4.1. Textual mode

Fanny primarily concentrated her DS on her writing and decided to add captions to her PowerPoint slides to reach both the L2 and L1 audience. She demonstrated knowledge of narratology and used writing strategies to communicate her story. She had higher L2 proficiency than her peers and was committed to mastering the writing portions of her digital story by submitting multiple drafts (4) to receive as much feedback as possible.

Conversely, Maïze made little use of the textual mode in her DS. She only used it to state credits and acknowledgments, which were displayed at the end of the project. She did not want to use English captions to reach a broader audience and advocated in her interview:

> "I think my message would reach more people if I also used the English language, but I also think sticking to the French language might intrigue more people and make them focus more on the actual video rather than the voiceover. ... I want [people] to watch the video, I don't really care if they don't understand, I want them to kind of see the feelings that they get when they watch it, just the video".

For Maïze, the use of French could carry her message not by conveying meaning but by intriguing people. The audience's inability to understand what she says strengthens other modes of communication. People could focus on visual and aural elements to negotiate meanings from the relationships of design elements. She wanted to awaken people's feelings through creativity, and she had found written texts to be merely informational and not sufficiently aesthetic.

4.2. Oral/aural mode

A piece of music and a recorded voiceover represent the aural mode of Maïze's project.

In her interviews, she explained that selecting music was difficult, and she had to change it twice. She avoided music with too fast or too slow a beat or lyrics that could distract her audience. She played one song throughout her project.

Her voiceover in French presents structured sentences to mitigate the language barrier. In the postquestionnaire, she wrote, "I didn't think complex ideas could be expressed in another language. Especially if that language was choppy and not fully developed. But then, I found a way to voice those complex ideas in a simpler manner". Maïze created short and concise sentences in L2 to deliver her message, and worked on her intonation to express rhythm, melody, and beat and emphasize the limited amount of words she used. She stated:

> "The tone of voice is crucial. I've always been so focused on pronouncing words right that I never really noticed the tone I was pronouncing them

in. I don't think you always need words to express something when your tone of voice can say everything for you".

Fanny put in a lot of work in the voiceover to improve her speaking skills. In her postquestionnaire, she explained:

> "The project helped me improve my speaking the most because I had to revisit my spoken portions numerous times. I feel that I spent about an even amount of time on making the auditory and visual components of the project, but I feel that I prepared the most for the auditory component".

In addition, she did not add any music to her final presentation. Instead, she wanted her audience to listen to the story, and "wake them up to their blessings, bring them to a humble state of being".

From the start of the project, she favored using both languages to fulfill her mission of becoming an inspiration for others. In her prequestionnaire, she explained, "I would like to have the whole project in French to improve my French but I am concerned about my subject becoming complex with tenses that I have not learned yet". Thus, Fanny focused her project on delivering her message rather than on improving her language proficiency or digital skills. Nonetheless, in her postquestionnaire, she confessed:

> "I used the online tool that speaks text for you. I used this tool to help improve my speaking skills [which] was improved by the project because I had to repeat saying words out loud over and over until they sounded correct. I had to listen to the online tools that speak text repeatedly in order to improve my speaking accuracy".

Despite her main determination to share her message, Fanny decided to select a digital tool to work on her L2 oral skills, and as a result she learned how to use it on her own.

Chapter 5

4.3. Visual mode

Both participants included visuals in their projects and used personal pictures to avoid any copyright issues. While Maïze spent a lot of time producing her visuals to make sure they would convey her story on their own, Fanny presented numerous pictures displayed in a collage form throughout her slideshow. These pictures were mostly used to illustrate her statements rather than to create specific meanings. Nonetheless, in an examination and comparison of the semiotics used by Fanny, some slides revealed disparities between the linguistics and the visuals. One slide in particular is analyzed more deeply in the second part of the findings section.

Maïze's entire project employed the visual mode. During an interview, Maïze explained, "I am a [sic] visual, so I really like the pictures, and like, the sounds or the subtitles kind of come second, so when I was working on it, I was try [sic] to, I just leave [sic] them out". Describing herself as a visually oriented person and a visual learner, she used images to share her message to others. For her project, she shot 14 different photos and 11 videos, and she explained: "I used my phone to take pictures and record most of the videos, two editing websites – Fotor.com and Ribbet.com – to edit the pictures so they would fit in the widescreen frame of the film, and Windows Movie Maker to bring it all together". In addition, she balanced still and moving images throughout the project by adding effects and transitions to maintain an aspect of fluidity.

These two participants made meaningful choices based on their digital skills and language confidence to deliver their stories. This underscores their determination to engage and play with design elements and shows autonomy and learning strategies.

The following section provides insights on how the participants arranged semiotics and 'translated' meanings in their digital stories, by using the concept of either transformation or transduction (Bezemer & Jewitt, 2009; Kress, 2003) as the design process.

4.4. Orchestration of semiotics

The chains of semiosis give particular attention to (1) the concept of transformation, defined as the process of shifting elements within a mode, and (2) the concept of transduction, which is "a process where something configured or formed in one modality is reconfigured or reformed into a different modality" (Kress, 2003, p. 47).

4.4.1. Maïze's case

The concept of transformation was particularly relevant when comparing Maïze's storyboard with her final project. She provided detailed explanations about her use of design elements and a fully developed French narrative. Figure 1 presents a sample of Maïze's storyboard. By capturing the visuals, she produced an original digital story and gave people "a sense of [her] own perspective, and what [she] believe[s] in".

Figure 1. Maïze's first slide of the storyboard

Images *(general or specific, location if known)*:

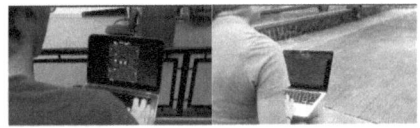

Design *(background color, font style, special effects)*:

(No title screen)

Transition into video from black screen.

Background image: Video of people on their computers.

Audio *(music, sound effects)*:

Music: Intro – The xx (song starts)

Narration *(the actual text that you would record to accompany this slide)*:

La technologie. Qu'est-que c'est la technologie?

Chapter 5

Maïze took multiple steps to achieve her goal. First, she selected pictures she liked from Google images and reproduced them. Her principal concern about using Google images involved the fact that the images were not hers and she did not know about their original purpose. Using an image that looked similar to what she was trying to convey was not enough. She needed to capture her environment and give her perspective. In her second interview, she explained, "I did not want random people, but people with whom I interacted and talked to them, and asked them to act for me to portray my experience and show my view within my environment". Inspired by images found online, Maïze reconfigured and rearranged her visuals. She staged scenes and made people act to "translate" her vision. Figure 2 presents one of the Google images selected by Maïze on the left[2], and the picture she recreated on the right. Her act of recontextualization and transformation within the same mode is incontestable. In setting the scene in her environment – the university – and in representing people who live around her in realistic outfits and attitudes, she showed ownership in the process of design.

Figure 2. Comparative table between the storyboard and the final project

Google Image (presented in storyboard)	Original Picture (drawn from Maize's DST)

Moreover, Maïze had a good sense of her storyline, and her storyboard provided fully structured sentences written in French. She produced short sentences and a redundant pattern to develop a melody and communicate her message. From the storyboard to the final version, the sentences did not change much and she only corrected lexico-grammatical mistakes based on feedback. Nonetheless, Maïze decided to stretch out some sentences across the slides. For instance, in

---

2. To the best of this researcher's knowledge this image is copyright free.

Table 1, the second sentence in bold of Slide 3 from the storyboard (Nous le/ la vérifions à chaque minute) was stretched out to Slide 4 in the final version. The rationale for adding images and stretching out sentences was to provide connections between images and words. During an interview, Maïze explained, "I kind of had really good pictures that I wanted definitively put in there, and some good lines that I wanted to put in there". Thus, Maïze had to stretch out sentences of the voiceover and played around with the aural and visual modes during the editing phase to finalize the project the way she envisioned it.

Table 1. Comparative table of narrative script and voiceover

Slides	Narration written in the storyboard over of the digital story	Slides	Narration transcribed from the voice
1	La technologie. Qu'est-que c'est la technologie?	1	La technologie, qu'est-ce que c'est la technologie?
2	Comment est-ce que nous l'utilisons?	2	Quand est-ce que nous l'utilisons?
3	Nous l'utilison [sic] tous les jours. Nous le vérifions chaque minute.	3	Nous l'utilisons tous les jours
		4	Nous la vérifions à chaque minute

Furthermore, Maïze emphasized her overall message within two or three modes of communication. For instance, one of Maïze's pictures represented "vanity", and the words she wanted to emphasize in her narration were the two adjectives "vain" and "negative". In order to highlight both words, she drastically accentuated her intonation when pronouncing them. Taken with TechSmith's software Camtasia, Figure 3 represents the transduction of meanings produced by Maïze from one mode – visual – to another – oral. As shown, the sentence "nous devenons [we become]" is presented by the two encircled longest audio tracks, while the shortest ones represent the adjectives "vain [vain]" and "négatif [negative]". The increase of the waveforms (encircled) shows the verbal/textual elements expressed by Maïze's voice. In contrast, the decrease in volume (almost nonexistent waveforms) presents the music piece she used. She faded it in and out to create negative space and lengthen her sentence, a strategy that provoked suspense for her audience.

Figure 3. Screenshot of the combination of image, audio track, and text

4.4.2. Fanny's case

By choosing a PowerPoint slideshow as her medium and selecting only specific design elements, Fanny engaged in transformation and transduction processes that were subtler and overlapping in her project. Her use of L1 and L2 to address her audience, her translation of the captions, and her image choices presented more complex engagement in the design process.

Fanny decided to use written captions to illustrate her story. However, she used both languages unevenly based on the message she conveyed and her target audience. At the beginning of her project (Slides 2 and 3), she stated, "Toute ma vie j'ai eu la famille et les amis qui m'ont supporté dans tous mes efforts. Je n'ai jamais été traité [sic] différemment parce que j'avais un bras [sic] [All my life,

I have had family and friends who supported me in all of my endeavors. I was never treated differently because I had one arm]". Whereas the translation is pulled from the storyboard, these two slides appeared exclusively in French in both modes, textual and oral, in Fanny's final project. She did not use English captions. Moreover, her statement is strong and frames her story. She carefully selected the French definite articles *la* and *les* in "J'ai eu la famille et les amis", excluding anyone who is not part of friends or family, and told her audience that she had not missed out on anything in her life: "Je n'ai jamais été traité [sic] différemment".

Yet, from Slides 4 to 6, she added English captions and used French only for the voiceover. To address the English audience, she started her story with a statement of uncertainty: "Sometimes I wondered if my parents knew that I had one arm" and illustrated both slides with a collage of pictures portraying herself with specific family members: her parents and grandparents. At this point, she spoke not only to an English audience, but a specific one: her family. She included them after presenting herself to the French audience, stating that she had what she needed and rejecting any compassion or judgment from them. Starting her story at different slides based on a specific audience underscored how she constructed meanings through the use of L1 and L2.

Moreover, from the proposal to the final version, she changed the title of her story from "One arm wonder" to "Ma vie [my life]", a more general title that addressed both the L1 and L2 audiences and encompassed anyone who would like to listen to her story. More importantly, she talked to her family and shared a more intimate story. Although Fanny's goal in her prequestionnaire was to give "a chance for the audience to be enlightened to a change in perspective", the findings highlighted layers of meanings developed in the arrangement of modes.

Furthermore, while at the beginning she firmly stated to the French audience that she had never been treated differently (Slide 3), she confessed later (Slide 6) to both audiences: "when I was young, I never imagined that people would treat me differently… As I grew older, I experienced many people who thought differently". This slide introduced a series of events in which she

Chapter 5

faced people who only saw her as a disabled person. She narrated these events in Slides 7, 8, 9, and 10, in which she displayed images and captions in both French and English. Fanny did not embed a voiceover in any of these four slides.

Findings revealed that Fanny had never provided Slides 7 and 8 as she turned in the different steps of her project. She added them in her final version. Without a postinterview, I could not explain the participant's choice to add these pieces to her story. Since she did not receive feedback on these oral parts, I could only suppose that Fanny did not embed them because of her lack of confidence in her speaking skills. Thus, she avoided recording them on her own, and instead, put captions in both languages.

Nevertheless, I believe that Fanny's decision was deliberate and carefully thought out. First, she chose to present all events without a voiceover even though she had recorded and received feedback for Slides 9 and 10. Then, she provided captions in the same order, French first and English second. Finally, she differentiated each language with a different color, red for French and green for English, and used this differentiation throughout the entire project.

Moreover, toward the end, Fanny continued to play with captions in French and/or English. Slides 11, 13, and 14 provide English captions, while Slide 12 does not. Slides 15, 16, and 20 present both languages. Slides 17 and 18 have English captions only, and Slide 19 is presented exclusively in French. At first glance, her choices are uneven and seem random, but an in-depth examination of how Fanny orchestrated elements of design revealed careful attention to detail and engagement in the design process. These disparities that emerged between and within modes point out meaningful decisions in her use of L1 and/or L2 based on (1) the audience(s) she targeted, (2) the message she conveyed and how she expressed it, and (3) the confidence she had with her own language proficiency.

Finally, the transduction process is particularly relevant in Fanny's selection of visual and linguistic elements. Two examples (Slides 7 and 8), in which

Fanny recounted two events, propose to examine how she constructed layers of meaning and developed agency.

Both experiences occurred during a trip to Australia in which she participated with a group of students. In Slide 7, she explained that she was not allowed to hold a koala, while other students did receive permission. Despite a detailed narration, she focused the audience's attention on one single picture to bring more meaning to her words (Figure 4).

Figure 4. Representation of Fanny's Slide 7

Every picture that Fanny chose throughout her DST portrayed her smiling and happy. Yet, for this particular moment, she informed her audience that she was frustrated. She was torn between the koala keeper's intention to keep the animal safe and her desire to prove her ability to hold the animal safely. According to the way she phrased it in both languages, her decision to not argue with the koala keeper showed her inner strength.

> "I had to try my hardest not to cry in this picture. I wanted to hold the koala and I knew that I could, I gave the koala keeper my peace because

Chapter 5

he simply did not understand. He was only protecting the koala. That I understand that".

In providing this afterthought, she maintained a positive attitude, avoiding blaming anyone who did not understand her, and preventing her audience from feeling uncomfortable or targeted. The adverbs 'simply' and 'only' and the redundancy of 'that' underscored self-reflection and her acceptance of the situation. Nonetheless, the disparity between her words "I had to try my hardest not to cry in this picture" and the picture displaying her smiling, encouraged the audience to think about the emotions she could feel as a disabled person. Through her words, she shared her feelings, while the visual showed the opposite. She smiled when posing for the photo; nevertheless, in her story, she meant to warn her audience about the ways people could act toward disabled people and the lack of understanding they could potentially demonstrate.

In the second example, Slide 8 (Figure 5), the concept of transduction occurred within the translation from L1 to L2. In the slide, she was describing outdoor activities such as zip-lining, surfing, and scuba diving in which she participated with her group and the coaches' attitude when giving safety instructions.

Figure 5. Representation of Fanny's Slide 8

During the narration, she decided to use a mini-dialogue happening between herself and her inner voice: "cette petite voix dans ma tête est venue disant quelque chose comme 'ouais ratée, va t'asseoir! Pour qui te prends-tu?' [that little voice in the back of my head came saying phrases similar to, 'Yeah go sit down, who are you kidding?']".

This dialogue, created when working on her project, never happened in real life, and her intention was merely to provide an example of how she was interpreting the coaches' thoughts about her disability. "They asked me several times questions like, 'Are you sure you can do it, have you done anything like this before'? Their faces expressed complete skepticism, pity, and extreme doubt". Her words "complete skepticism", "pity", and "extreme doubt" are striking, and by using all of them in one sentence, Fanny seemed to concentrate on the many feelings that she had seen in others' perceptions. They accentuated her disability and diminished her humanity. For the first time, she exposed some anger and frustration through the use of the "little voice".

Moreover, the expressions that Fanny used to make her inner voice speak were much more provocative in French than in English. She employed a familiar language register by saying, "ouais ratée" [yeah, failure] that she did not use in English. Also, she used the form "tu" which in the French context conveys familiarity between two interlocutors. She also used the imperative mode and an exclamation mark to communicate her perception of the coaches' command. Finally, the question "Pour qui te prends-tu?" is usually employed to recognize someone's inappropriate behavior in a given situation, or someone who is exceeding their rights.

By using these expressions in L2, Fanny demonstrated her ability to nuance what she would like to communicate in French and her native tongue. The French version seemed more bitter and heartless than the English version. Fanny may have deliberately softened her English version because of the broader or more intimate audience she anticipated to reach. Knowing that the French audience would only be restricted to her instructor and her classmates, who might not notice the differences as language learners, Fanny may have intended

Chapter 5

to (1) show some language proficiency by using some familiar expressions that she had learned during her semester abroad; and/or (2) express deeper feelings with no consideration toward the audience's (mainly my) reaction. Nonetheless, she developed her voice in her L2 as she made linguistic choices on how to share this particular event with her L2 audience, creating different feelings between the L1 and L2 messages.

5. Discussion

In this study, I did not analyze language proficiency and instead examined the use of the target language with equal attention to other semiotic resources. The study suggests that students made intentional language and semiotic choices to construct meanings and express opinions.

Maïze realized that sharing her point of view could be difficult in French despite her high proficiency. To mitigate challenges, she committed to work on diverse linguistic designs, including intonation, personal pronouns, and present tense. She chose to make short and well-structured sentences that she used as a pattern. Her vocabulary choices were selective and precise, which allowed her to sharpen her intonation and to emphasize specific words by stretching them out and orchestrating them with her visuals. She took the time to select music that supported her voiceover intonation and intertwined them. In addition, she shot her videos, choosing particular camera angles and movements. She stepped into the role of a director by interacting with people, explaining her project, deciding upon the setting, and directing them as actors. She used all the spatial and gestural design elements available to her and created new ones to design meanings.

Fanny used all the digital features required by the instructions, but her story was primarily based upon the writing and speaking portions. She carefully chose her words in both languages and worked on her intonation. She used informal discourse in which the French expressions were provocative and incisive. Whereas she selected the linguistic mode as the main design element, she carefully chose her pictures and thoughtfully displayed them to illustrate her narration, mixing slides with collage and slides with single photos as a focal point. She demonstrated her understanding of how the visual aspect of her storytelling embellished and supported her story and directed the way she represented herself.

As this study suggests, creating DS allows students to combine old and new literacies (Sylvester & Greenidge, 2009), which impact their language development (Hur & Suh, 2012). Through the creation of digital stories, students "articulate a complete, coherent story with a beginning, middle, and end in the target language using multiple media and multiple modalities" (Castañeda, 2013, p. 57). The benefits of integrating DS in FL classrooms relate to language production and practices. According to Smeda, Dakich, and Sharda (2014), digital narratives give students the opportunity to select and concentrate on the language modality(ies) they want to improve. They can also focus on specific tasks, such as structuring complete sentences, pronouncing high-level vocabulary, spelling words, and practicing intonation (Hur & Suh, 2012; Kim, 2014; Ramírez Verdugo & Alonso Belmonte, 2007; Smeda et al., 2014). Digital stories enhance language modalities that allow students to contextualize and construct their stories through the use of linguistic structures and visual and audio aids. As Darvin and Norton (2014) pointed out, "[w]hile some learners can be particularly skillful in crafting a story through words, others may be good at choosing images, finding the right music, matching the different elements, and using the digital tools" (p. 62).

6. Conclusion and implication for FL education

Today's necessity to integrate new literacy approaches (Cope & Kalantzis, 2015; Kern, 2015, Paesani, Allen, & Dupuy, 2016) into FL curricula to promote 21st century skills is clear and should not be overlooked by schools, administrators, and teachers. However, such curricular changes cannot be realized without urgently addressing the needs of FL teachers through quality professional development opportunities. Researchers have reported that teachers' lack of preparation, awareness, and familiarity with the ways a multimodal text works in its interplay between modes and meaning-making constructions prevents them from integrating and teaching multimodal literacy in their classrooms (Chandler, 2017).

Thus, through the lens of DS, this study illustrates the implementation of the multiliteracies pedagogy in an FL course and can serve as a potential model for FL teachers. DS is a tool that serves multiple teaching objectives and fosters numerous language modalities and learning strategies. Podkalicka and Campbell (2010) suggested that digital stories are more valuable to the process of learning than the final product itself. In developing personalized learning experiences (Smeda et al., 2014), DS invites students to become more aware of their language needs and skills and become proficient in technical aspects. In various studies (Robin, 2008; Smeda et al., 2014; VanderArk & Schneider, 2012, as mentioned in Smeda et al., 2014), teachers have reported that the 'learning by doing' approach fosters students' self-confidence to ask questions, participate in discussions, and express opinions.

Moreover, working with digital literacies increases students' motivation (Kim, 2014) and collaboration (Castañeda, 2013; Smeda et al., 2014), and helps them to remain engaged throughout the project (Sylvester & Greenidge, 2009). However, teachers who consider integrating digital stories into their curriculum must have clear goals and objectives. They need to know the reasons behind such a project, their expectations, and what they want to assess. They must be trained and prepared to support students' needs to achieve 21st century skills.

Future studies should take into account how a more extended period (i.e. several semesters) could impact students' performance, and consider students' level of language proficiency to understand how the learning process affects their semiotic awareness. In addition, future projects using DS could integrate into the curriculum (1) the editing phase to facilitate the creation process, and (2) a participative platform where students could post their productions, watch and comment on others' stories, and be involved in "real-world processes of language use" (Ollivier, 2018, p. 36), reaching communities beyond the FL classrooms.

References

Alismail, H. A. (2015). Integrate digital storytelling in education. *Journal of Education and Practice, 6*(9), 126-129.

Anderson, J., Chung, Y. C., & Macleroy, V. (2018). Creative and critical approaches to language learning and digital technology: findings from a multilingual digital storytelling project. *Language and Education, 32*(3), 195-211. https://doi.org/10.1080/09500782.2018.1430151

Bezemer, J., & Jewitt, C. (2009). Social semiotics. In J.-O. Östman, J. Verschueren & E. Versluys (Eds), *Handbook of pragmatics* (vol. 13, pp. 1-14). John Benjamins. https://doi.org/10.1075/hop.13.soc5

Blyth, C. (2014). Exploring the affordances of digital social reading for L2 literacy: the case of eComma. *Digital literacies in foreign and second language education, 12*, 201-226.

Bryant, A., & Charmaz, K. (2007). (Eds). *The Sage handbook of grounded theory*. Sage. https://doi.org/10.4135/9781848607941

Burgess, J. (2006). Hearing ordinary voices: cultural studies, vernacular creativity and digital storytelling. *Continuum: Journal of Media & Cultural Studies, 20*(2), 201-214. https://doi.org/10.1080/10304310600641737

Castañeda, M. E. (2013). "I am proud that I did it and it's a piece of me": digital storytelling in the foreign language classroom. *CALICO Journal, 30*(1), 44-62. https://doi.org/10.11139/cj.30.1.44-62

Chandler, P. D. (2017). To what extent are teachers well prepared to teach multimodal authoring? *Cogent Education, 4*(1), 1266820. https://doi.org/10.1080/2331186x.2016.1266820

Cope, B., & Kalantzis, M. (2009). "Multiliteracies": new literacies, new learning. *Pedagogies: An International Journal, 4*(3), 164-195. https://doi.org/10.1080/15544800903076044

Cope, B., & Kalantzis, M. (2015). (Eds). *A pedagogy of multiliteracies: learning by design*. Palgrave Macmillan.

Darvin, R., & Norton, B. (2014). Transnational identity and migrant language learners: the promise of digital storytelling. *Education Matters: The Journal of Teaching and Learning, 2*(1), 55-66.

Gee, J. P. (2008). Learning in semiotic domains. *Literacies, Global and Local, 2*, 137-149.

Hur, J. W., & Suh, S. (2012). Making learning active with interactive whiteboards, podcasts, and digital storytelling in ELL classrooms. *Computers in the Schools, 29*(4), 320-338. https://doi.org/10.1080/07380569.2012.734475

Jewitt, C. (2009). (Ed.). *The Routledge handbook of multimodal analysis* (pp. 28-39). Routledge.

Jiang, L. (2017). The affordances of digital multimodal composing for EFL learning. *ELT Journal, 71*(4), 413-422. https://doi.org/10.1093/elt/ccw098

Kern, R. (2000). *Literacy and language teaching*. Oxford University Press.

Kern, R. (2006). Perspectives on technology in learning and teaching languages. *TESOL Quarterly, 40*(1), 183-210. https://doi.org/10.2307/40264516

Kern, R. (2015). *Language, literacy, and technology*. Cambridge University Press.

Kim, S. (2014). Developing autonomous learning for oral proficiency using digital storytelling. *Language Learning & Technology, 18*(2), 20-35.

Kress, G. (2003). *Literacy in the new media age*. Routledge.

Kress, G. (2009). *Multimodality: a social semiotic approach to contemporary communication*. Routledge.

Kress, G., & van Leeuwen, T. (1996). Narrative representations: designing social action. In G. Kress & T. van Leeuwen (Eds), *Reading images: the grammar of visual design* (pp. 45-73). Routledge. https://doi.org/10.1075/fol.3.2.15vel

Lambert, J. (2002). *Digital storytelling: capturing lives, creating community*. Digital Diner.

Lambert, J. (2013). *Digital storytelling: capturing lives, creating community* (4th ed.). Routledge.

Lebrun, M., Lacelle, N., & Boutin, J.-F. (2012). Genèse et essor du concept de littératie médiatique multimodale. *Mémoires du livre / Studies in Book Culture, 3*(2), 1-19. https://doi.org/10.7202/1009351ar

Lemke, J. L. (1998). Metamedia literacy: transforming meanings and media. In D. Reinking, M. C. McKenna, L. D. Labbo & R. D. Kieffer (Eds), *Handbook of literacy and technology: transformations in a post-typographic world* (pp. 283-301). Erlbaum.

Lundby, K. (2008). Editorial: mediatized stories: mediation perspectives on digital storytelling. *New Media & Society, 10*(3), 363-371. https://doi.org/10.1177/1461444808089413

Lynch, T. (2007). Learning from the transcripts of an oral communication task. *ELT Journal, 61*(4), 311-320. https://doi.org/10.1093/elt/ccm050

Michelson, K., & Dupuy, B. (2014). Multi-storied lives: global simulation as an approach to developing multiliteracies in an intermediate French course. *L2 Journal, 6*(1), 21-49. https://doi.org/10.5070/l26119613

Miller, E. A. (2009). *Digital storytelling, in department of curriculum and instruction*. University of Iowa.

Nelson, M. (2006). Mode, meaning, and synaesthesia in multimedia L2 writing. *Language Learning & Technology, 10*(2), 56-76.

Nelson, M. E., & Kern, R. (2012). Language teaching and learning in the postlinguistic condition. In L. Asalgoff, S. L. Mckay, G. Hu & W. A. Renandya (Eds), *Principles and practices for teaching English as an international language* (pp. 47-66). Routledge.

New London Group. (1996). A pedagogy of multiliteracies: designing social futures. *Harvard Educational Review, 66*(1), 60-92. https://doi.org/10.17763/haer.66.1.17370n67v22j160u

Ollivier, C. (2018). Towards a socio-interactional approach to foster autonomy in language learners and users. eLANG project-Digital literacy for the teaching and learning of language. *Graz, Austria: European Center for Modern Languages.* https://www.ecml.at/Portals/1/documents/ECML-resources/elang-EN-A5_28112018_112721.pdf?ver=2018-11-28-112721-473

Oskoz, A., & Elola, I. (2016). Digital stories: overview. *Calico Journal, 33*(2), 157-173. https://doi.org/10.1558/cj.v33i2.29295

Paesani, K. W., Allen, H. W., Dupuy, B., (2016). *A multiliteracies framework for collegiate foreign language teaching.* Prentice Hall.

Paulus, T. M. (1999). The effect of peer and teacher feedback on student writing. *Journal of Second Language Writing, 8*(3), 265-289. https://doi.org/10.1016/s1060-3743(99)80117-9

Podkalicka, A., & Campbell, C. (2010, June). Understanding digital storytelling: individual 'voice' and community-building in youth media programs. *Seminar. Net: Media, Technology & Life-Long Learning, 6*(2), 1-10.

Ramírez Verdugo, D., & Alonso Belmonte, I. (2007). Using digital stories to improve listening comprehension with Spanish young learners of English. *Language Learning & Technology, 11*(1), 87- 101.

Reinhardt, J., Warner, C., & Lange, K. (2014). Digital games as practices and texts: new literacies and genres in an L2 German classroom. *Digital literacies in foreign and second language education, 12,* 159-177.

Reinhardt, J., & Zander, V. (2011). Social networking in an intensive English program classroom: a language socialization perspective. *Calico Journal, 28*(2), 326-344. https://doi.org/10.11139/cj.28.2.326-344

Robin, B. (2006). The educational uses of digital storytelling. *Technology and Teacher Education Annual, 1,* 709-716.

Robin, B. R. (2008). Digital storytelling: a powerful technology tool for the 21st century classroom. *Theory Into Practice, 47*(3), 220-228. https://doi.org/10.1080/00405840802153916

Smeda, N., Dakich, E., & Sharda, N. (2014). The effectiveness of digital storytelling in the classrooms: a comprehensive study. *Smart Learning Environments*, *1*(1), 1-21. https://doi.org/10.1186/s40561-014-0006-3

Sylvester, R., & Greenidge, W. L. (2009). Digital storytelling: extending the potential for struggling writers. *The Reading Teacher*, *63*(4), 284-295. https://doi.org/10.1598/rt.63.4.3

Unsworth, L. (2001). *Teaching multiliteracies across the curriculum. Changing contexts of text and image in classroom practice*. Open University Press.

Van Gils, F. (2005, June). Potential applications of digital storytelling in education. In *3rd twente student conference on IT* (Vol. 7). University of Twente, Faculty of Electrical Engineering, Mathematics and Computer Science Enschede.

VanderArk, T., & Schneider, C. (2012). *How digital learning contributes to deeper learning*. Getting Smart. http://www.worldwideworkshop.com/pdfs/GettingSmart_DigitalLearningDeeperLearning.pdf

Vinogradova, P., Linville, H. A., & Bickel, B. (2011). "Listen to my story and you will know me": digital stories as student-centered collaborative projects. *TESOL Journal*, *2*(2), 173-202. https://doi.org/10.5054/tj.2011.250380

Volle, L. M. (2005). Analyzing oral skills in voice e-mail and online interviews. *Language Learning and Technology*, *9*(3),146-163.

Yang, Y. F. D. (2012). Multimodal composing in digital storytelling. *Computers and Composition*, *29*(3), 221-238. https://doi.org/10.1016/j.compcom.2012.07.001

6. Telling stories multimodally: what observations of parent-child shared book-reading activities can bring to L2 kindergarten teachers' training

Pauline Beaupoil-Hourdel[1]

1. Introduction

In teacher training curricula, books are presented as an ideal material for building and enriching young children's language (Boisseau, 2005; Canut, 2001; Canut, Bruneseaux-Gauthier, Vertalier, & Lentin, 2012; Cellier, 2015). Cellier (2015, pp. 32-34) explained that there exists a strong link between book reading, story-telling, and the acquisition of vocabulary because teachers use narratives as a prop to give context to linguistic forms and to establish repetition routines of words or syntactic structures with the pupils. Preservice kindergarten teachers are therefore encouraged to use children's books to help their pupils acquire and master language. Most textbooks also warn teachers that they should carefully choose the children's books they want to present to the class, ensuring that the text is not too complex to understand for a child of three, four, or five years old (Canut et al., 2012, pp. 51-78; Cellier, 2015, p. 32). Canut et al. (2012) addressed one missing link in this training system, which is how teachers should be trained in using books to foster their learners' language acquisition. The authors show that teachers need to anticipate lexical and contextual difficulties. Cellier (2015) added that teachers need to ensure that the children understand the words and acquire them and will be able to later recall the new lexical items. Overall, books are presented as a rich support

---

1. Sorbonne Université and INSPE de Paris, CeLiSo (EA 7332), Paris, France; pauline.beaupoil-hourdel@espe-paris.fr; https://orcid.org/0000-0001-7245-8908

How to cite this chapter: Beaupoil-Hourdel, P. (2020). Telling stories multimodally: what observations of parent-child shared book-reading activities can bring to L2 kindergarten teachers' training. In B. Dupuy and M. Grosbois (Eds), *Language learning and professionalization in higher education: pathways to preparing learners and teachers in/for the 21st century* (pp. 167-198). Research-publishing.net. https://doi.org/10.14705/rpnet.2020.44.1105

material that can be used to elicit child-child and adult-child interactions, to enhance the children's language development, and to help widen their lexical repertoire (Canut, Masson, & Leroy, 2018).

Yet, the routine of reading at home with children is hardly ever mentioned. In a comparative study of book-reading activities with teachers in school and with low-income mothers at home, Dickinson, De Temple, Hirschler, and Smith (1992) showed that teachers should be aware of the social and cultural routines children may or may not be accustomed to before engaging in book-reading activities. The authors showed that the routines established at home are a prelude to the activities that teachers set up in class. However, if some pupils do not engage in Shared Book Reading (SBR) activities with a parent at home, these children are missing one piece of the puzzle. Taking into account the children's book-reading experience and observing how books are being used and how stories are being told at home in a highly multimodal and intimate situation could help teachers better adjust to children's needs in class and favor individual first and second language development.

In this chapter, I propose analyses of story-reading activities from a usage-based and first language acquisition perspective. The goal is to raise methodological questions for the professionalization of future kindergarten teachers who engage in L2 teaching with children aged three to six. This paper questions the links between the home and school environments in a context of L2 learning with beginners. The link between L1 and L2 acquisition is pertinent, as parents' practices and language use when interacting with children who do not master their mother tongue might inform the design of training programs for kindergarten teachers who teach a foreign language to pupils from three to six[2]. The chapter is organized as follows. First, I present a review of SBR activities and the use of books during adult-child interaction at home and in class. Second, I present my analytical approach to language use and development and its application to children's linguistic and

---

2. In France, kindergarten teachers can teach a second language, but it is not compulsory. Lately, parents of three to six year old children have been asking for early second language teaching at kindergarten schools. Consequently, some school directors and researchers are advocating for and implementing specific programs in early second language teaching (see Cnesco, 2019, and https://www.education.gouv.fr/bo/19/Hebdo22/MENE1915455N.htm).

interactional competences: I present results from my own projects on reading at home (Beaupoil-Hourdel, 2017; Beaupoil-Hourdel, Leroy-Collombel, & Morgenstern, 2019) and propose qualitative multimodal analyses of the data to account for the participation framework and content of SBR activities. Corpus-based analyses of parent-child SBR activities at home will contribute to show how the parents in the corpus naturally and spontaneously engaged in SBR activities with their children. Third, based on my analyses, I draw some guidelines for the professionalization of preservice teachers who are trained in universities, keeping in mind that the ecology of reading books at home significantly differs from that of reading books in class.

In this chapter I aim to theorize parents' spontaneous behavior in order to provide professional guidelines for teachers in the context of story-reading activities in a second language in class with children who cannot read yet. The analyses focus on how meaning is co-constructed by the adult, the child, the story in the book, and the surrounding environment by taking into consideration all the semiotic resources that the speakers have at their disposal (vocal productions, words, actions, gestures, and facial expressions). To analyze how meaning is constructed in this context, particular attention is paid to the book itself, its written and visual contents, as well as how it is manipulated by the participants.

2. Literature review

Research in first language acquisition has shown that routines are essential for children to develop language. Routines, or *scripts* (Bruner, 1983; Schank & Abelson, 1977), offer a format and a context for a specific action to develop along with language. Thanks to the repetition of such routines, children learn to behave as co-participants in interaction and to mobilize language in specific contexts while adjusting to the unfolding action and their speech partners. Thanks to routines and embodied social practices, children learn when and how to take a turn in interaction or what lexical forms are expected in a specific context; this is how they manage, at a very early age, to take part in activities like

Chapter 6

eating together, taking a bath, playing a board game, greetings, or telling stories and reading books (Snow & Goldfield, 1983).

Telling stories and reading books are common social practices in corpora of adult-child spontaneous interactions in families from an upper-middle-class background (as frequently evidenced in the CHILDES L1 Database). Interestingly, parents often use books with young children who cannot read. In these families, books are used for interaction and transmission of cultural knowledge about the world. Previous research has shown that routines of SBR activities (Beaupoil-Hourdel, 2017; Cameron-Faulkner & Noble, 2013; Noble, Cameron-Faulkner, & Lieven, 2018; Payne, Whitehurst, & Angell, 1994) trigger lexical development (Payne et al., 1994) and grammatical development (Cameron-Faulkner & Noble, 2013). Snow et al. (1976) and Hoff-Ginsberg (1992) have shown that language used during SBR involves a higher mean length of utterance than in spontaneous adult-child dyadic interactions, suggesting that both the parents and the child produce longer turns in the context of SBR than during spontaneous interactions. Parents' utterances are longer and grammatically richer during SBR because the stories have a different register from oral speech (Bus, van IJzendoorn, & Pellegrini, 1995; Cameron-Faulkner & Noble, 2013). Cameron-Faulkner and Noble (2013) observed a wider range of nouns and verbs and a more complex set of sentence types in SBR than in Child-Directed Speech (CDS) and oral speech in general. Their study relied on two types of books: books with pictures only and books with a written story. They expected that the first type of book would not alter the linguistic richness and complexity of the adults' utterances, but results showed that both types of books generate more complex constructions than free play CDS (Cameron-Faulkner & Noble, 2013). Therefore, books are often viewed as a form of enriched linguistic input (Cameron-Faulkner & Noble, 2013).

Other studies have shown that SBR activities help children develop narrative skills (Bamberg, 1987; Heath & Branscombe, 1986; Magee & Sutton-Smith, 1983) with the ability to adopt somebody else's perception (Leroy-Collombel, 2013; Lever & Sénéchal, 2011). They also enhance children's capacity to talk about themselves, their experiences, and others' feelings (Beaupoil-Hourdel,

2017). From a linguistic perspective, because the story in a book is not located in the here and now and does not focus on the child, SBR activities help young children develop skills for talking about displaced events and characters. Books offer a suitable context to mobilize the past, present, and future tenses as well as aspectual forms (Leroy-Collombel, 2013). SBR activities offer a favorable context for children to acquire oral language. The activity itself triggers a constant back-and-forth movement between children's daily lives and the work of fiction they are reading, but it also prompts displaced speech on the part of both parents and children. Storybooks add a new dimension to language itself since language is no longer used to carry out actions, but rather to talk about displaced events or imaginary characters (Beaupoil-Hourdel, 2017, pp. 56-57). This particular context may allow children to make sense of the world and to mobilize language to express their feelings, likes, and dislikes as well as to relate to the characters and the events encapsulated in the narrative (Beaupoil-Hourdel, 2017).

Children's books in SBR activities are multimodal objects since they make it possible for a written text to be oralized by the parent and embodied through prosody, rhythm, and added gestures or facial expressions (Beaupoil-Hourdel et al., 2019), but also because the text is usually accompanied with pictures that illustrate the narrative. The multimodal nature of books helps children build indexicality (i.e. the context-dependency of natural language), symbolization, intersubjectivity (Leroy-Collombel, 2013), and communication skills, as they learn to make sense of a text thanks to the visual cues at their disposal, be they pictures from the book or kinesic behavior used by the adult reading the story (Beaupoil-Hourdel, 2017; Beaupoil-Hourdel et al., 2019). A book is not a mere object with a text and pictures, it is "a game relevant semiotic object of a particular type" (Goodwin, 2003, p. 221) because the object is required for the activity and the interaction to develop.

In SBR activities at home, the adult takes the role of an intermediary who is the only one who can deliver the story to the child who cannot read (Frier, 2011). The adult is therefore crucial as well as the way they tell the story, modulate their voice, handle the book when reading the text, look at the child, and ensure joint attention. In this respect, when teachers read stories to pupils, they also take the role of an intermediary, and knowing the social practices the children are exposed to at home could help develop and enrich prospective teachers' training programs.

Books do not have the same status in all households. Bonnafé (2011) explained that although in some families, books are available for children, in others, books are absent or for adults only. Even among families from the same socioeconomic background, the frequency of book-reading activities varies (Beaupoil-Hourdel, 2017). These studies suggest that the social role of books differs between families, even those from similar socioeconomic backgrounds.

Shared book-reading activities have been studied in families of various socioeconomic status[3] and in school (Canut, 1997, 2001; Canut & Gauthier, 2009; Frier, 2011; Vertalier, 2009) and some research has compared book-reading practices and language development at home and in school (Frier, 2011; Heath, 1983; Payne et al., 1994). In the literature on teachers' professional acts in the context of book-reading activities, Canut and Gauthier (2009) provided advice to teachers on how to choose a children's book to read in class. They advocated using books (1) to which the children can easily relate as a way to prompt language production and help them understand the story, (2) with easily recognizable pictures, and (3) that meet specific learning goals that the teacher needs to establish before reading the book in class. These pieces of advice could easily be given to teachers who use books in an L2 context. Canut (1997) addressed the practice of telling the story of a book instead of reading the story. She mentioned that the two activities are different because the first one does not give access to the written material of the book. Boisseau (2005, pp. 140-141) described two types of oralization of a book: reading a story from beginning to end while sticking to the text and reading with pauses, enrichment, scaffolding, elicitations, and reformulations of the text. He explained that the first activity helps build linguistic skills in children. Teachers are advised to engage in this type of reading activity to help children distinguish between oral language and written

---

3. See, for example, Dickinson et al. (1992), Frier (2011), Payne et al. (1994), and Heath (1983) for studies on low-income families and Cameron-Faulkner and Noble (2013), Beaupoil-Hourdel (2017), and Leroy-Collombel (2013) among others for studies on families from the middle class.

language. He suggested that teachers stick to the text and use prosodic contours that mark the difference between spoken and written language. In this activity, the children are engaged in a comprehension task, and thus they are only listening to the teacher. Pictures are shown to them, but they are not commented upon. In the second reading-type activity, the book is used to foster children's language acquisition. The teacher may read the book once, twice, or more, and then the children are asked to tell the story or work on the narrative, react to the content, or make parallels with their own experience of the world. The children are active, and the book is a pretext for interaction. The pictures can be commented upon, and sometimes the story can emerge from the description of images. The text of the book is less important than the interaction the book yields. In a second language learning context with beginners and kindergarteners, the second type of oralization is mostly recommended to prospective teachers (Voise, 2018).

In parent-child interactions it seems that parents or children read a book for the story and the intimate moment that this activity creates. The two types of oralization presented by Boisseau are often intertwined in parent-child SBR activities. Indeed, the second type of reading often unexpectedly surfaces while the first type of reading activity is unfolding (Beaupoil-Hourdel et al., 2019). One major difference between school and home is the goal of the activity. In teacher-pupil interactions, reading books meets explicit goals, and the teacher chooses the book for specific reasons. In parent-child interactions, the activity is one among myriads of others and the reading of a book is only possible if both the child and the parent agree on engaging in the activity. Moreover, studies on parent-child interactions during SBR activities have shown that in this context, CDS is always within the child's Zone of Proximal Development (ZPD; Vygotsky, 1978). Vygotsky (1978, p. 87) defined the ZPD as the difference between what a child or a learner can do alone and what they could do with the help of an expert interlocutor, like a parent or a teacher. It appears that most parents naturally and spontaneously adjust to their child's ZPD, which enables the child to learn and acquire new words and knowledge. Teachers need to propose tasks that are provided within the children's ZPD if they want the pupils to learn. In the context of L2 SBR activities, teachers need to choose a book and to use it in class while ensuring that the task is within the children's ZPD.

This review of the literature highlights the fact that children learn language in situations that include 'joint attentional processes' (Tomasello, 1988). Research in first language acquisition often documents adult-child dyadic interactions as one of the situations in which children acquire language, but Goffman (1974) and cross-cultural studies of children's socialization indicate that they also learn language in multiparty interaction with other members of their community (Schieffelin & Ochs, 1986). These studies suggest that it is therefore interesting to look at children's language development in varied contexts and situations such as in dyadic interactions with a parent at home and in multiparty interaction with the teacher and other pupils at school.

Research on second language training programs for kindergarten teachers has shown that children between three and six learn foreign languages through immersion in a foreign-speaking context (Voise, 2018). It has been found that in foreign-speaking or multilingual learning contexts, young children's productions consist of exaggerated repetitions and transformation of language forms (phonetic, morphological, and syntactic features; Čekaitė & Evaldsson, 2019). The authors showed that learning a foreign language for children from three and six involved playing with languages. In this respect, instructional activities in a foreign language should be entertaining for the children and should add playful learning activities. Voise (2018) added that L2 teaching in a kindergarten context involves creating spaces for drama as both the teacher and the pupils need to enact the language verbally and nonverbally in order to build L2 linguistic competences. Research on professionalization for kindergarten and primary school teachers' advocates for the design of programs which train students in gesture studies (Tellier, 2006, 2008; Tellier & Yerian, 2018) and multimodality (Aden, Clark, & Potapushkina-Delfosse, 2019; Soulaine, 2018) in order to teach foreign languages to beginners. Similarly, teachers' training and professional practices could benefit from analyses of the social practices parents set up at home. Little research has been done on how parents' practices at home may be useful for kindergarten teacher training, and to what extent they could offer new perspectives on multimodal (verbal and nonverbal) construction of linguistic, narrative, and communication skills in young children at school.

3. Data collection and analysis

In this study I analyze the interaction framework of adult-child book reading situations at home and draw implications for teacher education. I use four longitudinal corpora of two monolingual French-speaking children (Madeleine and Anaé), and two monolingual English-speaking children (Ellie and Scarlett) filmed at home[4]. The goal of this study is to draw a link between routines of L1 story-reading activities at home and L2 teaching activities at school with children under the age of six.

The children filmed in their family in interaction with their parent were video-recorded one hour a month from ten months to four years old in spontaneous and natural interaction. I use three corpora from the Paris Corpus (Morgenstern, 2009; Morgenstern & Parisse, 2012, 2017) and one dataset collected in London by Sam Green (UCL ESRC). The French data were entirely transcribed using the CHAT format with the software CLAN (MacWhinney, 2000). The parents of the children signed a consent form and allowed us to transcribe and analyze the recordings, show them at conferences, and cite and show pictures of their interactions in academic papers. For the present study, I analyzed videos of the four children every six months. The home data is composed of 36 hours of videos, and SBR activities correspond to five hours of the overall data. In Madeleine's, Anaé's, and Scarlett's data, SBR context represents about 25% of the overall data. In Ellie's corpus the percentage is lower, with 6% of the time being devoted to reading books with a parent. Yet, Ellie and her mother engaged more often than the three other dyads in other types of activities, like cooking, that take time to develop. All the parents are educated middle-class adults. Books were present in their home environments and were available to the children. At the beginning of the data collection, the children were ten months old, they had access to board books, and the parents willingly read books to them.

This chapter falls in the field of interactional linguistics (Goodwin, 2017; Morgenstern, 2014; Morgenstern & Parisse, 2017) and considers language as

---

4. The children's parents allowed us to use their real names.

a system in which all modalities of expression play a role in the construction of meaning. Goodwin, Goodwin, and Yaeger-Dror (2002) showed that to express themselves, adults and children mobilize a variety of semiotic means they can combine or use in isolation. In line with this definition, this paper proposes qualitative analyses of excerpts from the corpus to analyze the adult-child interaction framework during story-reading and story-telling activities at home. In this study, none of the children are readers, and story-telling activities were therefore incorporated as part of a complete story-reading protocol. Using a constructivist, usage-based (Tomasello, 2003) and multimodal approach, I analyzed the vocal channel (speech and vocal productions) and the visual channel (actions, gestures, and facial expressions) and how the semiotic resources are mobilized by the speakers and contribute to the narrative that is oralized. To tag the story-reading activities in the data, I used transcriptions with CLAN and a spreadsheet grid to link the productions with the context. Detailed analyses of gestural forms were done using the software ELAN (Wittenburg et al., 2006) to focus both on the forms of the visual productions and the synchronization with other modalities of expression like speech or vocalizations. Prosodic analyses were also conducted with the software PRAAT. This methodology is based on the use of four compatible analytical tools (CLAN, EXCEL, PRAAT, and ELAN), which sustain fine-grained multilayered analyses. Coding the data in only one tool like ELAN would be time-saving, but the analyses would be less detailed.

4. Findings

4.1. Reading books with a parent at home

Children acquire language in a rich context composed of words, gestures, actions, vocalizations, facial expressions, and the objects they manipulate or talk about in interaction with others. The study of book-reading activities is therefore a useful means of analyzing the development of language in young children, as books are familiar objects in the home of the four children in the data and they are also education materials for teachers. Figure 1 presents eight pictures of book-reading activities in the home data. These pictures give a visual representation of shared book-reading activities at home.

Figure 1. Pictures of shared book-reading activities from the home data

Reading books at home first relies on choosing a book to read (Pictures b, c, and g). In the data the parents never chose a book to read without the child's approval. Before a child is two years old, the parents mostly choose a book and assess whether the child is willing to engage in the activity; after age two, children usually choose books and initiate reading activities.

Reading books at home with a parent for a child under four usually goes along with picture-pointing and picture-naming routines (Pictures d and e). Pointing gestures are frequent gestural forms in early children's language development (e.g. Bates, Camaioni, & Volterra, 1975; Goldin-Meadow & Butcher, 2003; Leroy, Mathiot, & Morgenstern, 2009; Morgenstern, Caët, & Limousin, 2016; Tomasello, Carpenter, & Liszkowski, 2007) and in book-reading situations, the parent and the child often point to the pictures of the book to name them or comment on them. Using a book sometimes creates explicit language teaching from the parent who can name the referent of the pictures the child points to or elicit specific spoken lexical productions from the child by asking what is in the picture, as in Example 1. In this example, Anaé is two years and one month old, and she is telling a story to her mother using a book. She describes the action of several animals climbing up a hill. She turns a page but stops speaking because she does not remember the noun *mouton* (*sheep*) or does not recognize that the drawing represents a sheep. The mother helps Anaé produce the target word by pointing to the picture (Appendix 1, Line 3), drawing a parallel with the experience of the child during her last holiday (Appendix 1, l. 4), by giving information about the grammatical gender of the animal in French with the article "le" (Appendix 1, Line 7) and finally by initiating the word when she utters the phoneme <m> for *mouton* (Appendix 1, Line 10). In Appendix 1 the mother uses the book to help the child recall a specific lexical item, and in doing so she builds lexical and phonological knowledge. Gestures are often mobilized in this type of context as the participants at times mimic the characters of the story (pouting, finger-wagging gestures for rejection, etc.), use metadiscursive gestures to react to or comment on the narrative (palm-up gestures to show absence, hands on the head to convey surprise; Figure 1, Picture h), draw attention to and name pictures (pointing gestures), and define words (iconic gestures, pointing gestures to objects in the environment, etc.). Gestures help the parent and the child create meaning thanks to shared attention during book-reading activities.

The pictures in Figure 1 also show that reading books at home with a parent is an intimate moment. The bodies of the participants are very close to each other (Pictures a, d, e, f, g, and h), and the parent often touches the child's body, with the child sitting close to the parent (Pictures e, f, g, h) or on her lap (Pictures a and d). Figure 1 thus shows that SBR at home is a highly multimodal routine in which the text of the book, the pictures, the spoken productions of the participants, their gestures, facial expressions, and vocalizations are all intertwined. These moments are not only intimate parent-child moments; they are also enjoyable moments (Pictures a and f), and they often establish implicit and explicit learning activities during which children learn new vocabulary and mobilize words and linguistic structures they already know in order to build a narrative with an adult. SBR activities are rich linguistic situations because of the participants' engagement and because books can be viewed as social objects that trigger and sustain interactions.

4.2. Books as social objects

Reading books with a parent is a frequent and recurrent activity in the data, and it happens spontaneously. The dyads were filmed in spontaneous daily activities at home, and they were not expected to engage in any specific interactions during the sessions. Therefore, all book-reading activities that developed were spontaneously initiated by the parent, the child, or both of them. In Appendix 2, Anaé is one year and four months old, and she has just taken up a book to read with her mother. At this age, Anaé cannot read, and it is her mother who usually reads stories to her. Yet, in this situation, the mother asks Anaé to tell the story herself ("Alors, tu nous racontes" / "So, tell us the story" Appendix 2, Line 8). The child immediately engages in the activity (Appendix 2, Line 10) and produces high-fall prosodic contours without words. At almost a year and a half, Anaé's speech is not developed enough for her to tell a story but her vocalizations with syllabic segmentation, and high-fall prosodic contours along with the handling of the book show that she has incorporated the script of the activity. She mimics her mother, and her embodied routine shows that SBR is a social practice she has been socialized in. Interestingly, the mother initiates the situation and positions Anaé as the reader or the storyteller right from the beginning, even though she knows that her child cannot tell a story from beginning to end or read. Appendix 2 illustrates that reading books at home is a complex activity that mobilizes the coordination and synchronization of speech, prosody, and specific actions of manipulation of the object, but before being able to use words to create a narrative, children need to understand the whole frame of the activity itself. In this excerpt Anaé's embodied routine of shared book activities highlights that she has incorporated the actions of reading a book (opening a book, putting it in front of her, turning the pages, and closing the book) and the prosodic structure of a narrative (prominent high-fall prosodic contours). Moreover, she can coordinate her actions and her vocalization and voice a story the way her mother would do it. Yet, the context of shared book-reading activities is not

Chapter 6

only crucial for children's language development, but also for the development of perspective and intersubjectivity.

4.2.1. Acquiring intersubjectivity

When they use a book, children and their parents focus on fictitious characters and their experience of the world. In adult-child data collected in the participants' homes, the center of attention and of the interaction was mostly the child. In the context of SBR activities, a shift occurred, and the characters of the story became the focus of attention. Children's books frequently address situations children experience in their everyday life, like refusing to eat, going to their grandparents', and going to nursery school. In this perspective, book-reading activities may help children learn to understand their own experience of the world through the characters in a book. The activity itself yields talk about others by using third-person pronouns and mobilizing verb endings that concord with these pronouns. They may also help children understand their own feelings by relating to the story and the characters. In this sense, reading books and relating to the characters may help develop theory of mind in young children along with affective stance and intersubjectivity (De Weck, 2005), as in Appendix 3, when Madeleine is one year and eleven months old. Her mother is reading *Le Petit Poucet* (*Hop-O'-My-Thumb*), and one picture in the book shows a crying mother of some children. Madeleine starts depicting the picture ("sa maman elle pleure", "his mother is crying"; Appendix 3, Line 1) and verbally and then physically offers her bunny to the character (Appendix 3, Lines 12 and 26). Madeleine's voice in Line 1 follows a rising intonation contour, and the mother immediately feels the need to offer an explanation to the child in Line 5. Madeleine and the mother discuss ways of comforting the character. The mother asks if she would like to give the character her bunny, and then Madeleine reuses the verb "consoler", "comfort", and repeats it three times. The mother's spoken production translates into words the affective stance Madeleine has conveyed with her actions, her gaze, the orientation of her body toward the book, and the prosody of her utterances. The mother offers linguistic scaffolding and a new word (Appendix 3, Line 20) that the child immediately takes up (Appendix 3, Line 22). In Line 26, Madeleine puts her bunny on the book and says "tiens", "there" (Appendix 3, Line 27) with a creaky voice. Her action of offering her bunny, the bunny itself, and the use of the creaky voice show that Madeleine is relating to the character and empathizing with her. She understands that the character is crying and that she needs comfort. When Madeleine is feeling sad and wants to cry in the data, she wants her bunny; her actions in this context constitute a multimodal way of taking the character's feelings into account and adjusting to them, without putting herself as the focal participant in the interaction. Even though Madeleine's mastery of language is not complex enough for her to use words spontaneously in this situation, she identifies with the character and manages to display an affective stance toward the object in a multimodal fashion (using not only language, but gestures and modified voice quality).

4.2.2. Multimodality during book-reading activities: giving body and voice to the characters

Examples 2 and 3 are instances of lexical enrichment provided by the mothers, but they also highlight that the parent or the child constantly sets a back-and-forth movement between the narrative and the child's sphere of experience. In Appendix 4, Scarlett is one year and five months old, and she is reading *The Very Hungry Caterpillar* with her mother (Figure 2).

Figure 2. Scarlett pointing to the 'Hungry Caterpillar' in the book

Figure 3. Scarlett's mother touches the child's stomach

In the narrative, the caterpillar eats too much during the day and feels sick. Scarlett knows the story; her mother often reads the book to her. In this excerpt the mother elicits the productions of "stomachache" (Line 1) with her prosody when she says "that night he had a" with a rising prosodic contour (Figure 3). Scarlett answers "stomachache" (Appendix 4, Line 3) and points to the caterpillar on the page (Appendix 4, Line 4). The combination of her spoken and gestural utterance indexes the reference (the caterpillar) and associates the sensation of stomachache to the drawing of the caterpillar feeling sick on the page. The mother gives positive feedback to her daughter by repeating the noun "stomachache" (Appendix 4, Line 5), touching Scarlett's stomach, and adding "his tummy hurt his tummy was owie" (Appendix 4, Line 5). In doing so, she enriches the child's spoken production and the narrative itself. The text of the narrative in the book stops after "that night he had a stomachache". The mother's multimodal explanation enriches both the narrative and the interaction. Her utterance builds upon Scarlett's pointing gesture synchronized with the word "stomachache" (Appendix 4, Lines 3 and 4) as she nonverbally explains to the child where the locus of the pain is, using the child's body when she touches Scarlett's stomach while explaining that the caterpillar had a sore stomach. The rubbing of the child's stomach and the use of a lexicon the child knows for pain ("hurt", "owie" Appendix 4, Line 5) not only contribute to the meaning but also explicitly add logical order to the events of the story: the mother makes the parallel between eating too much food and having a stomachache explicit. The mother's gaze also goes from the book to the child, illustrating that she is no longer reading and that she is redefining the focus of the story. At that moment, the mother puts Scarlett at the center of the interaction.

The child and the mother are taking part in a co-operative activity and building on each other's utterances and actions to tell the story of the caterpillar. They are engaged in co-operative semiosis in which they both build actions and utterances using the other's previous multimodal utterances to tell the story of the caterpillar (Goodwin, 2017). The shift of focus carried out by the mother, the enrichment of the narrative, and the routine of mapping the sensation onto the child's body are ways for the mother to give bodily form and substance to the narrative and to contextualize the narrative in order to help the child understand the story. The mother's scaffolding, contextualization, and recontextualization routine is apparently effective, since Scarlett easily retrieves the word stomachache at the beginning of the excerpt. Thanks to this routine, she mobilizes several modalities to say that the caterpillar had a stomachache. In the data, children under four usually describe what they see in pictures, and their mothers often verbalize what the characters' feelings and sensations are.

Embodying characters during story-reading activities is quite frequent in the data (Figure 4, below). In Appendix 5, Ellie is three years old and is reading *The Cat That Went Woof* with her mother. In the narrative, Patch is a puppy who is always cheerful and shows happiness by wagging his tail, and Tiger is a cat who is sad because she is no longer the only pet in the house.

In Appendix 5, anytime Ellie or the mother says "wagged his tail" Ellie moves her body as if she were the dog and smiles broadly. During this session, Ellie asks her mother to read the same book over and over, and either she incarnates the characters herself with her body to mimic the movements of the dog and the cat or she and her mother play with a toy dog and a toy cat to illustrate the narrative. The repeated reading and acting out of the same book and the playful routine of embodying the narrative with their body or with toys is a way for children to learn new vocabulary and syntactic structures and to develop the use of past tense and intersubjective and affective stance along with narrative skills. As a result of this repetitive routine, Ellie can almost tell the story herself, and she accompanies her mother in the process. This example illustrates Ellie's use of several parts of speech needed for the development of a narrative: she uses third-person pronouns ("she" [Appendix 5, Line 19] and "it" [Appendix 5, Line 21]), possessives ("his" [Appendix 5, Lines 8 and 13], "her" [Appendix 5, Line 25]), and preterit forms by adding -ed endings to lexical verbs ("barked" [Appendix 5, Line 3] and "wagged" [Appendix 5, Line 8 and Appendix 5, Line 13]), and she also uses the infinitive form with the verb "bark" (Appendix 5, Line 23) and the modal form "would" (Appendix 5, Line 25). She also uses a be+ing aspect when she says, "it's not having a fuss" (Appendix 5, Line 21). Ellie knows the narrative and she is able to tell parts of the story and explain to her mother why the cat is not happy. The activity encourages the child to use various words and grammatical structures as she and her mother explore the logic and causality of the story.

Figure 4. The mother enacts the story with toys

In Appendix 5 we observe that the mother's utterances serve different interactional functions: She reads the story (Appendix 5, Lines 1, 7, 22, and 24), illustrates meaning concretely by manipulating various toys (Appendix 5, Lines 4 and 10) and questions Ellie (Appendix 5, Line 15 to 22).

In the sequences presented, what makes the activity crucial for language acquisition is the agency of the children, who are not passively listening to the story. The children are linguistically – and even physically – active and with the mothers, they participate in the construction of the interaction framework. The role of the mother is crucial, as she visually checks that the child understands the story, enriches the narrative, defines words, and engages the child during the activity through multimodal elicitations. This analysis of at-home SBR illustrates that reading books and telling stories is a complex activity with a high level of engagement and shared attention by both participants. In our corpus, the children have all been socialized in reading books with a parent and in linguistically and physically engaging in the activity.

5. Some perspectives for professional language training

The analyses of the data show that interactions are crucial for children to acquire their mother tongue. Interactions develop thanks to linguistic and nonlinguistic features, and speakers use all the semiotic means at their disposal to communicate. This paper shows that the key feature that seems to sustain language acquisition and development in young children is the fact that they learn to express themselves in interaction with a competent other speaker. The role of the parent may shift from that of a co-participant in the interaction to an expert speaker who can repeat, explain, or define lexical or verbal items, contextualize meaning, and provide lexical, verbal, phonological, or morphological feedback to the child. As such, the role of the parent in the context of L1 acquisition may, to some extent, resemble that of a teacher. My claim is that knowing how a child acquires his or her mother tongue could inform and enrich kindergarten teachers' professional practice, especially when they engage in L2 teaching. Based on the analyses of the home data, this section will present some perspectives for professional language training for prospective kindergarten teachers on both theoretical and applied levels.

Chapter 6

5.1. Theoretical training: training program in conversation, CDS, and multimodality

Interacting with others in one's mother tongue or in a foreign language is a competence that students need to be trained in (Manoïlov, 2017, 2019). Manoïlov and Oursel (2019) advocated for the design of training programs prompting the development of L2 interactional skills at the university level. They explained that L2 learners need to be taught interaction skills to acquire a new language and to be able to speak the language. Yet, to train students, trainers need to be trained beforehand. Although the Common European Framework of Reference for Languages (Council of Europe, 2001) mentions that students should be able to interact with each other or with native speakers of their L2, L2 training programs in universities provide little knowledge and competences to trainers regarding interaction (Manoïlov & Oursel, 2019). The previous analyses of the home data show that children acquire language in interaction because their co-speaker provides scaffolding on various linguistic and nonlinguistic features. Training programs in higher education could therefore incorporate theoretical training regarding the notion of interaction and feedback and the factors that contribute to an interaction between speakers. For kindergarten preservice teachers, in particular, theoretical training in interaction, discourse analysis, conversation analysis, interaction analysis, CDS, and didactics of second/foreign languages and cultures could therefore enrich existing programs in higher education.

In the examples analyzed, the multimodal and plurisemiotic nature of language is also striking; adult-child interaction develops and is secured thanks to the constant efforts each speaker displays in order to make herself understood and to understand the other. For preservice teachers, developing explicit multimodal teaching practices could probably enhance their pupils' comprehension and learning in a foreign language. Peng (2019) showed that L2 teachers who exploit the potential of multimodal pedagogies promote students' motivation and willingness to participate in class. Tellier and Yerian (2018) suggested that prospective teachers be trained in gesture studies and the multimodal nature of language as part of their professional training. Learning to analyze video data of various types of human interaction ranging from home data with adult-child dyadic interactions to teacher-student interactions in class would probably help teachers develop a set of L2 pedagogic gestures.

There exist numerous typologies of gestures, but one goal of a research-based training design for kindergarten teachers in multimodality could consist in showing that gestures can be used in isolation or in coordination with speech and can perform a wide range of sociopragmatic functions. Teachers could be trained in using iconic gestures to make meaning or to visually represent an object and in using deictic gestures to locate objects in the environment, and they could be provided with guidance in the development of their own pedagogical gestural system to promote learning. In the context of L2 interaction, some gestures can take up a metadiscursive function and be used to comment on the linguistic aspects of a spoken utterance (Debras et al., 2020). Teachers could therefore be trained in using specific gestures to help their pupils with syntactic word order and phonological realization of words in an L2 learning context. They could for instance use a fixed and exaggerated set of gestures like the extension of the forefinger and the thumb in opposite directions to visually represent variations in vowel lengths or the use of beats to help students with the realization of stress patterns. Prosodic features at the sentence level could be performed visually with ample arm movements. Teachers are trained in breaking notions down for their pupils to understand, which helps them learn new knowledge and skills. Similarly, they could learn to identify the role and impact of their gestures when they teach a foreign language. They could learn to assess in what context they should better use words alone, words in combination with iconic gestures or embodied cognition, or when they should dissociate the use of iconic gestures and pedagogic gestures and use the spoken modality alone. The complementary nature of speech and gestures in interaction does exist, but speakers sometimes fail in mobilizing several modalities when expressing themselves (Throop & Duranti, 2015) and in professional settings, teachers should be trained in reflecting upon their use of semiosis when they are teaching. A gesture can be performed on the head or the hands, but also on the face, the shoulders, the arms, and the whole body, and higher education programs should include the training of teachers in using multimodality to promote learning and help their pupils develop language and communication skills.

5.2. From theory to practice: a multidisciplinary approach to language teaching and the role of context

The selection of examples presented in this chapter shows that before children can utter words and produce narratives using a book or toys, they are exposed to language. The input they get is linguistically rich and adapted to their level of understanding. The parents stay in the children's ZPD, and they do not expect their children to communicate with words at all times. Parents' postures may inform future L2 kindergarten teachers and encourage them to create opportunities for their pupils to listen to an L2 before being expected to produce words and short sentences. In this perspective, L2 kindergarten teachers could be trained in designing learning activities mostly based on comprehension skills and less on production skills.

In the home data, the role of the parent changed depending on the discourse context. Sometimes the parents provided linguistic feedback and corrected the children's previous oral production; sometimes they did not interfere. The parents did correct some mistakes and rephrase some utterances, but they seemed to favor the development of communication skills over linguistic correctness. Similarly, the role of the teacher as an expert in the language taught should also be addressed: Example 2 shows that before being able to tell a story with words, Anaé learned to tell a story with vocalizations. Before uttering their first words, babies learn to recognize and produce the prosodic contours or melody of their mother tongue (Martel & Dodane, 2012). In a school environment with children under six, having the pupils play with prosodic contours and more generally with phonological realization of the foreign language should be presented to prospective L2 teachers as part of the learning processes of a foreign language. Several researchers in early second language acquisition have advocated for teaching languages during music sessions in class because language and music share common features (Dodane, 2002; Voise, 2018). Dodane (2002) claimed that music could help train learners' vocalic and prosodic system for uttering words in a foreign language. Llorca (1992) explained that dancing and drama help incorporate prosodic contours. The role of repetition is also crucial in the process of learning languages (Examples 1, 2, 4, and 5), and Voise (2018) recommended that future kindergarten teachers be trained in teaching songs in a foreign language to enhance the acquisition of an L2 prosodic system in pupils. Therefore, professional language training should probably be built in coherence with professional music training in higher education. More generally, transversal courses could be implemented to train future teachers in multidisciplinary and soft skills.

The adult-child interactions in the examples analyzed previously developed in a specific context, and the meaning of each verbal, nonverbal, or multimodal utterance could be retrieved thanks to the discourse context in which it was produced. In the examples, all mothers drew an explicit parallel between the story and the child's life. These parents constantly contextualized, decontextualized, and recontextualized the situations depicted in the books to help their children understand the narrative and to make the depicted events meaningful to them (Example 4). Because the children related to the characters and their experiences, they were engaged and interested in the stories. The focus on story-reading activities illustrates that parents provide rich linguistic input that goes beyond the text written in the book.

In a school environment, learning contexts matter; contextualizing interactions in meaningful situations for the children appears to be a prerequisite for language development. Teachers can also be trained in designing learning situations that go beyond the material of a book with the use of games as learning practice in class. Figure 5 shows a kindergarten teacher in class. She is French and is teaching English to her pupils aged four and five[5]. She is telling the story of *the three little pigs* to her class. The teacher used a book to introduce the story earlier during the year. In the following lesson, the teacher decided to use flashcards for the three little pigs and their houses and a puppet for the wolf (Figure 5). She fully embodies the narrative, uses drama, and changes her voice to catch the children's attention. In the sequence, all children are engaged in the narrative and

---

5. This sequence comes from a classroom dataset collected as part of the IMAAJEE Project (Beaupoil-Hourdel, 2019), whose goal is to investigate the role of embodied cognition in second-language-learning kindergartners in France. The IMAAJEE corpus is still being collected and is currently composed of 17 hours of video data showing an experienced teacher teaching English to 27 pupils and seven preservice teachers who have accepted as part of their training education to take turns and teach English to the pupils one morning a week over a period of five weeks.

Chapter 6

contribute to the story with words and embodiment. The teacher tells the same story as the one written in the book, but she recontextualizes it differently, as she uses flashcards and a puppet to tell the story. After this session, the children were allowed to play with the puppet. Some of them used English and a hoarse voice and others gibbered in a husky voice. Playing with the material used during L2 teaching lessons could be presented in language teachers' training programs as a way to develop learning in doing. Contextualization, decontextualization, and recontextualization are processes for language learning. Knowing that, implementing a fully integrated multidisciplinary approach to L2 kindergarten teachers' training programs would probably help preservice teachers develop professional skills in L2 teaching.

Figure 5. The teacher telling the story of 'The Three Little Pigs'

6. Conclusion and directions

The present chapter presents analyses of at-home adult-child interactions during shared book-reading activities. The qualitative analyses of the data show that children learn their native language in interaction. More specifically, the analyses document the rich array of multimodal strategies used by the mothers to illustrate meaning, check comprehension, and elicit prior knowledge of the story being read and words previously used. In this context of shared attention and mutual engagement, children sometimes acquire new words and often use words and linguistic structures they already know in a new context. The role of the parent as a rich linguistic input provider is crucial. Knowledge of language development in adult-child interactions when children are not yet proficient speakers in their native language could thus inform training designs for preservice L2 kindergarten teachers in France, within the umbrella of the 21st century.

In an applied perspective, the analyses proposed in this chapter have implications for the training of future kindergarten teachers in order to ensure that they establish learning situations that favor language and individual development in young children. During SBR activities, children learn to talk about fictitious events and characters as well as displaced events. Parents linguistically enrich their children's productions by providing multimodal feedback. In this context, both CDS and the text of the book contribute to create a discourse context with enriched syntactic, lexical, and phonological content. The parents provide lexical and phonological input, syntactic repairs, and feedback. The parents' practices may thus inspire teachers' practices – the chapter thereby proposes guidelines for the design of training programs for preservice L2 kindergarten teachers on both theoretical and applied levels.

Higher education programs should develop courses and training on the notion of interaction in order to teach a second language to young children. Indeed, L2 kindergarten teachers need to take into account young children's communication skills as well as their mastery of their L1 in order to provide structured teaching adjusted for the linguistic, cognitive, and interactional developmental of children between three and six.

Prospective teachers could be trained in the use of multimodality in L2 teaching so as to promote L2 understanding and learning. Young children learn their native language in a holistic fashion, using all the semiotic resources they have at their disposal. Programs in higher education could thus be aligned with this natural language process that is at work in L1 acquisition. Courses on gestural modality and on how gestures contribute to meaning-making in interaction could be implemented.

This study also invites reconsideration of what learning a language means for beginners. L2 teaching should be contextualized, relying on activities that make sense to pupils. Moreover, learning a new language for young children raises the question of how this learning should be assessed, since comprehension activities should prevail over production activities. The home data may have implications for pedagogy in the sense that the analysis shows that before being able to speak a language, learners need to play with the language itself. Playing with words, prosodic patterns, and the sound of some phonemes is part of the language learning process – and should be implemented in L2 training programs in higher education. More and more researchers have advocated for multidisciplinary training designs in higher education to help L2 teachers thrive in school environments. Research in prosody has claimed that building L2 learning activities into music or drama sessions might help pupils acquire the prosodic structure of some sentences and enter into a new foreign language.

While the chapter highlights the crucial role of the parent or the teacher in the data when it comes to sparking language learning in young children, it also shows that multimodality is a medium for children to index meaning and express themselves. Training programs in pedagogy should therefore focus on the intricate relationship between interaction and multimodality in L2 teaching activities. My general objective in this chapter was to show that research in first language acquisition should not be completely separated from the field of second language acquisition. Detailed qualitative analyses of spontaneous adult-child interactions at home may be valuable for the design of training programs in higher education for preservice teachers.

7. Acknowledgments

I thank Aliyah Morgenstern and Marie Collombel for their contribution to the analyses of parent-child interactions during SBR activities at home. I am most indebted to Clélia Daniel for allowing me access to her kindergarten class, which made the comparison between home and classroom practices possible in this chapter. I thank the two editors, Muriel Grosbois and Beatrice Dupuy, the copy-editor, Nina Conrad, the reviewers, and my colleagues Camille Debras and Justine Paris for insightful and helpful comments on an earlier version of this chapter.

8. Supplementary materials

https://research-publishing.box.com/s/y1zepryvsvoai1vzeduadvazyx3u24gi

References

Aden, J., Clark, S., & Potapushkina-Delfosse, M. (2019). Éveiller le corps sensible pour entrer dans l'oralité des langues : une approche énactive de l'enseignement de l'oral. *Lidil. Revue de linguistique et de didactique des langues, 59*. https://doi.org/10.4000/lidil.6047

Bamberg, M. G. W. (1987). *The acquisition of narrative*. Mouton de Gruyter.

Bates, E., Camaioni, L., & Volterra, V. (1975). The acquisition of performatives prior to speech. *Merrill-Palmer Quarterly, 21*(3), 205-226.

Beaupoil-Hourdel, P. (2017). Expressing abstract notions in adult-child story-reading interactions. *Cycnos, 33*(1), 55-70.

Beaupoil-Hourdel, P. (2019). *Présentation du Projet IMAAJEE : corpus d'apprenants en maternelle*. https://je1-imaajee.sciencesconf.org/

Beaupoil-Hourdel, P., Leroy-Collombel, M., & Morgenstern, A. (2019). « Et tout un moment que c'était la nuit, Petit Soleil dorma à côté de Petit Lapin. » Rituel de lecture partagé à la maison. *Strenæ. Recherches sur les livres et objets culturels de l'enfance, 15*. https://doi.org/10.4000/strenae.3914

Boisseau, P. (2005). *Enseigner la langue orale en maternelle*. Retz. https://doi.org/10.14375/np.9782725624150

Bonnafé, M. (2011). *Les livres, c'est bon pour les bébés*. Fayard/Pluriel.

Bruner, J. S. (1983). *Le développement de l'enfant : savoir faire, savoir dire*. Presses Universitaires de France.

Bus, A. G., van IJzendoorn, M. H., & Pellegrini, A. D. (1995). Joint book reading makes for success in learning to read: a meta-analysis on intergenerational transmission of literacy. *Review of Educational Research, 65*(1), 1-21. https://doi.org/10.3102/00346543065001001

Cameron-Faulkner, T., & Noble, C. (2013). A comparison of book text and child directed speech. *First Language, 33*(3), 268-279. https://doi.org/10.1177/0142723713487613

Canut, E. (1997). Ajustements intuitifs d'un adulte lisant un livre illustré à un jeune enfant non lecteur. *L'Acquisition Du Langage Oral et Ecrit, AsFoReL, 39*, 37-45.

Canut, E. (2001). Raconter, c'est apprendre à parler. *Le Journal Des Professionnels de l'enfance, 9*, 50-51.

Canut, E., Bruneseaux-Gauthier, F., Vertalier, M., & Lentin, L. (2012). *Des albums pour apprendre à parler : les choisir, les utiliser en maternelle*. CRDP de Lorraine. https://doi.org/10.7202/1027630ar

Canut, E., & Gauthier, F. (2009). De quelques difficultés dans la compréhension des albums lus aux enfants non encore lecteurs. *Dyptique, 17*, 45-72.

Canut, E., Masson, C., & Leroy, M. (2018). *Accompagner l'enfant dans son apprentissage du langage : de la recherche en acquisition à l'intervention des professionnels*. Hachette Éducation.

Čekaitė, A., & Evaldsson, A.-C. (2019). Stance and footing in children's multilingual play: rescaling practices in a Swedish preschool. *Journal of Pragmatics, 144*, 127-140. https://doi.org/10.1016/j.pragma.2017.11.011

Cellier, M. (2015). *Guide pour enseigner le vocabulaire à l'école élémentaire + CD-Rom*. Retz.

Cnesco. (2019). Langue vivantes étrangères : comment l'école peut-elle mieux accompagner les élèves ? Dossier de synthèse. https://www.cnesco.fr/fr/langues-vivantes/

Council of Europe. (2001). *Common European framework of reference for languages: learning, teaching, assessment*. Cambridge University Press.

De Weck, G. (2005). L'appropriation des discours par les jeunes enfants. In B. Piérart (Ed.), *Le langage de l'enfant, comme l'évaluer ?* (pp. 179-193). De Boeck. https://doi.org/10.3917/dbu.piera.2005.01.0179

Debras, C., Beaupoil-Hourdel, P., Morgenstern, A., Horgues, C., & Scheuer, S. (2020). Corrective feedback sequences in tandem interactions: multimodal cues and speakers' positionings. In S. Raineri, M. Sekali & A. Leroux (Eds), *Linguistic correction/correctness* (pp. 91-116). Presses Universitaires de Paris Nanterre.

Dickinson, D. K., De Temple, J. M., Hirschler, J. A., & Smith, M. W. (1992). Book reading with preschoolers: coconstruction of text at home and at school. *Early Childhood Research Quarterly, 7*(3), 323-346. https://doi.org/10.1016/0885-2006(92)90025-T

Dodane, C. (2002). La langue en harmonie : influences de la formation musicale sur l'apprentissage précoce d'une langue étrangère. PhD dissertation. Besançon, France. https://www.theses.fr/2003BESA1007

Frier, C. (2011). (Ed.). *Passeurs de lecture : lire ensemble à la maison et à l'école*. Retz.

Goffman, E. (1974). *Frame analysis: an essay on the organization of experience*. Harvard University Press.

Goldin-Meadow, S., & Butcher, C. (2003). Pointing toward two-word speech in young children. In S. Kita (Ed.), *Pointing: where language, culture, and cognition meet* (pp. 85-107). Lawrence Erlbaum Associates.

Goodwin, C. (2003). Pointing as situated practice. In S. Kita (Ed.), *Pointing: where language, culture and cognition meet* (pp. 217-241). Lawrence Erlbaum Associates.

Goodwin, C. (2017). *Co-operative action*. Cambridge University Press.

Goodwin, M. H., Goodwin, C., & Yaeger-Dror, M. (2002). Multi-modality in girls' game disputes. *Journal of Pragmatics, 34*(10-11), 1621-1649. https://doi.org/10.1016/S0378-2166(02)00078-4

Heath, S. B. (1983). W*ays with words: language, life and work in communities and classrooms*. Cambridge University Press.

Heath, S. B., & Branscombe, A. (1986). The book as narrative prop in language acquisition. In B. B. Schieffelin & P. Gilmore (Eds), *The acquisition of literacy: ethnographic perspectives* (vol. 21, pp. 16-34). Ablex.

Hoff-Ginsberg, E. (1992). How should frequency in input be measured? *First Language, 12*(36), 233-244. https://doi.org/10.1177/014272379201203601

Leroy, M., Mathiot, E., & Morgenstern, A. (2009). Pointing gestures and demonstrative words: deixis between the ages of one and three. In J. Zlatev, M. Johansson Falck, C. Lundmark & M. Andrén (Eds), *Studies in language and cognition* (pp. 386-404). Cambridge Scholars Publishing.

Leroy-Collombel, M. (2013). Développement des compétences narratives : analyse longitudinale des récits d'un enfant entre 2 et 4 ans. *ANAE. Approche neuropsychologique des apprentissages chez l'enfant, 124*, 247-253.

Lever, R., & Sénéchal, M. (2011). Discussing stories: on how a dialogic reading intervention improves kindergartners' oral narrative construction. *Journal of Experimental Child Psychology, 108*(1), 1-24. https://doi.org/10.1016/j.jecp.2010.07.002

Llorca, R. (1992). Le rôle de la mémoire musicale dans la perception d'une langue étrangère. *Revue de Phonétique Appliquée, 102*, 45-67.

MacWhinney, B. (2000). *The CHILDES project: tools for analyzing talk. Volume 1: transcription format and programs. Volume 2: the database.* Lawrence Erlbaum Associates.

Magee, M. A., & Sutton-Smith, B. (1983). The art of storytelling: how do children learn it? *Young Children, 38*(4), 4-12.

Manoïlov, P. (2017). *L'interaction orale entre pairs en classe d'anglais LV2 : analyse didactique et linguistique de la construction et du développement des compétences des apprenants.* PhD thesis. Sorbonne Paris Cité. http://www.theses.fr/2017USPCA162

Manoïlov, P. (2019). Repenser l'organisation des tâches pour favoriser le développement des interactions orales entre pairs. *Langues modernes, 3.*

Manoïlov, P., & Oursel, E. (2019). Analyse des interactions et didactique des langues : tour d'horizon des relations. *Linx. Revue des linguistes de l'université Paris X Nanterre, 79.* https://doi.org/10.4000/linx.3399

Martel, K., & Dodane, C. (2012). Le rôle de la prosodie dans les premières constructions grammaticales : étude de cas d'un enfant français monolingue. *Journal of French Language Studies, 22*(Special Issue 01), 13-35. https://doi.org/10.1017/S0959269511000561

Morgenstern, A. (2009). *L'Enfant dans la langue.* Presses de la Sorbonne Nouvelle.

Morgenstern, A. (2014). Children's multimodal language development. In C. Fäcke (Ed.), *Manual of Language Acquisition* (pp. 123-142). De Gruyter.

Morgenstern, A., Caët, S., & Limousin, F. (2016). Pointing and self-reference in French and French Sign Language. *Open Linguistics, 2*(1), 768-787. https://doi.org/10.1515/opli-2016-0003

Morgenstern, A., & Parisse, C. (2012). The Paris corpus. *Journal of French Language Studies, 22*(1), 7-12.

Morgenstern, A., & Parisse, C. (2017). (Eds). *Le langage de l'enfant de l'éclosion à l'explosion.* Presses de la Sorbonne Nouvelle.

Morgenstern, A., & Sekali, M. (2009). What can child language tell us about prepositions? In J. Zlatev, M. Andrén, M. Johansson Falck & C. Lundmark (Eds), *Studies in language and cognition* (pp. 272-286). Cambridge Scholars Publishing.

Noble, C. H., Cameron-Faulkner, T., & Lieven, E. (2018). Keeping it simple: the grammatical properties of shared book reading. *Journal of Child Language, 45*(3), 753-766. https://doi.org/10.1017/S0305000917000447

Payne, A. C., Whitehurst, G. J., & Angell, A. L. (1994). The role of home literacy environment in the development of language ability in preschool children from low-income families. *Early Childhood Research Quarterly, 9*(3-4), 427-440. https://doi.org/10.1016/0885-2006(94)90018-3

Peng, J.-E. (2019). The roles of multimodal pedagogic effects and classroom environment in willingness to communicate in English. *System*, *82*, 161-173. https://doi.org/10.1016/j.system.2019.04.006

Schank, R. C., & Abelson, R. P. (1977). *Plans, scripts, goals and understanding*. Lawrence Erlbaum Associates.

Schieffelin, B. B., & Ochs, E. (1986). *Language socialization across cultures*. Cambridge University Press.

Snow, C. E., Arlman-Rupp, A., Hassing, Y., Jobse, J., Joosten, J., & Vorster, J. (1976). Mothers' speech in three social classes. *Journal of Psycholinguistic Research*, *5*(1), 1-20. https://doi.org/10.1007/BF01067944

Snow, C. E., & Goldfield, B. A. (1983). Turn the page please: situation-specific language acquisition. *Journal of Child Language*, *10*(3), 551-569. https://doi.org/10.1017/S0305000900005365

Soulaine, S. (2018). Une approche énactive de l'enseignement-apprentissage des langues : le corps au centre de la formation des futurs enseignants. *Recherches & éducations*, HS. https://doi.org/10.4000/rechercheseducations.6086

Tellier, M. (2006). *L'impact du geste pédagogique sur l'enseignement/apprentissage des langues étrangères : étude sur des enfants de 5 ans*. PhD dissertation. Université Paris-Diderot - Paris VII. https://tel.archives-ouvertes.fr/tel-00371041

Tellier, M. (2008). The effect of gestures on second language memorisation by young children. *Gesture*, *8*(2), 219-235. https://doi.org/10.1075/gest.8.2.06tel

Tellier, M., & Yerian, K. (2018). Mettre du corps à l'ouvrage : travailler sur la mise en scène du corps du jeune enseignant en formation universitaire. *Recherche et Pratiques Pédagogiques En Langues de Spécialité - Cahiers de l'APLIUT, Association Des Professeurs de Langues Des Instituts Universitaires de Technologie (APLIUT)*, *37*(2). https://doi.org/10.4000/apliut.6079

Throop, J. C., & Duranti, A. (2015). Attention, ritual glitches, and attentional pull: the president and the queen. *Phenomenology and the Cognitive Sciences*, *14*, 1055-1082. https://doi.org/10.1007/s11097-014-9397-4

Tomasello, M. (1988). The role of joint attentional processes in early language development. *Language Sciences*, *10*(1), 69-88. https://doi.org/10.1016/0388-0001(88)90006-X

Tomasello, M. (2003). *Constructing a language: a usage-based theory of language acquisition*. Harvard University Press.

Tomasello, M., Carpenter, M., & Liszkowski, U. (2007). A new look at infant pointing. *Child Development*, *78*(3), 705-722. https://doi.org/10.1111/j.1467-8624.2007.01025.x

Vertalier, M. (2009). L'activité narrative avec des livres illustrés. Contribution à l'apprentissage du langage oral et préparation au statut de lecteur. In E. Canut & M. Vertalier (Eds), *L'apprentissage du langage. Une approche interactionnelle. Réflexions théoriques et pratiques de terrain. Mélanges offerts par ses collègues, ses élèves et ses amis en hommage à Laurence Lentin.* L'Harmattan.

Voise, A.-M. (2018). Corps - accords : une approche holistique et transdisciplinaire des langues à l'école maternelle. *Recherche et pratiques pédagogiques en langues de spécialité. Cahiers de l'Apliut, 37*(2). https://doi.org/10.4000/apliut.6345

Vygotsky, L. S. (1978). *Mind in society: the development of higher psychological processes.* Harvard University Press.

Wittenburg, P., Brugman, H., Russel, A., Klassmann, A., & Sloetjes, H. (2006). ELAN: a professional framework for multimodality research. *Proceedings of the Fifth International Conference of Language Resources and Evaluation (LREC'06).*

7 Informing language training with multimodal analysis: insights from the use of gesture in tandem interactions

Camille Debras[1]

1. Introduction

In the 21st century, increased mobility, internationalization, and technical innovations define our professional world. Learning and training have become lifelong processes, and skills that were once considered 'soft' are now a must. This chapter focuses on the multimodal, interactional, and intercultural aspects of communicative competence, which have yet to gain institutional recognition. For instance, the Common European Framework of Reference for languages (CEFR) tends to marginalize the role of gesture in the acquisition and mastery of a language (Council of Europe, 2001). CEFR descriptors consider gestures to be a mere paralinguistic, compensatory strategy used by beginners: a beginner 'below A1' can "make simple purchases where pointing or other gesture can support the verbal reference" (Council of Europe, 2001, p. 32); an A2 speaker "can use an inadequate word from his/her repertoire and use gesture to clarify what he/she wants to say" (Council of Europe, 2001, p. 64). In curriculum scenarios, "attention paid to body language and gestures" (Council of Europe, 2001, p. 172) is restricted to primary school. Conversely, I draw from linguistics research on the multimodality of tandem interactions so as to provide evidence for the crucial communicative and linguistic functions of gesture during exolingual interactions (i.e. between native and nonnative speakers of a language). This chapter addresses the following questions: how can future professionals learn to

---

1. Université Paris Nanterre, CREA (EA 370) and MoDyCo (UMR 7114), Nanterre, France; cdebras@parisnanterre.fr; https://orcid.org/0000-0002-2308-7052

How to cite this chapter: Debras, C. (2020). Informing language training with multimodal analysis: insights from the use of gesture in tandem interactions. In B. Dupuy and M. Grosbois (Eds), *Language learning and professionalization in higher education: pathways to preparing learners and teachers in/for the 21st century* (pp. 199-228). Research-publishing.net. https://doi.org/10.14705/rpnet.2020.44.1106

Chapter 7

communicate as part of exolingual interactions? How can they learn to interact efficiently, notably by combining speech with gesture? More broadly, how do the results of this research inform language learning and professionalization in higher education?

This chapter offers an overview of four multimodal studies of language use in a videotaped corpus of tandem interactions in French and English. These studies capture the contribution of gesture with a focus on (1) corrective feedback, (2) alignment, (3) reference tracking, and (4) foreigner talk. These four topics correspond to essential issues and strategies at stake in tandem communication, namely providing each other with feedback, ensuring mutual comprehension and engagement, stabilizing referential meaning, and adjusting to a nonnative interlocutor. After laying out the basics of tandem learning and the multimodal approach, I present the corpus and methodology. I then present each study's main findings, before synthesizing their relevance for language learning and professionalization in higher education.

2. Language learning in tandem

Originally developed in the 1960's so as to complement formal classroom language teaching, tandem learning is "an arrangement in which two native speakers of different languages communicate regularly with one another, each with the purpose of learning the other's language" (O'Rourke, 2005, p. 434). Language tandems provide a unique collaborative learning environment based on solidarity and reciprocity (Brammerts & Calvert, 2003); while aiming to learn a target foreign language, participants also engage in helping partners learn their own mother tongue (Helming, 2002).

Linguistic tandems provide a favorable socioaffective context for L2 learning (Horgues & Scheuer, 2015). Tandem learning is based on role reversibility and peer symmetry, in which the asymmetry of language expertise is contextual and temporary. Peer empathy and mutual commitment are central, and each participant has something to learn. Tandems breed trust and motivation because participants often perceive native speakers as trustworthy representatives of the target language community, and participants become interested in getting to know their partners as "individuals and not just as sources of language input" (O'Rourke, 2005, p. 434).

During tandem interactions, learners are exposed to spoken and contextualized L2 input that is extensive and authentic. Tandems provide learners with 'positive' and 'negative' evidence of the target foreign language (Gass, 2003; Mackey, 2006), respectively defined as "the set of well-formed sentences to which learners are exposed" and "the type of information that is provided to learners concerning the incorrectness of an utterance" (Gass, 2003, p. 225), across all dimensions of a language, from pronunciation to syntax. Crucially, face-to-face tandems allow participants to share the same interaction space and to rely on nonverbal cues like gestures, facial expressions, and the articulation of pronunciation (jaw, mouth, and lip placements).

3. A multimodal approach to language tandems, with a focus on gesture

The construction of meaning in interaction is by essence multimodal, intersubjective, and sequential. Participants mobilize a variety of semiotic modes and resources, one of which is language. Their actions are inscribed in time, one after the other or simultaneously; they alternately react to and project others' actions (Sacks, Schegloff, & Jefferson, 1974), providing new communication material or reusing material provided by others (Goodwin, 2013). Face-to-face communication is multimodal by nature (Argyle, 1972; Norris, 2004); multiple semiotic modes are used by participants to communicate (Bezemer & Jewitt, 2010; Kress & van Leeuwen, 2001), including speech and gestures. Gestures are bodily actions that "[belong] to the 'story line' of the interaction" (Kendon, 1986, p. 6) and that are inscribed in its sequentiality; they coincide with other actions in the construction of meaning, rather than being there by mere coincidence (Schegloff, 1984). Gesture is here understood as a large category for communicative kinesic resources, including hand gestures, head and shoulder movements, facial expressions, and body posture (Allwood et al., 2007).

Speech and gesture are tightly coupled in interactional communication (Kendon, 2000). Gesture can fulfill a variety of communicative functions, among which linguistic ones (Cienki, 2017; Müller, Ladewig, & Bressem, 2013). Gesture is a resource that plays a crucial role in second language acquisition, for instance in classroom settings (McCafferty & Stam, 2008). In face-to-face tandems, gesture is a shared resource that participants can mobilize so as to bridge the L1/L2 language and culture gap. The four studies presented here provide insights into how tandem participants use gesture to collaborate, adjust to their interlocutor, negotiate and secure meaning, and make communicative progress.

Study 1 (Debras et al., 2020) focuses on Corrective Feedback (CF, after Lyster & Ranta, 1997; Sheen & Ellis, 2011), understood as an equivalent of negative evidence – that is, "the type of information that is provided to learners concerning the incorrectness of an utterance" (Gass, 2003, p. 225). It shows how tandem participants mobilize gesture during CF sequences (Graziano & Gullberg, 2013) and what cultural differences can be observed in the way native speakers of French and of English position themselves as experts or learners.

Study 2 spells out the functions of gestural alignment (i.e. the cross-speaker repetition of a gesture form; Atkinson, Churchill, Nishino, & Okada, 2007; Kimbara, 2006) during metalinguistic sequences. During communication breakdowns, tandem participants engage in metalinguistic sequences in which gestural alignment plays a key role.

Study 3 (Debras & Beaupoil-Hourdel, 2019) documents the key contribution of gesture to anaphora, or reference tracking (Gullberg, 2006). When participants mention a given referent multiple times as the interaction unfolds, the form of the referent's successive mentions (which form a reference chain) can change. Since tandem interactions are characterized by referential instability and linguistic insecurity, gesture is crucial as a shared resource used to secure reference chains.

Study 4 documents how native speakers adapt their gestures when addressing L2 learners as part of foreigner talk in the tandem data. Indeed, foreigner talk (i.e. the linguistic and conversational adjustments made by native speakers who address nonnative speakers, after Ferguson, 1975) affects gestures as well (Adams, 1998).

4. Corpus and methodology

The studies reviewed in this chapter are based on data from the SITAF project (*Spécificités des interactions verbales dans le cadre de tandems linguistiques Anglais-Français*) coordinated by Céline Horgues and Sylwia Scheuer at Sorbonne Nouvelle University (Horgues & Scheuer, 2015). This project was created with two main goals: first, to provide students with the opportunity to improve their language, communication, and intercultural skills by participating in language tandems, and second, to collect language tandem data to create a learner corpus (Gilquin, Granger, & Paquot, 2007; Granger, Gilquin, & Meunier, 2015) in order to analyse the participants' practices and measure their progress. The project paired up undergraduate students who were native speakers of French and English and were learning each other's language as an L2. The French participants were undergraduate students from Sorbonne Nouvelle University, and the English-speaking participants were exchange students at this university who came from the United States, United Kingdom, Australia, Ireland, and Canada. Participants were paired up on the suggestion of the coordination team after filling out an online questionnaire about their linguistic background and level of L2 proficiency as well as their interests and preferred conversation topics. The participants' spoken language proficiency was not formally evaluated other than by self-assessment for L2 oral comprehension and expression as part of the online questionnaire. Their language proficiency varies from level B1 to C1 according to the CEFR (Council of Europe, 2001).

The corpus collected as part of the project is a 25-hour collection of videotaped interactions in 21 tandems (42 participants). Two sessions of each tandem were video-recorded in the university's recording studio at a three-month interval in February and May 2013. Partners were encouraged to hold unsupervised meetings once a week between the two recording sessions, and each pair met an average of 12 times. In each recording session, participants engaged in three tasks: a reading task and two game-like communicative activities aiming at eliciting storytelling and argumentation, respectively. The four studies presented in the chapter are based on the second recording session of the storytelling game *Liar, Liar*, in which the nonnative speaker tells a personal story to the native speaker and hides three lies in it. A discussion ensues during which the native speaker has to guess the lies. To allow comparisons of the ways a speaker communicates during exolingual (L1/L2) and intralingual (L1/L1) interaction, an extra round of recording was done during the May session, in which all the participants performed the three tasks addressing a native speaker. Study 4 is based on a comparison between the L1/L2 and the L1/L1 data.

The technical setup was well suited for the study of nonverbal cues: three cameras were used (one aimed at each participant and one capturing the whole set), allowing a rich capture of the various dimensions of gestural output (Mondada, 2006). Although the interactions were constrained in some respects (i.e. participating in a task, sitting on stools in the university recording studio, the presence of recording devices), they remained spontaneous in character. Sitting on chairs did not prevent participants from moving freely from the waist up, where most gesture articulators are located.

The method used in the four studies is rooted in multimodal interaction analysis (Ferré, 2019; Norris, 2004) and the linguistic analysis of gesture (Müller et al., 2013). The discourse content of the tandem interactions was transcribed, and the transcriptions were aligned with the video recordings in the software ELAN (Wittenburg et al., 2006). The analyses relied on either:

- the systematic annotation of gesture forms and functions (Bressem, Ladewig, & Müller, 2014; Kendon, 2004;) in ELAN (Wittenburg et al., 2006) to provide a quantitative overview of gesture use in the data; and

- the moment-to-moment, qualitative analysis of interaction sequences (Goodwin, 2013) to provide insight into the variety of observable processes at play, or a combination of both.

Table 1 presents the corpus data and the method used in each study.

Table 1. Corpus data and method used in the four studies

Study	Corpus (Session 2, storytelling game Liar, Liar)	Method
Study 1 – corrective feedback	Eight recordings (four in French, four in English) with the most occurrences of CF; 58 min of footage	Annotation and qualitative analysis
Study 2 – gesture alignment	Collection of excerpts from recordings of two tandems (Session 2)	Qualitative analysis
Study 3 – reference tracking	Collection of excerpts from the recording of one tandem (Session 2)	Qualitative analysis
Study 4 – foreigner talk	Ten recordings in French: five participants paired with a native speaker of English and five with a native speaker of French (L1/L2 compared with L1/L1); 58 min of footage	Annotation and qualitative analysis

5. Analyses and findings

5.1. Study 1: the multimodality of CF

Repairs proposed by more skilled speakers play a key role in L2 learners' acquisition of a language (Gass, 2003; Long, 2007; Sato & Lyster, 2012). Interactions with expert speakers allow language learners to notice the gap between their L2 production and the target form (Schmidt, 1990; Mackey, 2006), enabling them to adjust mental representations of the target forms, reshape hypotheses about them, and modify their output accordingly.

Study 1 (Debras et al., 2020) pertains to a sample of the corpus data that includes the eight recordings (four in French, four in English) with the most occurrences of CF. In the 58 minutes and 37 seconds of total footage selected, the coding yielded 128 occurrences of CF. Out of the 128 occurrences of CF, 91 were in French and 37 in English: In this data, 72% of the CF is given by French native speakers.

CF is an interactional process organized in different phases: (1) request (by the nonnative speaker), (2) provision (by the native speaker), and (3) uptake (by the nonnative speaker). Phase 2 (CF provision) is always present, but Phases 1 and 3 (request and uptake) are optional.

In study 1, the 128 occurrences of CF collected in the eight recordings were double-coded in ELAN for the following features:

- CF type: recast, explicit correction, clarification request, suggestion, etc., based on existing categories described in the literature;

- CF request: requested, not requested, request unclear;

- CF uptake: uptake, partial uptake, acknowledgment, no uptake; and

- semiotic resources mobilized for each phase of CF: (1) verbal: discourse; (2) vocal: intonation, hyper articulation; and (3) visual: manual gestures, gaze, head movements, and facial variations (smile, frowning, squinting eyes…).

The visual modality is used very frequently in all three sequential phases of CF: 96% of the time during request, 93% during provision, and 87.5% during uptake. During CF provision, the majority of head nods and metadiscursive hand gestures are produced by French native speakers when providing normative CF (i.e. an explicit correction or a recast). Their preferred kinesic forms point to a more professorial positioning on the part of French native speakers: They visually confirm the 'right', target-like form with a nod of the head or embody their expert's stance by literally manipulating the target language through metadiscursive gestures.

English native speakers provide fewer normative forms of CF than French natives and use more lifted eyebrows to do so. This type of facial display can serve "to signal and monitor affective cues between the participants" (Peräkylä & Ruusuvuori, 2006, p. 132) or mark the reception of information as unexpected, with possible nuances such as signifying that something is new, interesting, surprising, worthy of notice. English natives thus attend to affective relations with the interlocutor by marking the reception of the learner's production as worthy of notice or interesting. This gesture could be interpreted as a strategy for toning down the normativity of CF by emphasizing friendliness toward and interest in the interlocutor.

During CF requests, English learners of French account for the most metadiscursive gestures, thereby displaying more metalinguistic awareness of the learning process. They make more frequent use of frowning or squinting eyes, which display uncertainty or distance from the discourse they are producing. These visual cues can be taken up as appeals for the French native to provide a more target-like form. English learners of French not only request more feedback than French learners of English but also mobilize more visual resources to make it visually more obvious and explicit that they are doing so. Overall, because of their physical behavior during CF requests, English natives can appear more proactive in the role of learner than French natives do.

Most CF uptakes are performed by English learners of French. They use visual resources more often than French learners to do so, mostly in the form of metadiscursive gestures, head nods, and lifted eyebrows. These kinesic forms all participate in expressing the learners' metalinguistic awareness; learners explicitly inform native speakers that they are involved in taking up the CF provided. For instance, lifted eyebrows can be used to receive CF as new information, while head nods can indicate affiliation (Stivers, 2008), signaling that the CF is understood and accepted. Conversely, French learners of English more rarely respond to CF and more rarely accompany their response with gestures than English learners of French do. The fuller kinesic involvement of English learners of French suggests that they position themselves as more eager students, whereas French learners of English appear more passive.

The multimodal analysis of CF sequences showed different strategies on the part of French and English native speakers. French native speakers provided more CF, gave more normative CF, and used more visual cues during CF provision. Conversely, English natives provided less CF, gave less normative CF, made more CF requests and uptakes as learners, and used more visual cues for request and uptake. Based on these observations, French speakers may appear more proactive as experts, whereas English speakers could be perceived more proactive as learners. These results might be due to a variety of factors, namely different sociocultural orientations to CF with varyingly prescriptive conceptions of what it means to learn and to speak a language as well as the fact that the interactions are taking place in France.

5.2. Study 2: gestural alignment in the negotiation of meaning

Study 2 (Debras & Beaupoil-Hourdel, forthcoming) focuses on gestural alignment (Atkinson et al., 2007), which can be used by the L2 learner to bridge lexical gaps, with the native speaker's subsequent aligned gesture enabling the participants to secure the referent. Aligned representational gestures can also be used by the L2 learner to display understanding by securing the referent. Gestures can also scaffold the L2 learner's appropriation of new vocabulary. When gesture is sufficient to ensure mutual understanding, the visual modality can take over from speech, with neither participant ending up naming the referent that has been identified visually, as shown in Table 2. In this excerpt, the native speaker asks the language learner for further detail about a Christmas tree that she made. The nonnative speaker explains that she made it out of twisted wire – a challenge because neither *twist* nor *wire* is part of her vocabulary. She hence resorts to the visual modality, combining a gestural enactment of twisting a wire, using speech only to specify the material she used ("I made it with iron").

The learner's multimodal utterance integrates gesture into the linearity of speech (Ladewig, 2014). The missing lexeme *twist* is specified by multimodal clues: the nonnative speaker's gesture fills the gap of a predicate after the generic subject pronoun *you*, indicating that the missing lexeme is a verb. The gestural enactment (circular gestures, holding a thin object) indicates that the unnamed referent is a durative action, thereby the lexical aspect of the missing dynamic verb (*twist*). *Wire* can be retrieved by the metonymic specification of the material used (*iron*) as well as by the hand shape (folded fingers as if holding a long, thin object). The native speaker immediately takes up the language learner's gesture, showing her understanding of the whole complex predicate *twisting the wire*: Her mirroring circular gestures indicate the understanding of *twist*, and the imitated hand shape with folded fingers shows understanding of what is twisted (*wire*). The two participants utter *yeah* simultaneously, thereby confirming mutual understanding. This sequence shows that gesture can take over from speech in conveying the main information of an utterance. It also shows how 'gesture-craft' (Streeck, 2009) is a highly efficient modality for representing the activity of hand-crafting an object.

Table 2. Excerpt

1-ENG native: Gesture:	*and what did you make it with?* [left hand pointing gesture with movement from the left to the right
2-FR native: Gesture:	*hum I made it with [iron* [Open hand facing each other and moving top and down and away from each other, representing a triangle. Iconic gesture for Christmas tree.
3-ENG native: Gesture:	*really?* [raised eyebrows and head nod
4-FR native: Gesture:	*yeah (.) [with iron and (.) you know you take iron* [moving her hands in circular gestures

Chapter 7

5-FR native:	*and [you*
Gesture:	[moving her hands in circular gestures
6-ENG native:	*[and you ...*
Gesture:	[moving her hands in circular gestures similarly to the interlocutor

7-FR native:	*yeah.*
8-ENG native:	*okay.*

Gestural alignment can even be used in metalinguistic sequences where the vocabulary is fairly transparent. Gestural alignment is transferred from discourse objects to discourse as an object; gesture forms with attitudinal and interpersonal functions are used to secure the participants' mutual engagement in the metalinguistic sequence itself. For instance, in a sequence in English, a native speaker provides feedback on the plural form of the noun *goose*. To do so, he identifies the target of his feedback both in speech (*you can say for uh there's more than one goose, there're geese*) and by lengthening the vocal sound [i:] of *geese*, and in gesture, by virtually holding the word between his extended thumb and index finger. The nonnative speaker immediately takes up the target word, mirroring the native speaker's visual and vocal exaggeration. The native speaker then provides further explanations on grammar and irregular spelling (*yeah it changes to E E in the middle*), combined with a representational gesture that indexes the activity of writing. With his index finger, he traces the letter 'e' twice in the upper center of his gesture space, high enough to meet the nonnative speaker's gaze and catch her attention (Figure 1). Again, the nonnative speaker immediately aligns with the native speaker, mimicking the writing of 'e' twice with her index finger high up at gaze level (Figure 2), while repeating the target word *geese* with visual and vocal exaggeration to show that she has taken in the target form.

This metalinguistic sequence targets phonology, grammar, and spelling – not vocabulary; visual alignment is used so as to secure the participants' shared awareness of being involved in a metalinguistic sequence.

Figure 1. French learner of English aligning visually by tracing the spelling as well

Figure 2. English native speaker representing the spelling 'ee' in geese visually

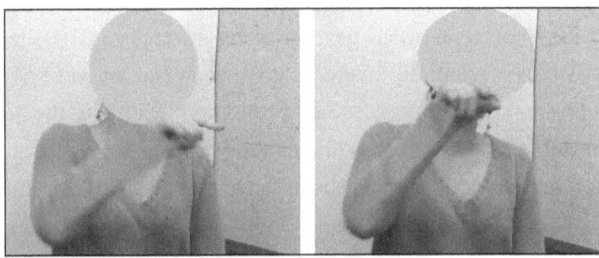

Gestural alignment is a crucial locus of interpersonal resonance and the collaboration of speakers in interaction. Tandem participants use it for various interactional goals, from mutual understanding to language learning. The gradual stabilization of referents through speech and gestures shows how meaning is an unfolding process that relies on the accumulation of forms, which, once used, become part of a public substrate (Goodwin, 2013), namely the collection of semiotic forms used by speakers that constitute a common set of reusable, decomposable, and transformable resources for the intersubjective construction of meaning in interaction.

5.3. Study 3: the use of gesture in reference tracking

Study 3 is a detailed qualitative analysis of interaction sequences rooted in a formal approach to gesture analysis (Boutet, 2015). It shows how chains of reference (Schnedecker & Landragin, 2014) are constructed sequentially, multimodally, and interactively during tandem conversations. Reference stability and co-referentiality are key issues for mutual comprehension and for the co-construction of meaning in conversation, all the more so during exolingual interactions. Gestures can contribute to the construction of referents by fulfilling anaphoric functions (Navarretta, 2011), deictic ones (Kita, 2003), or representational ones (Müller, 2014).

Exolingual interactions have a direct effect on the formal characteristics of gestures. Native speakers tend to use more gestures, and their gestures are extended in time and space (they last longer and are ampler, and iconic gestures are more frequent; Adams, 1998; Tellier & Stam, 2012; Study 4). Language learners can use representational gesture to fill lexical gaps (Ladewig, 2014) and tend to use co-referentially overexplicit speech (i.e. overuse of full lexical nominal expressions but limited use of pronouns). Visually, the repetition of full noun phrases is synchronized with anaphoric gestures (Gullberg, 2006) that maintain a referential locus in the gesture space (Perniss, 2012).

When gesture forms are repeated by the speaker or taken up by the interlocutor (Bressem, 2014; Study 2), participants never actually reproduce a gesture in its exact same form. Formal variations in the gesture's realization are often meaningful in terms of the referent's informational status (i.e. as new/foregrounded or old/backgrounded information). For that reason, the term 'gesture reiteration' is preferred to 'gesture repetition'. Study 3 shows how these reiterations of the speech of self and others are concatenated and combined with gesture to sequentially co-construct chains of referents that evolve as the conversation unfolds, in a context of referential instability and linguistic insecurity that is typical of tandem interactions.

Study 3 shows that links of one and the same reference chain can be expressed monomodally in speech or gesture only, or multimodally, in a combination of both. Multimodal referential expressions can combine mentions from different reference chains that can be expressed simultaneously with each hand representing a distinct referent, as illustrated in Figure 4: the native speaker of English represents a Christmas tree with one forearm and hand and a Christmas bauble hanging from it with the other hand. Two different gesture forms can be combined with the same lexical form in speech to highlight different characteristics of the referent; in that case, maintaining the same locus in the gesture space (Perniss, 2012) or an object of similar size helps identify two different gestures as being related to one and the same referent.

Figure 3. Third mention of the referent 'Christmas tree', native English speaker (from Debras & Beaupoil-Hourdel, 2019)

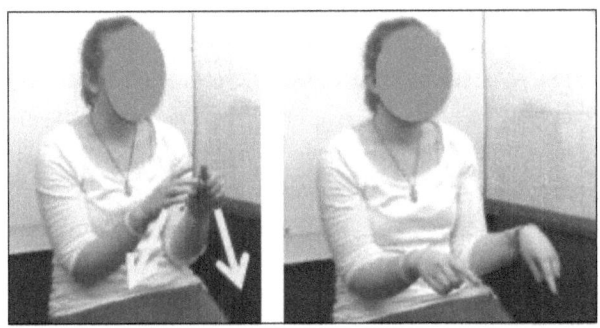

Figure 4. Fourth mention of the referent 'Christmas tree', third mention of the referent 'Christmas bauble', native English speaker (from Debras & Beaupoil-Hourdel, 2019)

Gesture reiterations involve two major processes, namely the reduction or the expansion of the reiterated form. Reduced forms imply the reduction of one or many formal features: The reiterated gesture can be faster, smaller in amplitude, or less articulated, or it can involve one hand only when both hands have been used previously. A referent that has first been presented in three dimensions (modeling as per Müller, 2014) or two (*tracing*), can be taken up in a more schematic way that involves fewer dimensions. Formal reduction can involve only one modality at a time. When an already established referent is used as visual background for another, it can be sketchier (e.g. fourth mention of the Christmas tree, Figure 4) than a more detailed, previous mention (third mention of the Christmas tree, Figure 3; see also Holler & Bavelas, 2017). A sketchier gesture form can also be used when it is repeated by the interlocutor to confirm understanding. The development of common ground (Clark, 1996) between the participants as the interaction unfolds is a factor that explains the formal reduction of gesture reiterations. The reduction of subsequent visual reiterations can also be analyzed as a process of gesture conventionalization at the scale of an interactional sequence (LeBaron & Streeck, 2000). In all, gesture reiterations display features similar to proforms in speech, reflecting the accessibility of referents (Ariel, 1990): More reduced forms can be used once the referent's status has shifted to known information (Gundel, Hedberg, & Zacharski, 1993).

Gesture reiterations can also involve formal expansion: they can last longer, be ampler, or be more precise. For instance, a representational gesture can go from tracing to modeling, or from two to three dimensions, as exemplified by the first and second representations of a Christmas bauble (respectively in Figure 5 and Figure 6), by the French native, who is speaking in English and filling a lexical gap with gestures to refer to a 'bauble'.

Figure 5. First mention of the referent 'bauble', French native compensating for a lexical gap – tracing gesture (from Debras & Beaupoil-Hourdel, 2019)

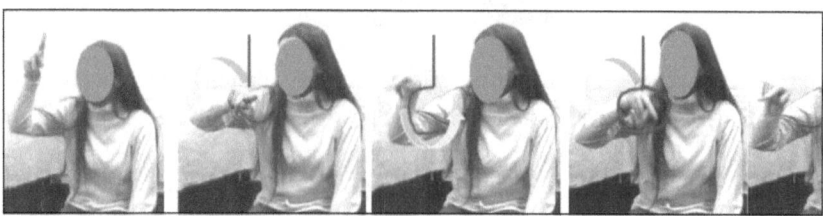

Figure 6. Second mention of the referent 'bauble', French native compensating for a lexical gap – modeling gesture, expansion to three dimensions (from Debras & Beaupoil-Hourdel, 2019)

A first, sketchier representation in gesture only can anticipate a fuller speech and gesture representation. Articulatory efforts aiming to produce a more developed gestural representation are typically used by native speakers adapting their communication style to facilitate nonnative speakers' understanding (Adams, 1998). More broadly, expanded gesture reiterations show how gestures belong in the 'public substrate' (Goodwin, 2013): the dynamic production of new forms based on shared ones enables structure-preserving transformations that are necessary for future actions to unfold.

5.4. Study 4: gestures of foreigner talk

Foreigner talk encompasses all the linguistic and conversational adjustments made by native speakers when speaking to nonnative speakers (Ferguson, 1975). It can involve syntactic changes (e.g. shorter, less complex sentences), semantic ones (e.g. simpler lexicon), and articulatory ones (e.g. slower flow of speech). As shown by Adams (1998), foreigner talk affects gesture as well. Adams's (1998) study compared the use of gestures by native speakers of American English when addressing Korean students versus when addressing other native speakers. When addressing language learners, native speakers used more pantomime, iconic (representational) gestures, and deictic gestures (pointing), although only the higher rate of deictic gestures proved statistically significant. Possibly because the participants had no metalinguistic awareness of their own use of gesture, they did not use fewer metaphorical (more abstract) gestures or emblems (more conventionalized) with language learners (see McNeill, 1992, for detailed definitions of these gesture functions).

Tellier and Stam (2012) studied the use of gesture by students who were training to become teachers of French as a foreign language when they explained action verbs to Erasmus students who were learners of French versus other native speakers of French. As future teachers, they were more sensitized to the needs of language learners; they did not use significantly more gestures, but their gestures were significantly longer and ampler when addressing learners. The rate of iconic gestures was significantly higher when addressing learners, while the rate of metaphorical gestures was significantly higher when addressing native speakers.

Study 4 (conducted by Léa Baldran and myself) focuses on the kinesic behavior of five native speakers of French participating in the storytelling game *Liar, Liar* with a native speaker of English who was learning French versus a native speaker of French. The ten video recordings amount to a total length of 58 minutes. Systematic annotation was made in ELAN (Wittenburg et al., 2006) to quantify various features of the gestures used, including the use of nonmanual gestures (head gestures as per McClave, 2000, and facial gestures of the mouth and eyebrows as per Bavelas & Chovil, 2018). Double coding was made on a portion of the annotations so as to ensure their reliability.

Study 4 yielded the annotation of 1,018 gestures of the hands, head, and face (269 manual gestures and 749 nonmanual gestures). The frequency of gestures produced was overall higher when addressing a nonnative speaker (18.4 gestures/minute on average) than a native speaker (14.9 gestures/minute on average). Participants produced far more nonmanual gestures than manual ones in both conditions, yet the proportion of manual gestures increased when addressing a nonnative speaker. Indeed, out of the 285 gestures addressed to native speakers, 230 were nonmanual (81%) and 55 were manual (19%); out of the 733 gestures addressed to nonnative speakers, 519 (71%) were nonmanual and 214 (29%) were manual (see Figure 7 for the distribution of nonmanual gestures in the data). This suggests that tandem participants who are not training to become foreign language teachers but are sensitive to the language gap when addressing a nonnative speaker spontaneously intensify the use of markers of affect and interpersonal relations (e.g. eyebrow movements, smiling, head nods).

Figure 7. Distribution of nonmanual gestures when addressing a native or nonnative speaker

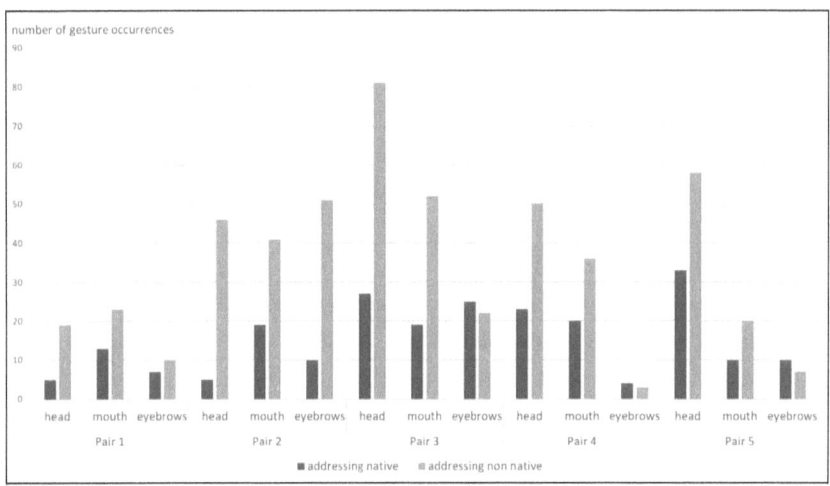

In contrast to Tellier and Stam's (2012) findings, there was no drastic change in the duration of manual gestures depending on whether the interlocutor addressed a native speaker (2.4 seconds on average) or a nonnative speaker (2.3 seconds on average). No striking change was observed either in the gestures' amplitudes, annotated in terms of their realization in the center or periphery of the gesture space, following a simplified, two-fold partition of the gesture space inspired by McNeill's (1992, p. 89) model. This could be due to the fact that participants in Tellier and Stam's (2012) study are future teachers sensitized to the needs of language learners, contrary to the tandem participants in the data. Gesture functions were grouped in terms of cultural functions (including emblems and metaphorical gestures) and referential ones (including deictic and iconic gestures). Although the participants in the data set did use more referential gestures in the presence of nonnative speakers, they used far more cultural gestures overall in both conditions. Again, this result contrasts with Tellier and Stam's (2012) finding that future language teachers use more iconic gestures when addressing nonnative speakers. Being professionally trained to address native speakers seems to be a crucial differentiating factor in this case as well. And yet, the participants use a more varied repertoire of manual gesture functions when addressing a nonnative speaker than a native speaker; again, this suggests an attempt on their part to adjust their communication to a nonnative interlocutor.

6. Perspectives for higher education language training and professionalization

The research presented above has shown how gesture plays a central communicative role in interactional contexts (Goodwin, 2013; Kendon, 2000), especially in exolingual ones (McCafferty & Stam, 2008). Language tandem participants use gesture for a variety of purposes: notably to collaborate, stabilize referential meaning, ensure discourse cohesion and mutual comprehension, scaffold language learning, provide feedback, adjust to their interlocutor, secure mutual engagement, and develop interpersonal relations. The use of gesture also mirrors how participants spontaneously adapt to the intercultural aspect of the language tandem. Gestures are more frequent (especially nonmanual ones) and their functions are more varied when addressing a nonnative speaker. The use of gesture also reveals differences in sociocultural positionings toward what it means to speak a target language, to learn it, and to help others learn one's mother tongue. Based on this research, I propose recommendations for the professionalization of language learning in higher education. I focus on language learning, teacher training, and the institutional recognition of the relationship between research, pedagogy, and innovation.

6.1. Language learning and professionalization

Universities are becoming increasingly international places, with a substantial potential for preparing students for the international workplace. Although students and faculty from all over the world make universities places of cultural diversity, this cultural diversity could often be more recognized or valued. Exchange students often stay for a short period of time, and often end up socializing mostly among themselves. Study abroad offices could collaborate more systematically with faculty so as to facilitate links between exchange students and local ones who volunteer for intercultural meetings, exchanges, and projects, of which the language tandem is just one example among many. While the European Commission (2012) remarks that "not all languages are equally valuable on the labour market" (p. 13), linguistic diversity remains absolutely vital for cultural and personal development.

The research on language tandems presented above shows the considerable potential of intercultural settings during which university students of diverse backgrounds interact as peer partners to achieve a common goal. Student projects with a core intercultural component should be more systematically included in university curricula in order for all students to develop, value, and learn to integrate 'soft' skills which have now become a must, namely intercultural and interactional ones. More specifically, intercultural collaborative learning projects can help students develop the following skills: becoming sensitized to openness and diversity, becoming more open and responsive to new and diverse perspectives, bridging cultural differences, using differing perspectives to increase the quality of work, and using appropriate sociolinguistic skills in order to function in diverse cultural and linguistic contexts (ACTFL, 2011). Intercultural collaborative learning projects can include more than two participants, and they can aim at personalized real-world tasks to ensure motivation and/or a specific domain to develop expertise. Another benefit is that they can be included in lifelong learning programs (EUA, 2008). They can also take the form of online collaborations if opportunities to be in the same room are limited (Guth & Helm, 2012). Whether face-to-face or online, collaborative learning arrangements will give university students opportunities to develop their communicative competence as well as a large array of other skills: responsibility and autonomy, creativity and innovation, problem-solving, and social and cross-cultural skills. By developing intercultural collaborative projects in their curricula, universities can at once professionalize students and promote an inclusive learning society.

6.2. Language teaching, teacher training

The research presented above can also inform teacher training in two main directions: developing more learner-centered approaches to language learning, and including more multimodal, interactional, and intercultural aspects of communicative competence in both teacher training and language teaching. Although the language tandem was invented to complement language learning in the classroom, it is today closer to what is considered the essence of language learning: the learner is active in a learner-centered arrangement, developing personal skills in the context of an authentic exchange, while the language teacher remains at the periphery as a facilitator (ACTFL, 2011). Future higher education language teachers could be trained to set up language tandems so as to diversify opportunities for learners to use language beyond the classroom, but they could also be encouraged and trained to develop their students' interactional skills in the classroom directly. As facilitators supervising language tandems, teachers should be trained to develop specific know-how, such as ways to be available to students, means of securing students' motivation, and forms of nonintrusive verification that tandem meetings are taking place. If assessment of students' progress is planned, it will require careful design and the targeted skills (language, communication, and intercultural competence) will need to be made explicit.

Language teacher training should also more systematically include research-based modules on how to develop the multimodal, interactional, and intercultural aspects of learners' communicative competence. As Tellier and Yerian (2018) suggested, the training of future language teachers should cover multimodal communication (e.g. topics such as the role of gestures in the multimodal co-construction of meaning, gesture functions, manual and nonmanual gestures, gestural alignment, and gestures related with foreigner talk), so that language teachers become more aware of the multimodal resources that are (literally!) at hand to enhance their communication and teaching skills. A key tool for future teachers' development of communicational self-awareness is retrospective reflection sessions based on videotaped recordings of their performance, for instance as part of exolingual interactions (Rivière & Guichon, 2014).

This method from applied research on online exolingual interactions can be transposed to in-class interactions by filming future teachers in training; seeing themselves teach allows them to study their own performance from an analytical and more distanced standpoint, as they go through past interactions again (Guth & Helm, 2012).

Teachers whose training has sensitized them to the multimodal dimension of exolingual interaction can, in turn, sensitize their students to the role of gesture. Two basic pedagogical goals come to mind: first, encouraging students to go beyond stereotyped perceptions of gesture, whose functions are usually broader and more complex that they might think, and second, helping them develop self-awareness of their own bodies in communication, and an awareness of how gesture can enhance or hinder communication. From the perspective of intercultural interaction, it will be especially useful for students to learn to distinguish between the idiosyncratic, cultural, and iconic dimensions of gesture but also to become aware that these dimensions are not always easy to tease apart. Interactional exercises (e.g. role-play, theater exercises, and public speaking) followed by reflective discussion can be used to help students pinpoint differences in the ways language users communicate in intralingual and exolingual contexts. Interactional exercises can be used to discuss sociocultural variation in the use of speech and gesture and cover notions like foreigner talk or the functions of other-repetition. During reflective sessions, language learners can for instance become aware that they already use gestural alignment and reiteration when speaking in their native tongue, and they can be encouraged to transpose this strategy to exolingual or L2 interactions so to secure meaning and interpersonal relationships.

6.3. Institutional recognition of the relationship between research, pedagogy, and innovation

As a learner corpus (Gilquin et al., 2007; Granger et al., 2015), the SITAF data shows the need for gesture to be more systematically included in language class curricula, language teachers' training, and language evaluation frameworks. Gestural cues should not be relegated to compensatory strategies used by pupils and/or beginners (although they can fill that purpose as well); gesturing skills are closely intertwined with spoken language skills, which should be recognized in levels B and C of *CEFR* descriptors (Council of Europe, 2001), when it comes to speaking, understanding, and interactional skills.

Interactional and intercultural competences are transversal to all domains, both at university and throughout professional life. As such, they could become core topics in lifelong learning in higher education. As the European Universities' *Charter on Lifelong learning* (EUA, 2008) suggests, successful lifelong learning will rely on a strengthened relationship between research, teaching, and innovation – an idea that this chapter has, I hope, exemplified to some extent. A research perspective on multimodal interaction shows that the contribution of gesture is at once essential, subtle, and complex, at the crossroads of culture, language, and communication. More broadly, lifelong learning opportunities developed by universities can provide uniquely innovative training based on research – and, in turn, lifelong learning can itself be a great source of new research methodologies and topics. After all, university researchers themselves are a fine example of lifelong learners whose own educational needs are continually evolving (EUA, 2008).

7.   Conclusion

Taking research on the use of gesture in language tandems as a point of entry, this chapter has proposed directions for training future professionals who communicate in exolingual interactions. It draws on research findings to inform pedagogy and innovation in higher education, and advocates for an increased institutional recognition of multimodal, communicative, and intercultural skills. These soft skills are central in today's internationalized professional life and for that reason they need to become core features of language and communication training for future professionals, among whom future language teachers. On a final note, one can say that preparing university students for the professional world is at once a fundamental mission of higher education and a continuous and exciting challenge, that of constantly adjusting to the transformations of the professional world of today and tomorrow.

References

ACTFL. (2011). *The 21st century skills map*. American Council on the Teaching of Foreign Languages. https://www.actfl.org/sites/default/files/resources/21st%20Century%20Skills%20Map-World%20Languages.pdf

Adams, T. W. (1998). *Gesture in foreigner talk*. Unpublished doctoral dissertation. University of Pennsylvania.

Allwood, J., Cerrato, L., Jokinen, K., Navarretta, C., & Paggio, P. (2007). The MUMIN coding scheme for the annotation of feedback, turn management and sequencing phenomena. *International Journal of Language Resources and Evaluation, 41*(3), 273-287. https://doi.org/10.1007/s10579-007-9061-5

Argyle, M. (1972). *The psychology of interpersonal behaviour*. Penguin.

Ariel, M. (1990). *Accessing noun-phrase antecedents*. Routledge.

Atkinson, D., Churchill, E., Nishino, T., & Okada, H. (2007). Alignment and interaction in a sociocognitive approach to second language acquisition. *The Modern Language Journal, 91*(2), 169-188. https://doi.org/10.1111/j.1540-4781.2007.00539.x

Bavelas, J., & Chovil, N. (2018). Some pragmatic functions of conversational facial gestures. *Gesture, 17*(1), 98-127. https://doi.org/10.1075/gest.00012.bav

Bezemer, J., & Jewitt, C. (2010). Multimodal analysis: key issues. In L. Litosseliti (Ed.), *Research methods in linguistics* (pp. 180-197). Continuum.

Boutet, D. (2015). Conditions formelles d'une analyse de la négation gestuelle. *Vestnik of Moscow State Linguistic University, Discourse as social practice: Priorities and prospects, 6*(717), 116-129.

Brammerts, H., & Calvert, M. (2003). Learning by communicating in tandem. In T. Lewis & L. Walker (Eds), *Autonomous language learning in tandem* (pp. 45-59). Academy Electronic Publications.

Bressem, J. (2014). Repetitions in gesture. In C. Müller, A. Cienki, E. Fricke, S. Ladewig, D. McNeill & J. Bressem (Eds), *Body-language-communication: an international handbook on multimodality in human interaction* (pp. 1641-1649). De Gruyter Mouton.

Bressem, J., Ladewig, S., & Müller, C. (2014). Linguistic annotation system for gestures (LASG). In C. Müller, A. Cienki, E. Fricke, S. Ladewig, D. McNeill & S. Teßendorf (Eds), *Body - language - communication* (vol. 2, pp. 1098-1124). De Gruyter Mouton.

Cienki, A. (2017). Lecture 9: language as a prototype category. In A. Cienki, *Ten lectures on spoken language and gesture from the perspective of cognitive linguistics: issues of dynamicity and multimodality*. Brill. https://doi.org/10.1163/9789004336230_002

Clark, H. (1996). *Using language*. Cambridge University Press.

Council of Europe. (2001). *Common European framework of reference for languages (CEFR)*. Cambridge University Press.

Debras, C., & Beaupoil-Hourdel, P. (2019). Gestualité et construction des chaînes de référence dans un corpus d'interactions tandem. *Cahiers de praxématique [Online] 72*. https://doi.org/10.4000/praxematique.5576

Debras, C., & Beaupoil-Hourdel, P. (forthcoming). Gestural alignment in metalinguistic sequences during tandem interactions. *Multimodal Communication*.

Debras, C., Beaupoil-Hourdel, P., Morgenstern, A., Horgues, C., & Scheuer, S. (2020). Corrective feedback sequences in tandem interactions: multimodal cues and speakers' positionings. In S. Raineri, M. Sekali & A. Leroux (Eds), *La correction en langue(s) – linguistic correction/correctness*. Presses de l'Université Paris Nanterre.

EUA. (2008). *European universities' charter on lifelong learning*. European University Association. https://eua.eu/downloads/publications/european%20universities%20charter%20on%20lifelong%20learning%202008.pdf

European Commission. (2012). *First European survey on language competences. Final report*. http://www.surveylang.org/media/ExecutivesummaryoftheESLC_210612.pdf

Ferguson, C. A. (1975). Toward a characterization of English foreigner talk. *Anthropological Linguistics*, *17*(1), 1-14.

Ferré, G. (2019). *Analyse de discours multimodale*. Editions de l'Université Grenoble Alpes.

Gass, S. M. (2003). Input and interaction. In C. J. Doughty & M. H. Long (Eds), *The handbook of second language acquisition* (pp 224-255). Blackwell.

Gilquin, G., Granger, S., & Paquot, M. (2007). Learner corpora: the missing link in EAP pedagogy. *Journal of English for Academic Purposes*, *6*(4), 319-335. https://doi.org/10.1016/j.jeap.2007.09.007

Goodwin, C. (2013). The co-operative, transformative organization of human action and knowledge. *Journal of Pragmatics*, *46*(1), 8-23. https://doi.org/10.1016/j.pragma.2012.09.003

Granger, S., Gilquin, G., & Meunier, F. (2015). *The Cambridge handbook of learner corpus research*. Cambridge University Press. https://doi.org/10.1017/cbo9781139649414

Graziano, M., & Gullberg, M. (2013). Gesture production and speech fluency in competent speakers and language learners. *Proceedings of the Tilburg Gesture Research Meeting (TiGeR)*. http://tiger.uvt.nl/pdf/papers/graziano.pdf

Gullberg, M. (2006). Handling discourse: gestures, reference tracking, and communication strategies in early L2. *Language Learning, 56*(1), 155-196. https://doi.org/10.1111/j.0023-8333.2006.00344.x

Gundel, J., Hedberg, N., & Zacharski, R. (1993). Cognitive status and the form of referring expressions in discourse. *Language, 69*(2), 274-307. https://doi.org/10.2307/416535

Guth, S., & Helm, F. (2012). Developing multiliteracies in ELT through telecollaboration. *ELT Journal, 66*(1), 42-51. https://doi.org/10.1093/elt/ccr027

Helming, B. (2002). *L'apprentissage autonome des langues en tandem*. Didier.

Holler, J., & Bavelas, J. B. (2017). On the multi-modal communication of common ground - a review and examination of social functions. In R. B. Church, M. W. Alibali & S. Kelly (Eds), *Why gesture? How the hands function in speaking, thinking, and communicating* (pp. 213-240). John Benjamins.

Horgues, C., & Scheuer, S. (2015) Why some things are better done in tandem. In J. A. Mompeán & J. Fouz-González (Eds), *Investigating English pronunciation: current trends and directions* (pp. 47-82). Palgrave Macmillan. https://doi.org/10.1057/9781137509437_3

Kendon, A. (1986). Some reasons for studying gesture. *Semiotica, 62*(1-2), 3-28. https://doi.org/10.1515/semi.1986.62.1-2.3

Kendon, A. (2000). Gesture and speech: unity or duality. In D. McNeill (Ed.), *Language and gesture* (pp. 47-63). Cambridge University Press.

Kendon, A. (2004). *Gesture: visible action as utterance*. Cambridge University Press.

Kimbara, I. (2006). On gestural mimicry. *Gesture, 6*, 39-61.

Kita, S. (2003). (Ed.). *Pointing: where language, culture, and cognition meet*. Lawrence Erlbaum.

Kress, G., & van Leeuwen, T. (2001). *Multimodal discourse: the modes and media of contemporary communication*. Arnold.

Ladewig, S. H. (2014). Creating multimodal utterances: the linear integration of gesture into speech. In C. Müller, A. Cienki, E. Fricke, S. Ladewig, D. McNeill & S. Teßendorf (Eds), *Body - language - communication: an international handbook on multimodality in human interaction* (pp. 1662-1677). De Gruyter Mouton.

LeBaron, C., & Streeck, J. (2000). Gesture, knowledge, and the world. In D. McNeill (Ed.), *Language and gesture* (pp. 118-138). Cambridge University Press.

Long, M. H. (2007). *Problems in SLA*. Lawrence Erlbaum.

Lyster, R., & Ranta, L. (1997). Corrective feedback and learner uptake. *Studies in Second Language Acquisition, 19*(1), 37-66. https://doi.org/10.1017/s0272263197001034

Mackey, A. (2006). Feedback, noticing and instructed second language learning. *Applied Linguistics, 27*(3), 405-430. https://doi.org/10.1093/applin/ami051

McCafferty, S., & Stam, G. (2008). (Eds). *Gesture: second language acquisition and classroom research*. Routledge.

McClave, E. (2000). Linguistic functions of head movements in the context of speech. *Journal of Pragmatics, 32*(7), 855-878. https://doi.org/10.1016/s0378-2166(99)00079-x

McNeill, D. (1992). *Hand and mind*. University of Chicago Press.

Mondada, L. (2006). Video recording as the preservation of fundamental features for analysis. In H. Knoblauch, J. Raab, H. Soeffner & B. Schnettler (Eds), *Video analysis: methodology and methods* (pp. 51-68). Peter Lang. https://doi.org/10.3726/978-3-653-02667-2

Müller, C., Ladewig, S. H., & Bressem, J. (2013). Gesture and speech from a linguistic perspective: a new field and its history. In C. Müller, A. Cienki, E. Fricke, S. Ladewig, D. McNeill & S. Teβendorf (Eds), *Body - language - communication: an international handbook on multimodality in human interaction* (vol. 1, pp. 55-81). Walter de Gruyter. Mouton. https://doi.org/10.1515/9783110302028

Müller, C. (2014). Gestural modes of representation as techniques of depiction. In C. Müller, A. Cienki, E. Fricke, S. Ladewig, D. McNeill & S. Teβendorf (Eds), *Body - language - communication: an international handbook on multimodality in human interaction* (pp. 1687-1702). De Gruyter

Navarretta, C. (2011). Anaphora and gestures in multimodal communication. *Proceedings of the 8th Discourse Anaphora and Anaphor Resolution Colloquium* (DAARC 2011) (pp. 171-181). Edições Colibri.

Norris, S. (2004). *Analyzing multimodal interaction: a methodological framework*. Routledge.

O'Rourke, B. (2005). Form-focused interaction in online tandem learning. *CALICO Journal, 22*(3), 433-466. https://doi.org/10.1558/cj.v22i3.433-466

Peräkylä, A., & Ruusuvuori J. (2006). Facial expression in an assessment. In H. Knoblauch, B. Schnettler, J. Raab & H. Soeffner (Eds), *Video-analysis, methodology and methods: qualitative audiovisual data analysis in sociology* (pp. 127-142). Peter Lang. https://doi.org/10.3726/978-3-653-02667-2

Perniss, P. (2012) Use of sign space. In R. Pfau, M. Steinbach & B. Woll (Eds), *Sign language: an international handbook* (pp. 412-431). Mouton de Gruyter. https://doi.org/10.1515/9783110261325

Rivière, V., & Guichon, N. (2014). Construction de bilans rétroactifs par des apprentis tuteurs langue en ligne : essai de caractérisation discursive de la dynamique socio-cognitive. *Recherches et Applications*, 56.

Sacks, H., Schegloff, E., & Jefferson, G. (1974). A simplest systematics for the organization of turn-taking for conversation. *Language 50*(4), 696-735. https://doi.org/10.1353/lan.1974.0010

Sato, M., & Lyster, R. (2012). Peer interaction and corrective feedback for accuracy and fluency development. *Studies in Second Language Acquisition, 34*(4), 591-626. https://doi.org/10.1017/s0272263112000356

Schegloff, E. A. (1984). On some gestures' relation to talk. In J. M. Atkinson & J. Heritage (Eds), *Structures of social action: studies in conversation analysis* (pp. 266-296). Cambridge University Press & Editions de la Maison des Sciences de l'Homme.

Schmidt, R. (1990). The role of consciousness in second language learning. *Applied Linguistics*, *11*, 129-158.

Schnedecker, C., & Landragin F. (2014). Les chaînes de référence. Présentation. *Langages*, *195*, 3-22.

Sheen, Y., & Ellis, R. (2011). Corrective feedback in language teaching. In E. Hinkel (Ed.), *Handbook of research in second language teaching and learning* (vol. 2, pp. 593-610). Routledge. https://doi.org/10.4324/9780203836507.ch36

Stivers, T. (2008). Stance, alignment, and affiliation during storytelling: when nodding is a token of affiliation. *Research on Language and Social Interaction*, *41*(1), 31-57. https://doi.org/10.1080/08351810701691123

Streeck, J. (2009). *Gesturecraft: the manu-facture of meaning*. John Benjamins.

Tellier, M., & Stam, G. (2012). Stratégies verbales et gestuelles dans l'explication lexicale d'un verbe d'action. In V. Rivière (Ed.), *Spécificités et diversité des interactions didactiques* (pp. 357-374). Riveneuve.

Tellier, M., & Yerian, K. (2018). Mettre du corps à l'ouvrage : travailler sur la mise en scène du corps du jeune enseignant en formation universitaire. *Recherche et Pratiques Pédagogiques En Langues de Spécialité - Cahiers de l'APLIUT, Association Des Professeurs de Langues Des Instituts Universitaires de Technologie (APLIUT), 37*(2). https://doi.org/10.4000/apliut.6079

Chapter 7

Wittenburg, P., Brugman, H., Russel, A., Klassman, A., & Sloetjes, H. (2006). ELAN: a professional framework for multimodality research. *Proceedings of the Fifth International Conference of Language Resources and Evaluation* (LREC'06), Genova, Italy.

8. The social dimension of learner autonomy in a telecollaborative project: a Russian course for apprentice engineers

Elsa Chachkine[1]

1. Introduction

According to the International Labour Organisation (ILO, 2019), many of today's skills will not match the jobs of tomorrow. Lifelong learning and learning to learn are thus crucial. The Conservatoire des arts et métiers (Cnam) language centre has for a long time had this ambition. Although the approach was at first learner-centred and based on individual-focused learning processes (social support being provided solely by teacher-advisers), current research has shown a social shift (Cappellini, Lewis, & Mompean, 2017; Lantolf, 2013; Little, 2000) with the rediscovery of social theories on learning (Bruner, 1975; Clot, 1999; Lantolf & Thorne, 2007; Vygotsky, 1978). In addition, the social web offers new affordances such as "commenting, linking, co-authoring, revising, remixing, sharing, [and] liking" (Blin, 2012, p. 79), thus providing new forms of online interaction and possibilities for collective activities. However, students need to be prepared for online participation, as "processes, methods, and strategies of effective language learning should be taught more explicitly in order to improve self-directed learning" (Vandergriff, 2016, p. 241).

The main objective of this exploratory research is to investigate how the social dimension of the Russian course sustains autonomisation and whether

---

1. Conservatoire National des Arts et Métiers (Cnam), FoAP (EA 7529), Paris, France; elsa.chachkine@lecnam.net; https://orcid.org/0000-0002-1484-5915

How to cite this chapter: Chachkine, E. (2020). The social dimension of learner autonomy in a telecollaborative project: a Russian course for apprentice engineers. In B. Dupuy and M. Grosbois (Eds), *Language learning and professionalization in higher education: pathways to preparing learners and teachers in/for the 21st century* (pp. 229-261). Research-publishing.net. https://doi.org/10.14705/rpnet.2020.44.1107

it supports the development of language, cultural, and other skills needed by 21st century apprentice engineers. The aim is also to enrich practices and try to improve the course in terms of student guidance, learning, and well-being, following an action research process that seeks transformative change through the simultaneous process of taking action and conducting research (Stringer, 2008). To do so, I will first examine the rationale of the course in light of the literature, combining sociocultural theory with the paradigm of autonomous learning through the lens of self-determination, self-regulation, and self-efficacy theories, which is an original theoretical basis for language learning research in France. Following a qualitative approach, I will then analyse the data collected to explore how the social dimension manifests itself and its impact in terms of learning.

2. Theoretical anchoring of the Russian course

2.1. Socio-Cultural Theory (SCT)

According to SCT (Vygotsky, 1978), human developmental processes take place

> "through participation in cultural, linguistic, and historically formed settings such as family life and peer group interaction, and in institutional contexts like schooling" (Lantolf & Thorne, 2007, p. 197).

The Zone of Proximal Development (ZPD) is "the distance between the actual developmental level as determined by independent problem solving and the level of potential development as determined through problem solving under adult guidance or in collaboration with more capable peers" (Vygotsky, 1978, p. 86). For Vygotsky (1978), "human learning presupposes a specific social nature and a process by which children grow into the intellectual life of those around them" (p. 88). Learning collaboratively with others in instructional settings precedes and shapes development, hence the importance of educational mediation by peers and experts in the Russian course for the apprentice engineers' development of language skills and learner autonomy.

2.2. Learner autonomy

Since Holec (1981) first described learner autonomy as "the ability to take charge of one's own learning" (p. 3), it has been generally agreed that conscious, critical reflection, choice, and decision-making are key elements (Little, 2000; Murphy, 2014). A major criticism of this position is its reliance on an individual perspective. To address this, I introduced reflective peer group workshops and one-to-one counselling sessions with myself as a teacher-counsellor (henceforth referred to as learner-tutor scaffolding exchange sessions). Moreover, the emotional and relational aspects of the learning process need to be taken into account. Indeed, autonomy depends on the development of a learner's psychological and emotional ability to monitor their own and others' emotions (O'Leary, 2014; Salovey & Mayer, 1990), the ability to cooperate with others and solve conflicts in a constructive way (Kohonen, 1992; O'Leary, 2014), and the value of responsibility to others in a social context (Kohonen, 1992; O'Leary, 2014), in addition to displaying empathetic behaviours, controlling one's anxiety, and encouraging oneself and others. Taking emotions into account in autonomous learning therefore requires metacognitive skills but also meta-emotional skills (O'Leary, 2014); these types of skills are highly valuable in the professional world (Cherniss & Goleman, 2001; Sackett & Walmsley, 2014) and are described as key competences for the 21st century to be promoted in the framework of language training (ACTFL, 2011).

2.3. Self-Determination Theory (SDT)

SDT (Deci & Ryan, 2002), a theory of motivation and human development, provides an explanation regarding the power of active learner involvement. In this theory, the notion of 'choice' is central to autonomous behaviour. Motivation is underpinned by three basic psychological needs: autonomy, competence, and relatedness (Niemiec & Ryan, 2009). Freedom of choice is fundamental and is supported by the desire to be at the origin of one's own behaviour, the need for effectiveness, and the need to have confidence in achieving desired outcomes. It is also supported by the need for learners to experience "positive and mutually satisfying relationships, characterized by a sense of closeness and trust" (Haerens, n.d., para 3). In the Russian course under study, a great freedom of choice was offered, as well as the possibility of being in contact with speakers of the target language and culture of about the same age.

2.4. Self-Regulated Learning (SRL) and sense of self-efficacy

Motivation, however, is not enough. According to Schunk and Zimmerman (2008), post-decision processes require that action be regulated until the goal is achieved. SRL refers to the process by which learners personally activate and sustain cognition, affects, and behaviors that are oriented toward the attainment of learning goals (Shunk & Zimmerman, 2008). A common and crucial factor in both initiating learning and persisting is Bandura's (1986, 2001) self-efficacy theory. If people do not think they can produce the results they want by their actions, they have little reason to act or persevere in the face of difficulties (Bandura, 1986). Personal self-efficacy judgements are primarily derived from lived or vicarious experiences and, to a lesser extent, from verbal persuasion. Consequently, seeing peers succeed, receiving encouragement from them, and encouraging other learners to make their learning experience a positive one can enhance learners' senses of personal self-efficacy.

Having shown in our theoretical anchoring how the combination of sociocultural theory, motivational theory, and a theory of human agency are important when considering learner autonomy, I now turn to telecollaborative learning – a pedagogical approach that encompasses many online exchange practices for language learning.

2.5. Telecollaborative learning

Pedagogically structured online collaborative learning initiatives between learners in different geographical locations are known as telecollaborative learning (Dooly, 2017; Dooly & O'Dowd, 2018). Language learning in tandem is well-founded in theory and well-researched (Brammerts et al., 2002; Lewis &

Walker, 2003; Tardieu & Horgues, 2020), and today teletandem exchanges allow virtual exchanges as part of telecollaboration. The relationship between tandem and self-study learning was established in the late 1980's. Autonomous tandem language learning in the context of self-training language learning trends was then enriched by scaffolding exchanges with a tutor to support tandem language learning at the organisational, educational, and social levels (Brammerts et al., 2002; Lewis & Walker, 2003).

Technological accessibility has contributed to an increase in telecollaboration, but other factors also justify its success, namely

> "the widespread acceptance that intercultural awareness and intercultural and interpersonal communicative competences are extremely important for foreign language learning; the need for an interactive approach through cognitively challenging, meaningful use of language that goes beyond the classroom walls; and thirdly, the fact that language learners must gain combined skills of communicating in multiple languages and through multiple modalities" (Dooly & O'Dowd, 2018, p. 21).

Developing cultural references about other cultures and putting one's own culture at a distance (Zarate, 1986), being curious and prepared to suspend disbelief about others' cultures and belief about one's own (Byram, 1997), learning to organise exchanges in a multicultural environment and being able to make them last, and maintaining contact are important skills for learning how to learn a language throughout life and are core work skills, according to the ILO.

Telecollaborative projects require practitioners to coherently sequence both in-class and out-of-class activities and ensure appropriate metacognitive scaffolding. This implies designing appropriate, interconnected tasks (Dooly & O'Dowd, 2018).

In light of these theoretical issues, this exploratory research sets out to investigate the extent to which the social dimension of the Russian course facilitates learning.

3. Russian course under study

3.1. Participants

On the French side they were students from the Cnam (*n*=8), most of them apprentice engineers, who were getting ready to spend six months in Siberia. On the Russian side, the Novosibirsk State University (NSU) students were either future teachers of French or Russian, or students majoring in biology, mathematics, or physics who were going to spend a mobility period in France the following year.

For the Cnam apprentice engineers, learning a second foreign language was optional, but taking the Russian course was highly recommended for those who would study in Russia because they were complete beginners in Russian. On the Russian side, the students were of at least B1 level in French, and their participation in the telecollaborations was optional; Russian students chose their course from among several options, and their work was graded. I am aware that telecollaborations are based on mutual exchanges, but within the limits of this chapter, only data from the Cnam students are analysed.

In addition to being the designer of the course, I was also the tutor trainer and researcher who collected and analysed the data. The immersion of the researcher in the context in order to understand the actors is a strength of this study. So is my ability to distance myself from the analysis (Groulx, 1999). The researcher involved in action research is aware of the necessity for distancing and can observe an empathic neutrality (Patton, 1990).

3.2. Learning objectives

The learning objectives were multiple: develop the learners' language skills as well as their knowledge of Russian culture, provide them with intercultural experiences, and prepare them for their mobility period in Siberia and future professional lives. Following the tradition of self-access centres (Kronenberg, 2017; Little, 2015; Rivens Mompean, 2013), another objective was to develop the learners' skills in learning a language autonomously. The approach was expanded to social networks and telecollaboration with speakers of the target language.

The Cnam students were free to choose their learning objectives, but the majority wanted to learn how to read Cyrillic, be able to communicate in simple everyday situations, and develop some knowledge of the culture. Therefore, the following were required: a basic mastery of Russian pronunciation (stressed and unstressed vowels for words of more than two syllables, learning of velar phonemes [hard] or palatalised phonemes [soft]; Cubberley, 2002), a minimal understanding of inflexional morphology, and acquisition of everyday vocabulary.

3.3. Course organisation

For their one-semester period of self-directed learning, students were provided with a supportive social environment, metacognitive support, and educational resources (as summarised in Figure 1):

- three 45-minute learner-tutor scaffolding exchange sessions organised throughout the semester;

- two reflective workshops, each lasting two hours – one at the beginning of the semester and one at the end;

- five teletandem sessions of 50 min with a Russian student at the Russian partner university, which the students will attend during their mobility period;

- a Facebook page for all Cnam students ($n=8$) and Russian students ($n=8$) who participate in teletandems, where they can share and exchange cultural information; and

- educational resources such as Russian language textbooks, a logbook, and sheets designed to help structure teletandems.

Figure 1. Self-directed learning in one's social environment

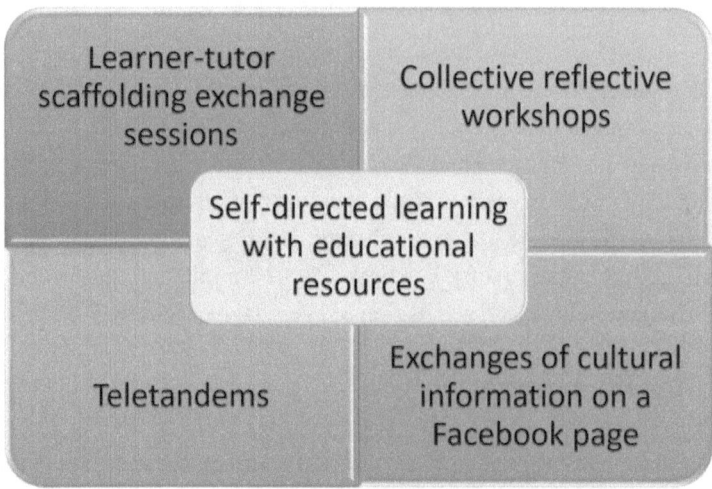

3.4. Learner-tutor scaffolding exchange sessions

Scaffolding exchange sessions were usually face-to-face with me as a tutor, held at regular intervals, and 'non-decision-making' (Gremmo, 1995). In line with the self-determination theory and without prior knowledge of the learners' needs and desires, as teacher-counsellor, I helped the learners make choices and would not make choices on their behalf.

During the first session, the learners were asked to:

- assess their knowledge of the target language and culture;

- identify realistic learning objectives;

- think about how to schedule the teletandem sessions;

- choose educational resources with respect to the objectives;

- reflect upon the organisation of their self-study (time slots dedicated to self-study, place where self-study will be performed); and

- reflect upon learning strategies they have used, implement personal tricks for learning better, in line with learning self-regulation.

In Sessions 2 and 3, the learners were asked to:

- talk about the educational resources they have used for self-study;

- discuss the teletandem sessions carried out, the information shared on the collective Facebook page;

- evaluate learning outcomes and the strategies implemented to learn;

- set new objectives;

- choose new educational resources; and

- test new learning strategies that I suggested as teacher-counsellor.

Through attentive listening, I invited the learner to speak about their learning and the learning processes in which they were involved. A number of tips were provided so as to support the learners' motivation, to help ensure the exchanges with the tandem partner would last, or to help decipher posts from Russian students on the Facebook social page. I also gave a great amount of encouragement to the learners.

3.5. Collective reflective workshops

Two reflective workshops were scheduled, one at the beginning and one at the end of the semester. The first workshop was designed to present the different elements of the project to the Cnam students ($n=8$), introduce the Russian students to the French students via a videoconferencing tool, and start

Chapter 8

thinking collectively about how to learn a language in a self-training setting, working on the basis of recommendations (identified and shared by students who experienced a similar training arrangement the year before, collected and edited beforehand).

During the second workshop, every student wrote out an assessment of their learning and the learning processes they had experienced, specifying what had been achieved and what was less successful, and presented this orally. The students then collectively developed a recommendation sheet for future students in the course with tips about how to avoid pitfalls. This allowed every participant to formalise the experience, share learning strategies, and promote vicarious experiences (Bandura, 1986, 2001). The second part of the workshop was dedicated to a collective analysis of the cultural information exchanged on Facebook, to further students' reflection on how to learn a language in a self-training setting as well as in the teletandem arrangement and how to take advantage of social networks.

3.6. Telecollaboration

In this context, Cnam students and students from the NSU in Russia cooperated to learn each other's native tongues, gain knowledge of both cultures, and gain from an intercultural experience.

For the Cnam students, the teletandem exchanges would later be followed by face-to-face exchanges, as they would be moving to Siberia. On the French side of the arrangement, students had several supporting elements to sustain their learning: the two reflective workshops, the individual scaffolding sessions with me, a logbook, and worksheets they could complete with their Russian tandem partner. The sheets, designed for complete beginners in Russian, provided activities to help them develop their ability to read and pronounce words with their partner, suggest dialogue simulations, ask questions about student life in Siberia or questions on differences in 'ways of being' and attitudes (e.g. what is the rudest thing for you: smoking in someone's home, not taking off your shoes when you are invited in someone's house, or not saying thank you?). Teletandem partners were asked to consult each other to choose the videoconferencing tool they would use. Students could decide to use audio communication only. They could also use text chat to complement oral communication.

All participants also shared information on a Facebook page. Students took turns posting cultural information (a film, text, video, photo, song, etc.) from their home country that they considered important and then justifying their choice. Each post was either about an element of culture shared by most people or about an element of culture personally valued by individual students. An explanation was expected. Great freedom of choice was offered in this activity, which is consistent with Deci and Ryan's (2002) self-determination theory.

Posts could give rise to asynchronous written comments asking for additional information or expressing analogies or dissimilarities. Students were strongly encouraged to comment on posts published by others. This space was intended to federate all students and expand their network of contacts so that exchanges with native speakers would not be limited to their tandem partners. It was also intended to encourage collaboration with more capable peers in the target language and culture, in line with sociocultural theory.

Such activities were designed to foster meaningful use of language that goes beyond classroom use of participants' interpersonal and existing intercultural skills. They also provided opportunities for developing a combination of skills in communicating in multiple languages and through multiple modalities (oral communication by videoconference, text and asynchronous text writing on Facebook), as well as learning to learn a language with a speaker of the target language, which is consistent with the core competencies for lifelong learning identified by the ILO.

3.7. Educational resources

Textbooks could be borrowed for the duration of the training period. Selected learning sites and language learning applications were also suggested.

Chapter 8

A logbook given during the first exchange session included several sections to be completed by the student during the sessions and throughout the semester:

- self-assessment of Russian language skills, knowledge at the beginning of the course, and prior self-directed language learning experiences;

- learning objectives and resources used, to be completed during the sessions;

- a schedule of teletandem sessions to be carried out over the semester;

- a section on strengths and weaknesses, successes and difficulties experienced; and

- a 'validation' section, which includes all the elements that are required for the course to be validated; this helps students to ensure their 'training contract' is fulfilled.

The logbook was to be brought to the scaffolding sessions. It was shared with me and constituted an essential element of the learner-tutor sessions. It helped raise awareness and promoted the diversity of contexts and uses of language appropriation by promoting reflection on them.

4. Methodology

The course design, in connection with the theories presented, will now be explored through the two research questions that resulted from the theoretical construct.

- How does the social dimension of the course manifest itself? How does it sustain autonomisation?

- How does the social dimension support the development of language skills, as well as cultural and relational knowledge?

I present the data collected in an attempt to provide answers to these questions.

4.1. Data collection

The approach is qualitative: the research is designed to come as close as possible to an accurate understanding of autonomisation and of learning processes made possible by the course design. It also aims, with an interpretative perspective, to ensure that the experimentation is understandable by taking into account meanings given by the actors (the students; Paquay, 2006). Data obtained during the course (logbooks, learner-teacher Sessions 2 and 3, the last reflexive collective workshop, exchanges on the Facebook page) and data generated for the purpose of the study (an anonymous questionnaire at the end of the training, an anonymous questionnaire administered four months post training) were used. I worked from:

- logbooks (8);

- transcriptions of learner-teacher scaffolding exchange Sessions 2 and 3 (16)

- anonymous Questionnaire 1, given at the end of the course (eight responses),

- transcriptions of the last reflexive collective workshop discussions; and

- anonymous Questionnaire 2, given four months after the end of the course asking students about their feeling of personal effectiveness in learning languages after this experience, their practice of self-directed learning, tandems, and Russian social networks (seven responses).

4.2. Method

A semantic analysis (Bardin, 1997) of the exchange sessions and reflective workshop was conducted, and the presence or absence of the following elements was checked:

- traces of motivation, satisfaction, and self-regulation. Particular attention was paid to identifying traces of social motivation, intrinsic motivation, emotional well-being, volition, how an activity was made more meaningful, and self-efficacy, in line with the self-determination theory (Reeve, Ryan, Deci, & Jang, 2008) and self-regulation theory (Zimmerman & Schunk, 2008);

- traces of autonomous learner actions (setting goals, planning learning activities, selecting relevant resources, evaluating resources and strategies, keeping track of time and place of learning), in line with research on learner autonomy (Holec, 1981; Lewis, 2014; Nogueira, O'Connor, & Cappellini, 2017); and

- traces of emotional involvement and, in particular, how the students exercised control over the affective dimension (O'Leary, 2014, p. 20), their ability to monitor their emotions and others' emotions (O'Leary, 2014, p. 20), how they empathised with others, their ability to cooperate with others and solve conflicts in a constructive way (Kohonen, 1992, p. 19), how they lowered their anxiety, and how they self-encouraged (Oxford, 1990, p. 21).

The anonymous questionnaire administered following the training period provided information on:

- self-efficacy belief[2]; and
- self-directed learning with teletandems.

In order to understand the learning potential (as regards language skills, cultural knowledge, intercultural awareness, and interpersonal skills), data from the following were explored:

- logbooks;

---

2. Questionnaires 1 and 2 are given in supplementary materials, Appendix 1.

- scaffolding exchange sessions: analyses of students' ability to read, stress syllables and reduce nonstressed syllables, very basically communicate, and demonstrate cultural and intercultural awareness, as well as the relationships they built and the network they developed or did not develop;

- Questionnaire 1 at the end of the course: impressions on the different components of the course, learning; and

- Questionnaire 2, given four months after the end of the course, also provides information about interpersonal skills (are you still in contact with your tandem partner? If so, have you already met your tandem partner)?

Some results are discussed in the following section in relation to the research questions.

5. How does the social dimension manifest itself? Does it support autonomisation?

5.1. Main indicators of a social dimension of autonomy

5.1.1. Teletandems: social motivation and intrinsic motivation for the activity

During the individual exchange Sessions 2 and 3, when the students were invited to report on their learning and I asked them, "tell me about what you have learned over the past few weeks", the eight students all immediately talked about the teletandems: "uh... I'm on my third exchange with my tandem partner... We completed the sheet, the second one, we went over the pronunciation and introducing oneself again"[3] (Student 1 [ST1], Session 2). And if a teletandem had to be cancelled for technical reasons or because of organisational problems

---
3. The students' quotations were translated from French into English. The quotations in their original French are shown in supplementary materials, Appendix 2.

either on the French or Russian side, the student would be frustrated and lose motivation, which was the case for two students: "I haven't heard from him for a while, he stood me up two or three times, well [laughs] it did affect my motivation a bit, I wasted some time as I spent an afternoon waiting, so I didn't do a tandem" (ST8, Session 2).

For students who practised teletandems ($n=6$ at the beginning, $n=7$ at the end of the course), the tandem partners helped them work on their reading and pronunciation, and they simulated short dialogues and helped students develop knowledge about culture. This is shown by the logbooks and questionnaires: "during the tandems, she really helps me to correct my pronunciation, she tells me how to stress words correctly... We also spoke with Russian ST1 (ST_RUS1) about the mentality of young people in Russia nowadays" (ST1, logbook); "list of learning with the teletandem partner: sheets (reading, pronunciation and basic communication) and cultural exchange with my Russian tandem" (ST3, logbook).

The practice of teletandems seemed to be an essential social motivation factor for the students. It was recognised as both a precursor to self-regulatory development and a vital component of students' current efforts to self-regulate (adaptive forms of help seeking; e.g. Ryan & Deci, 2000). The relationship with the tandem partner seemed to play a strong motivational role and also had a regulating effect. This, however, seemed to be dependent on a positive relationship that the students managed to maintain (or not) with their partners. It is reflected in the scaffolding sessions and some logbooks that when the relationship had been friendly, warm, and lasting, the students described their experience positively, expressing the desire to continue once the course was over. Otherwise, they tended to lose motivation, even interrupting their self-directed learning:

> "I was lucky to have a friendly tandem partner; it is a very interesting way of exchanging because we have the opportunity of communicating with a person whose mother tongue is Russian. Moreover, we gain confidence and learning becomes more interesting and unconventional. I intend to continue to keep in touch with my partner. It is a perfect method for me" (ST2, logbook).

The social motivation that made it possible to seek help or support, as well as to be and remain motivated, also provided the pleasure of being able to help and cooperate: "I had asked her for short expressions and short sentences, 'how much does it cost', everyday sentences, and then she asked me to train her a bit because she had an oral test, a French test, she often asked me 'is it correct to say it that way', it was nice, it was really both ways" (ST6, session 2).

Teletandems also seemed to be a strong source of intrinsic motivation, as the notions of "pleasure" and "interest" were frequently mentioned in the exchange sessions or in the reflective workshop:

> "she's great, she's highly reactive, in fact she's the one that helps me practise, she helps me practise pronunciation THOROUGHLY, she's good at challenging me, we're going to have our third teletandem on Sunday, it's once a week, no, it's GREAT" (ST8, Session 3).

The question of strong motivation provided by these exchanges was expressed by seven out of eight students in their answers to Questionnaire 1. To the question "how would you describe the exchanges with your tandem partner", the terms "fun" and "enriching" are both given four times each, most often together, or they are qualified as "positive", "warm", "friendly", or "stimulating".

Finally, the experience of managing teletandems generated many emotions. Beyond the pleasure they had in cooperating, the fondness they had of their tandem partner, or the pleasure they had in helping, students learned to "monitor their emotions" and "to lower their anxiety" when it came to having their first tandem meeting with a stranger: "it's a bit, uh… unsettling to find yourself facing a person you don't know. At first it feels a bit weird as you click and then ALL OF A SUDDEN he answers!" (ST5, Session 2).

5.1.2. *Oral cognitive and metacognitive reflection*

Only the list of points that were completed with students' tandem and the teaching resources used for self-directed learning were noted in the logbooks.

Chapter 8

There was no mention of new objectives, no evaluation of progress, and not even any assessment of their learning strategies or their ability to organise their learning. It was only in the context of exchange sessions or during reflective workshops that, at my request, students evaluated their learning and the teaching resources they had used, expressed their new learning objectives, and sometimes evaluated learning strategies they had applied.

ST6 and tutor, Session 2:

> T: Fine, and what are your goals?
>
> ST6: Well, uh, to be able to read some signs when we get there. To be able to get by with the little vocabulary I have without uh... having to use English to make myself understood.

ST3 and tutor, Session 3:

> Yes, by the way, I had a manual that you sent in pdf format, it's good, that one helped me a little, it's well done, it guides you step by step, it avoids going too fast right away, whereas I had a textbook with vocabulary but as it doesn't give pronunciations, it's not really... the best.

Similarly, reflections on cultural information that was posted, cultural comparisons, or intercultural awareness were never written down in the logbooks or in the comments of Facebook posts. Instead, reflections were expressed verbally during the exchange sessions after I invited students to do so.

ST4 and tutor, Session 3:

> T: There was a sign that I found interesting in the demonstration. There was a young girl who wrote [on a sign]: "I love my mother, but she didn't come [to the demonstration against the government in office]". That means...

> ST4: Her mother doesn't agree with that. Both generations disagree, the daughter protests, the mother doesn't.

Or the following discussion that invites the student to compare cultural aspects, ST5 and tutor, Session 2:

> T: So it's true that almost all Russians have seen this film. Would there be an equivalent in France or in the French-speaking world?
>
> ST5: Uh there's *Les Visiteurs* or *Les Bronzés* or *Brice de Nice*...

It is through dialogue, through sustained guidance, and through oral verbalisation that learning processes can become conscious – that choices, decision-making, and incipient critical reflection are made possible. It is reasonable to assume that without this personalised support, no cognitive or metacognitive thinking would have taken place, which demonstrates the importance of intentionally designed learning environments to stimulate qualitative developmental changes.

5.2. From external regulation to integrated regulation

Finally, it is interesting to note that organisational or metacognitive suggestions, as well as recommendations related to the evaluation of learning resources that I may have mentioned during exchange sessions, were integrated by the students: students recommended to other students the suggestions I had previously given. This occurred during the activity that aimed to draw up a list of recommendations to be communicated to future students who would take the course the following semester. During the final workshop, in response to the question "What advice would you give to students who, like you, will take this course, and on the other hand what would you recommend they should avoid?" they answered as below.

> "Don't let the deadline approach, be persistently self-disciplined in your work".

> "Don't focus 100% on tandems. You still have to take time to work on your own".
>
> "To plan them [teletandem sessions] from the beginning and to have good quality internet connection".
>
> "One thing to do is to prepare the sheets well before the tandem".

I made all of these recommendations during scaffolding exchange sessions (Session 2 with ST2, ST3, ST7, ST8; Session 3 with ST1, ST6), as illustrated in this exchange between a student and me: "It might be worth working on your sheets before you get on the tandem" (tutor to ST6, Session 2).

5.3. Intrinsic motivation for cultural information exchange on Facebook

All the posts made on the Facebook page were viewed in turn and seemed to be very much appreciated by the students. In Questionnaire 1, the following terms were used to characterise them: "interesting", "enriching", or "constructive" together with the term "fun" in five out of eight answers. It was also confirmed during the exchange sessions that the posts were considered genuinely interesting: as ST7 stated, "yes, it's interesting to know what software Russians use". The notions of interest, pleasure, and lightness of the posts appeared most important to them. However, as noted previously, very few comments were posted in reaction to posts on the Facebook page, for drawing comparisons, asking for additional information, analysing the post. Facebook posts were used as a support for teletandem discussions, as shown in this excerpt from an exchange session in which ST6 talked about how his partner gave him explanations on a post during a teletandem:

ST6 and tutor, Session 2:

> T: It's a pity, they didn't say how things were going in Russia, it would have been interesting to know.

ST6: I asked ST_RUS6 and she told me that it's not easy to practise sports in Russia, that they don't have many sports facilities there, that's what she told me.

Even though the material posted on the Facebook page shared by all the French and Russian students was only followed by a few written comments, the space provided and the sharing of cultural information played important roles in the students' intrinsic motivation. The choice of information to be posted was carefully thought out and may have been prepared at length (ST2, for example, specifically took a tour-boat cruise on the Seine river in Paris and found out information about the monuments so as to be able to comment on the main buildings, and then filmed and commented on the tour to share the video with the group on the Facebook page). Freedom of choice combined with the desire to please seemed to motivate the posting.

5.4. Does this social environment sustain autonomisation?

The social environment proposed in this course, in particular teletandems and to some extent telecollaborations via Facebook, seemed to have a catalytic effect on learner motivation. The exchanges between learners had an impact on social motivation (Zimmerman & Schunk, 2008, p. 19) by nurturing the basic psychological need for relatedness – that is, the need for learners to experience positive and mutually satisfying relationships, characterised by a sense of closeness and trust and allowing students to live human experiences and to engage in affects (friendship, cooperation, reciprocity, altruism), which is a source of pleasure and recognition. The other effect of social motivation was the impact it had on self-regulation, helping to maintain efforts during the course but also the wish to continue self-directed learning and learning through teletandems once the course had ended (seven out of eight wished to continue learning through tandems, Questionnaire 1; four out of seven continued self-directed learning four months after the end of the training period, Questionnaire 2). It would seem, therefore, that social processes were recognised as both precursors of human self-regulatory development (Schunk & Zimmerman, 1997; Zimmerman & Schunk, 2008) and as vital components of current efforts to self-regulate (Karabenick, 1998).

Chapter 8

On the other hand, the inherent interest that students seemed to have in telecollaboration activities, as well as the great freedom of choice offered (choice of goals, resources, learning times, places, and cultural information posted, etc.) can be regarded as a form of intrinsic motivation, given the expressions of interest, pleasure and light-heartedness associated with these activities. Intrinsic motivation is based on students' inherent interest in the activity itself and is associated with enjoyment and inherent satisfaction in a task activity. "Intrinsic motivation can strengthen students' sense of autonomy" (Zimmerman & Schunk, 2008, p. 16), their need to feel for example a sense of personal control or self-agency, and their willingness to learn in a self-regulated way. The students' intrinsic motivation was also fostered by my support as the teacher, through which I sought to develop their autonomy rather than to control their behaviour. According to Deci, Schwartz, Sheinman, and Ryan (1981, p. 16) when teachers provide significant autonomy support but little behavioural control, their students become more intrinsically motivated for learning, feel more competent at learning, and develop a higher level of self-esteem. This could explain why six out of seven students felt more competent in learning a language after their learning experience (Questionnaire 2).

With regard to cognitive and metacognitive skills, the students experienced self-directed learning, organised their teletandems, cooperated, managed their emotions, reflected on the organisation of their learning, set achievable goals with my help, chose resources, and looked for strategies to learn better and to stay motivated. It is important to note that prior to this experience, none of the students at the Cnam had experienced self-directed language learning, and none had used social networks to learn a foreign language, nor foreign-language networking sites or social networking sites for language learning (Questionnaire 1). The guidance offered (exchange sessions, reflective workshops) to support self-directed learning was essential. Indeed, the lack of previous experience, combined with the fact that many students lacked confidence in writing in French (despite my encouragement, there were no written records in the logbooks and few written comments on the Facebook page) made the support essential to initiate reflection. Educational mediation and guidance by an expert and peers did at least allow students to orally verbalise choices, decision-making, critical reflection, and learning processes. The verbalisations of learning processes may have contributed to giving learners a sense of greater control over their learning process and encouraged them to continue learning.

6. Does the social dimension sustain learning?

6.1. Language learning

The students engaged cognitively and emotionally in group activities. Indeed, a majority continued learning Russian after the course and felt more confident in learning a language, but their language learning was limited. Six out of eight students had great difficulty reading Cyrillic at the end of the course. During the last exchange session, when they were asked to read in order to assess their learning, students had difficulty in deciphering Cyrillic. However, the two students who went through self-directed learning before starting their teletandems very late in the course (ST4), or even only at the end of their training period (ST8), read Cyrillic well and had mastered very basic communication (greeting; introducing oneself very simply; asking where a monument, a bus, or a subway station is; understanding numbers from 0 to 20). This shows that self-directed learning is crucial and that without it, learning outcomes are limited; in addition, with teletandems alone, language learning is not sufficient. However, we note that the students who participated in teletandems had good pronunciation (properly stressed vowels in particular), probably due to the fact that they had worked on their oral expression with their Russian partners. It is also worth noting that three students who, in addition to French and English knew another language (Tamil, Bantu languages) that was spoken by their parents, were at ease in pronouncing Russian (ST1, ST2, ST4), see Table 1.

It seems that self-directed learning was largely overlooked by six out of eight students, and five out of eight students focused only on teletandems and seemed to be working on their Russian only on this occasion. In the recommendations they give during the last reflexive workshop, they suggested, "do not focus

100% on tandems" or "before the exchange, train properly for the exchange, for example if you are working on reading, start by first working on your reading alone, do not start during the tandem". I also note that some students who chose not to follow the teletandem sheets (ST5 and ST6) did overly complicated tasks in Russian and were not able to remember the sentences suggested by their Russian partner (ST6) or completed tasks at much too fast a pace (ST5).

Table 1. Overview of student learning in Russian

Students	Teletandem practice	Self-directed learning	Easy reading (without help and reading after less than 5 s of reflection)	Basic mastery of Russian pronunciation (stressed and unstressed vowels, etc.)	Communicate VERY simply
ST1	YES	Little work	NO	YES	YES
ST2	YES	Little work	NO	YES	YES
ST3	YES	Very little work	NO	YES	NO
ST4	Started late, after 2 months	YES	YES	YES	YES
ST5	YES	Very little work	NO	YES	NO
ST6	YES	Little work	NO	YES	NO
ST7	NO	Very little work	NO	NO	NO
ST8	Started at the end of the course	YES	YES	NO	YES

6.2. Cultural and intercultural learning

With regard to the opportunities to learn about Russian culture and French students' own culture made possible by the exchange of cultural information on the Facebook page and by the teletandems, seven out of eight said they developed their knowledge of Russian culture (Questionnaire 1; workshop; exchange sessions). Knowledge shared on the Facebook page included landscapes, food and cooking, the fact that some Soviet films are still important references in today's cinema, the absurd tone of 'Art Freedom Cats', and the political activity of young Russians through an event called 'Monstration', which is a parody of May 1st with fairly explicit banners such as "further north than Korea". The post that was an explicit criticism of the current regime helped Cnam students to realise during the workshop that speech is not totally muzzled in Russia: it is a mocking way to say "will Russia turn into a sort of North Korea or the other is more explicit [laughs] it's starting to stink [laughs]" (workshop).

It should be noted that these exchanges of cultural information and teletandems gave rise to some intercultural awareness. Three students out of eight said that after the course they had a different representation of Russians and that they no longer had negative misconceptions about them: "Russians are not as cold as they seem", "I saw that they were very open" (Questionnaire 1), or that the course had helped them change their representation of Russia, initially imagined as a dark country where the sun never shines: "Otherwise they do have sunshine despite all the rest [laughs], he [his tandem partner] was clearly in the sunlight!" (workshop).

Finally, as students were asked to post cultural information that they considered important to share, the choice of the information to be published caused some cultural awareness during exchange sessions or during the workshop: Students in France did not easily find French-speaking cultural references to share, and their musical references, series, films, etc., were more naturally drawn toward Anglo-Saxon cultural references. They also become aware of the preeminence of American culture, unlike Russians, who had their own search engines, social networks, etc.: "It's different from here, it's not Google in the lead" (workshop).

6.3. Relational learning

As previously mentioned, the relationship with the tandem was the first point raised by the students during the scaffolding sessions. There was a constant assessment of the quality of the relationship with their partner: "he's pretty nice [laughs] we HIT IT OFF really well" (ST5) or "it's good to have a tandem partner that you get along with… You enjoy what you're doing" (ST2). As Nogueira et al. (2017) observed, it seems that "for the tandem to be successful in terms of learning, it should be also successful on the social level of the partnership" (p. 81). The fact that a 'successful tandem relationship' has an impact on 'successful tandem learning' was discussed during the exchange sessions and reflective workshops in order to mitigate this dependence. This is a point of particular attention worth discussing at the very beginning of the course.

Nevertheless, the dependence on the tandem partner did not prevent students from extending their network to other French and Russian students. Students became 'friends' with Russian students on their personal Facebook pages. As I suggested or at the request of their Russian tandem partner, the Cnam students also joined the Russian social network VK, an equivalent of the Russian Facebook site, in order to build a network of Siberian 'friends', a network in which Russian students were much more active. Three out of eight students were registered on VK at the end of the training period, and five out of seven were registered four months after the training ended (including three active students with 20 'friends'). I also note that half the students are still in contact with their tandem partners four months after the end of the training period (four out of seven; Questionnaire 2), but the students no longer carry out teletandems. The objective of broadening the network of relationships between Russian and French students was therefore a success that led students to implement the professional skill of 'learning to learn' a language by relying on the network of relationships and also, for those who would spend time in Russia, to facilitate their integration.

7. Discussion

While aware of the limitations of this study due to the fact that Russian student data were not included in the analysis, I consider the study to reveal that the telecollaboration environment, individual and collective guidance, freedom of choice, and availability of educational resources enabled students to engage cognitively and emotionally in their learning; to reflect on learning processes, organisational processes, language, and culture; and to develop moderate language and cultural skills, as well as to have their first intercultural experiences.

What seems most striking is that the young adults had the desire to continue learning by themselves and with their tandem partners after the end of the course: More than half of them said they continued learning (four out of seven), and six out of seven a few months after the course felt more confident in learning a language. It seems that the freedom offered and the social environment proposed, as well as the guidance they received, helped to motivate the students intrinsically, provided a positive experience in which the students were the main actors of their learning, and helped them feel competent and experience relatedness. These results are consistent with the work of Deci and Ryan (2002) and Deci and Flaste (1996) on the theory of self-determination, for whom autonomy is one of the three basic needs that must be satisfied to achieve a sense of self-fulfilment and to embrace an activity with a sense of interest and commitment. The other two basic needs are competence and relatedness. People have a feeling of competence when they confront and successfully overcome "optimal challenges" (Deci & Flaste, 1996, p. 66), and they experience relatedness when they love and are loved by others (Deci & Flaste, 1996, p. 88). Achieving the three needs not only provides a feeling of self-fulfilment, but also seems to have an impact on learning regulation and the sense of self-efficacy.

In our study, we also observed that students strongly focused on their tandem partners, the question of language learning in self-study being placed in the background and individual cognitive involvement noticeably neglected by six out of eight learners. Students concentrated their attention on the telecollaboration, teletandems in particular. It is likely that the self-directed learning of Russian went beyond their ZPD and that they had entrusted the regulation of their learning to the tandem partner. As Kohonen (2010) clearly notes, "[t]he tasks that pupils can do on their own are within their area of self-regulation. The development in the zone thus proceeds from other-regulation to self-regulation, towards increased autonomy" (p. 6). Since the students were complete beginners in the target language, self-directed learning certainly made learning more complex.

Chapter 8

This is confirmed by Little, Dam, and Legenhausen (2007), for whom "learner autonomy is inseparable from the learner gradually developing target language proficiency" (pp. 16-17), meaning that "the development of learner autonomy and the growth of target language proficiency are not only mutually supporting but fully integrated with each other" (p. 15). This is an improvement to be made to the course so that telecollaboration does not replace self-directed learning but remains complementary. This can be achieved by either strengthening guidance at the beginning of the course or offering an online training course for an introduction to Russian that would leave freedom of choice, continue to allow students to manage their learning, and be just as flexible as the current course.

In terms of professionalisation, the Russian course and its social multicultural environment allow the development of linguistic and cultural skills required in a globalised world. The course also teaches valuable 21st century skills that include promoting initiative and self-direction, seeking opportunities to use language beyond the classroom, and social and cross-cultural skills (ACTFL, 2011), which include emotional skills (e.g. self-knowledge, empathy, self-control, helping others) that are essential for cooperating with others and solving conflicts in a constructive way (Cherniss & Goleman, 2001; Sackett & Walmsley, 2014). These skills will be put to the test during the professional training in Russia.

8. Conclusion

Despite its limitations, this study tends to show that training in a language and culture and learning autonomy in language learning in a supportive social environment are beneficial. It also supports the need to refocus on autonomous learning and to reconsider the concept in light of technological developments.

The questions this study raises are twofold: praxeological and methodological. The first would aim to understand (via a longitudinal study and more precisely than through a questionnaire) how students continue self-directed learning or do not, with or without the help of tandems and social networks, for Russian as well as for other languages or subjects. Another avenue for future research would be to analyse the path that leads French students from the Facebook network to the Russian social network VK and, once they are on VK or on another Russian social network, the activities they carry out and how they take or do not take advantage of the network to learn. Another future research perspective would be to measure the impact of the course when on work placement abroad.

In terms of methodologically related research questions, addressing the issue of autonomisation in relation to social environments seems the obvious perspective to adopt, although it is methodologically complex to apprehend. I chose to combine self-determination, self-regulation, and self-efficacy theories (which are very seldom used in language teaching in France) with the paradigms of autonomous learning and emotion management. This interweaving of complementary theories is an approach I wish to further develop.

9. Supplementary materials

https://research-publishing.box.com/s/uitubpqofbx3h2okqbxjr2rq283jjtod

References

ACTFL. (2011). *The 21st century skills map*. American Council on the Teaching of Foreign Languages. https://www.actfl.org/sites/default/files/resources/21st%20Century%20Skills%20Map-World%20Languages.pdf

Bandura, A. (1986). *Social foundations of thought and action, a social-cognitive theory*. Prentice Hall.

Bandura, A. (2001). Social cognitive theory: an agentic perspective. *Annual Review of Psychology, 52*, 1-26. https://doi.org/10.1146/annurev.psych.52.1.1

Bardin, L. (1997). *L'analyse de contenu*. Presse Universitaire de France.

Blin, F. (2012). Introducing cultural historical activity theory for researching CMC in foreign language education. In M. Dooly & R. O'Dowd (Eds), *Theories, methods and challenges. Telecollaboration in education* (pp. 79-106). Peter Lang.

Brammerts, H., Little, D., Calvert, M., Otto, E., & Woodin, J. (2002). Introduction. In B. Helmling (Ed.), *L'apprentissage autonome des langues en tandem* (pp. 19-24). Didier.

Bruner, J. S. (1975). The ontogenesis of speech acts. *Journal of Child Language, 2*, 1-19.

Byram, M. (1997). *Teaching and assessing intercultural communicative competence.* Multilingual Matters.

Cappellini, M., Lewis, T., & Mompean, A. R. (2017). (Eds). *Learner autonomy and Web 2.0.* Equinox.

Cherniss, C., & Goleman, D. (2001). (Eds). *The emotionally intelligent workplace.* Jossey-Bass.

Clot, Y. (1999). *Avec Vygotski.* La dispute.

Cubberley, P. (2002). *Russian: a linguistic introduction.* Cambridge University Press.

Deci, E. L., & Flaste, R. (1996). *Why we do what we do: understanding self-motivation.* Penguin.

Deci, E. L., & Ryan, R. M. (2002). (Eds). *Self-determination theory in human behavior.* Plenum Press.

Deci, E. L., Schwartz, A. J., Sheinman, L., & Ryan, R. M. (1981). An instrument to assess adults' orientations toward control versus autonomy with children: reflections on intrinsic motivation and perceived competence. *Journal of Educational Psychology, 73*(5), 642-650. https://doi.org/10.1037/0022-0663.73.5.642

Dooly, M. (2017). Telecollaboration. In C. A. Chapelle & S. Sauro (Eds), *The handbook of technology in second language teaching and learning* (pp. 169-183). Wiley-Blackwell. https://doi.org/10.1002/9781118914069.ch12

Dooly, M., & O'Dowd, R. (2018). Telecollaboration in the foreign language classroom: a review of its origins and its application to langue teaching practice. In M. Dooly & R. O'Dowd (Eds), *In this together: teachers'experiences with transnational, telecollaborative language learning projects* (pp. 11-34). Peter Lang.

Gremmo, M.-J. (1995). Conseiller n'est pas enseigner : le rôle du conseiller dans l'entretien de conseil. *Mélanges CRAPEL, 22*, 33-62.

Groulx, L. H. (1999). Le pluralisme en recherche qualitative : essai de typologie. *Revue suisse de sociologie, 25*(2), 317-339.

Haerens, L. (n.d.). *Supporting educational professionals and optimizing student motivation.* Center for self-determination theory. https://selfdeterminationtheory.org/application-education/?

Holec, H. (1981). *Autonomy and foreign language learning.* Pergamon Press.

ILO. (2019). *Lifelong learning and the future of work: challenges and opportunities*. International Labour Organization.

Karabenick, S. A. (1998). (Ed.). *Strategic help seeking: implications for learning and teaching*. Erlbaum.

Kohonen, V. (1992). Experiential language learning: second language learning as cooperative learner education. In D. Nunan (Ed.), *Collaborative language learning and teaching* (pp. 14-39). Cambridge University Press.

Kohonen, V. (2010). Autonomy, agency and community in FL education: developing site-based understanding through a university and school partnership. In B. O'Rourke & L. Carson (Eds), *Language learner autonomy: policy, curriculum, classroom* (pp. 3-28). Peter Lang.

Kronenberg, F. A. (2017). From language lab to language center and beyond: the past, present, and future of language learning center design. *Apprentissage des langues et systèmes d'information et de communication (Alsic), 20*(3). https://doi.org/10.4000/alsic.3172

Lantolf, J. (2013). Sociocultural theory and the dialectics of learner autonomy/agency. In P. Benson & L. Cooker (Eds), *The applied linguistic individual: sociocultural approaches to autonomy, agency, and identity* (pp. 17-31). Equinox.

Lantolf, J., & Thorne, S. L. (2007). Sociocultural theory and second language learning. In. B. van Patten & J. Williams (Eds), *Theories in second language acquisition* (pp. 201-224). Lawrence Erlbaum.

Lewis, T. (2014). Learner autonomy and the theory of sociality. In G. Murray (Ed.), *Social dimensions of autonomy in language learning* (pp. 37-59). Palgrave Macmillan. https://doi.org/10.1057/9781137290243_3

Lewis, T., & Walker, L. (2003). (Eds). *Autonomous language learning in tandem*. Academy Electronic Press.

Little, D. (2000). Learner autonomy and human interdependence: some theoretical and practical consequences of a social interactive view of cognition, learning, and language. In B. Sinclair, I. McGrath & T. Lamb (Eds), *Learner autonomy, teacher autonomy: future directions* (pp. 15-23). Pearson.

Little, D. (2015). Language learner autonomy, Vygotsky and sociocultural theory: some theoretical and pedagogical reflections. In K. Schwienhorst (Ed.), *Learner autonomy in second language pedagogy and research: challenges and issues* (pp. 5-28). Candlin & Mynarde Publishing.

Little, D., Dam, L., & Legenhausen, L. (2007). *Language learner autonomy: a guide for teachers, teacher educators and researchers*. Multilingual Matters.

Murphy, L. (2014). Autonomy, social interaction, and community: a distant language learning perspective. In G. Murray (Ed.), *Social dimensions of autonomy in language learning* (pp. 119-134). Palgrave Macmillan. https://doi.org/10.1057/9781137290243_7

Niemiec, C. P., & Ryan, R. M. (2009). Autonomy, competence, and relatedness in the classroom: applying self-determination theory to educational practice. *Theory and Research in Education, 7*(2), 133-144. https://doi.org/10.1177/1477878509104318

Nogueira, D., O'Connor, K. M., & Cappellini, M. (2017). A typology of metacognition: examining autonomy in a collective blog compiled in a teletandem environment. In M. Cappellini, T. Lewis & A. Rivens Mompean (Eds), *Learner autonomy and Web 2.0* (pp. 67-90). Equinox.

O'Leary, C. (2014). Developing autonomous language learners in HE: a social constructivist perspective. In G. Murray (Ed.), *Social dimensions of autonomy in language learning* (pp. 15-36). Palgrave Macmillan. https://doi.org/10.1057/9781137290243_2

Oxford, R. (1990). *Language learning strategies: what every teacher should know*. Heinley and Heinley.

Paquay, L. (2006). Introduction. In L. Paquay, M. Crahay & J.-M. De Ketele (Eds), *L'analyse qualitative en éducation. Des pratiques de recherche aux critères de qualité* (pp. 13-29). De Boeck.

Patton, M. Q. (1990). *Qualitative evaluation and research methods* (2nd ed.). Sage Publications.

Reeve, J., Ryan, R., Deci, E. L., & Jang, H. (2008). Understanding and promoting autonomous self-regulation: a self-determination theory perspective. In D. H. Schunk & B. J. Zimmerman (Eds), *Motivation and self-regulated learning* (pp. 223-244). Routledge.

Rivens Mompean, A. (2013). *Le centre de ressources en langues : vers la modélisation du dispositif d'apprentissage*. Presse universitaire du Septentrion. https://doi.org/10.4000/books.septentrion.16720

Ryan, R. M., & Deci, E. L. (2000). Self-determination theory and the facilitation of intrinsic motivation, social development, and well being. *American Psychologist, 55*(1), 68-78. https://doi.org/10.1037/0003-066x.55.1.68

Sackett, P., & Walmsley, P. (2014). Which personality attributes are most important in the workplace? *Perspective in Psychological Science, 9*(5), 538-551. https://doi.org/10.1177/1745691614543972

Salovey, P., & Mayer, J. (1990). Emotional intelligence. *Imagination, Cognition, and Personality, 9*(3), 185-211. https://doi.org/10.2190/dugg-p24e-52wk-6cdg

Schunk, D., & Zimmerman, B. (1997). Social origins of self-regulatory competence. *Educational Psychologist, 32*(4), 195-208. https://doi.org/10.1207/s15326985ep3204_1

Schunk, D., & Zimmerman, B. (2008). *Motivation and self-regulated learning*: Lawrence Erlbaum Associates.

Stringer, E. (2008). *Action research in education*. Pearson.

Tardieu, C., & Horgues, C. (2020). *Redefining tandem language and culture learning in higher education*. Routledge. https://doi.org/10.4324/9780429505898

Vandergriff, I. (2016). *Second language discourse in the digital world. Linguistic and social practices in and beyond the networked classroom*. John Benjamins Publishing Company. https://doi.org/10.1075/lllt.46

Vygotsky, L. S. (1978). *Mind in society. The development of higher psychological processes*. Harvard University Press.

Zarate, G. (1986). *Enseigner une culture étrangère*. Hachette.

Zimmerman, B. J., & Schunk, D. H. (2008). Motivation. An essential dimension of self-regulated learning. In D. H. Schunk & B. J. Zimmerman (Eds), *Motivation and self-regulated learning: theory, research, and applications* (pp. 1-30). Routledge. https://doi.org/10.4324/9780203831076

Coda – opportunities and challenges in language learning and professionalization in higher education: the road ahead

Béatrice Dupuy[1] and Muriel Grosbois[2]

1. Introduction

In considering theoretical, methodological, and pedagogical perspectives for preparing language learners and teachers in/for the 21st century, the preceding chapters have sought to highlight how research findings could/should inform curriculum, instruction, and professional development in higher education so as to promote language learning and sustain its link to professionalization in today's and tomorrow's society. Language learning and professionalization have been explored here through researches focusing on: university students who need to learn to communicate in one or more foreign languages to both interact as global citizens and increase their chances of employability; professionals who, on their lifelong learning journey, study foreign languages to enrich or develop (new) skills for a variety of reasons, including the need to meet evolving work requirements and adapt to an ever changing society; and (pre-service) language teachers who need to learn how best to meet the needs of learners. In this brief coda, we synthesize the major points from the chapters included in this book and highlight the opportunities that exist and the challenges that must be addressed if we want the opportunities not to remain just that.

---

1. University of Arizona, Tucson, Arizona, United States; bdupuy@email.arizona.edu; https://orcid.org/0000-0003-1122-4264

2. Conservatoire National des Arts et Métiers (Cnam), Paris, France; muriel.grosbois@lecnam.net; https://orcid.org/0000-0003-2258-8733

How to cite: Dupuy, B., & Grosbois, M. (2020). Coda – opportunities and challenges in language learning and professionalization in higher education: the road ahead. In B. Dupuy and M. Grosbois (Eds), *Language learning and professionalization in higher education: pathways to preparing learners and teachers in/for the 21st century* (pp. 263-268). Research-publishing.net. https://doi.org/10.14705/rpnet.2020.44.1108

Coda

2. Expanding understandings of communication

For over two decades, scholars have recognized and theorized the multilingual and multimodal communication landscapes in which we live and work, and the connectedness of language and culture. Already in 1996, The New London Group was arguing that the multiplicity of texts resulting from increased cultural and linguistic diversity but also increased diversity in modes of meaning-making in the world called for a broader understanding of literacy. Since then, society has changed even more: it is much more digital and the forces of globalization are different. The nature of diversity is no longer understood as it was in the mid-1990's. Enabled by digital media, people from all over the world now come together for a variety of purposes both social and professional and interact in new ways.

Communication can no longer be considered as anchored in the linguistic dimension only, but rather crosses different modes that promote multiliteracies (see Betül Czerkawski and Margherita Berti, Chapter 1). Audio, visual, gestural, and spatial modes of communication are not only integrated within, but often supplant, traditional spoken and written linguistic ones as modes of meaning-making in texts. In this respect, Elyse Petit (Chapter 5) stresses the necessity to go beyond just language by illustrating how in communication, multiple modes co-operate in the creation of meanings, including but not limited to the linguistic mode. Camille Debras (Chapter 7) also insists on the role played by multimodality in communication: focusing on the multimodal, interactional, and intercultural aspects of communicative competence that are key elements of international professional life in the 21st century, she emphasizes the crucial communicative functions of gesture during exolingual interactions. Elsa Chachkine (Chapter 8) explores communication with technology through a telecollaborative project that goes beyond the classroom walls and gives French apprentice-engineers the opportunity to communicate multimodally with their Russian partners. In the process, the French students become familiarized with the Russian language and culture prior to their mobility period, while developing their autonomy as learners, a skill also valuable for their lifelong learning journey.

The expanding understandings of communication illustrated in the book call for a fundamental transformation of foreign language curricula and require a major paradigm shift if the objective of higher education is to foster effective communication to respond to the demands of and changes in the world of work and beyond.

3. Transforming the curriculum

There is a broad consensus that lifelong learning opportunities are needed for professionals across all disciplinary areas, including languages and cultures, and for people at all stages of their careers. The resulting implication is that learner-centered programs, flexible learning paths, and assessment and recognition of prior learning are required for language learning. Faced with this imperative, institutions of higher education need to be agile and committed enough to meet this challenge.

Words such as active, applied, and evidence-based are currently framing conversations related to transforming curricula, pedagogies, and spaces (physical or virtual, at home or abroad) in which learning takes place and knowledge is developed (Brooks, 2010). In this book, Betül Czerkawski and Margherita Berti (Chapter 1) underscore the necessity to transform current FL curricula so they can foster 21st century skills and lifelong learning. They make the case for using instructional design guidelines to create meaningful learning experiences that meet people's communication needs in environments in constant evolution. Aude Labetoulle (Chapter 3) explains how complex it can be to design an English curriculum that is relevant to students' future professional needs in French universities when their disciplines are varied. She proposed a diversified and flexible syllabus organized around meaningful tasks for students. Individual needs were taken into consideration and students had the opportunity to select tasks based on needs and a personal project activity was introduced. The objective was to individualize the degree of professionalization by allowing students to tailor the course to their specific needs. The course also put emphasis on learner autonomy when completing the tasks. Naouel Zoghlami (Chapter 2) suggests that needs analysis could provide the necessary data to inform the design of a curriculum and pedagogical tasks that are responsive to learners' needs in a French public institution dedicated to lifelong learning.

The challenge inherent to instructional design is strengthened by the fact that in today's society, circumstances change rapidly (social, economic…) and learners are diverse; as The Douglas Fir Group (2016) reminds us, "[i]ncreasingly numerous and more diverse populations of adults and youth become multilingual and transcultural later in life, either by elective choice or by forced circumstances, or for a mixture of reasons" (p. 19). Learners also tend to make the most of formal as well as non-formal and informal learning opportunities on their lifelong learning journeys. As noted by Toffoli (2020) learners may "engage in totally independent journeys, in entirely informal contexts and media, while others choose trajectories marked by institutional constraints, and still others pursue journeys somewhere between these two extremes" (p.186). Furthermore, their trajectories are likely to evolve over time on an individual basis.

The diversity of learning paths sustains the relevance of the shift from instructional design to learning design, a distinction established in the literature to underscore the importance of learner-centeredness in the design process. This change of focus actually goes as far as to raise the question of adult learners as course designers, a perspective which gives learners great freedom of choice. Learning centered on the learner's needs does not necessarily follow a previously established path and is partly shaped by 'organizing circumstances' (Spear & Mocker, 1984) as suggested by Narcy-Combes (2018). This change of perspective, with a more or less loosely structured framework, calls for a shift in language teacher education.

4. Rethinking the role and preparation of language teachers

The need to both expand current understandings of communication and reconsider the very principles of instructional design underscores the urgency to rethink the education and professional development of language teachers. Betül Czerkawski and Margherita Berti (Chapter 1) emphasize the importance for teachers to go beyond a curriculum that often privileges linguistic aspects of language rather than meaning and explore the complementarity that exists between more or less formal settings to create learning opportunities that align with students' needs. Tara Hashemi (Chapter 4) highlights the need to provide pre-service language teachers with relevant professional development opportunities so that they understand the complex notions that undergird the multiliteracies framework and multiliteracies pedagogy and are better able to facilitate the meaning-making process as students read and produce multimodal texts. When implemented, a multiliteracies-oriented approach may help overcome the challenges that language and culture might bring, as illustrated by Elyse Petit (Chapter 5). This line of research aligns well with the call for a broader understanding of literacy and literacy teaching to better support learners as they design their social and professional futures (The New London Group, 1996). Pauline Beaupoil-Hourdel (Chapter 6) also argues that the multimodal interactions that take place in the home during literacy events should inform the professional development of kindergarten and primary school teachers. Blurring the frontiers between learning environments, she invites (pre-service) teachers to make the most of the home/school link with respect to new multimodal perspectives on fostering communicative competence.

Given the evolving nature and complexity of communication and learning environments as well as the diversity of learners and the conception of language teachers as facilitators of learning, we consider that the way forward is for language researchers-teachers and learners to be partners in shaping the curriculum so it is best suited to meet the needs of professionals in the 21st century.

What started as a two-day symposium co-organized by the Cnam and the University of Arizona in January 2019 triggered our reflection on language learning and professionalization and laid the groundwork for this volume. We hope that the cases under study in this book will lead the profession to reflect on language learning and professionalization in higher education with a view of how to best prepare learners and teachers in/for the 21st century, especially at a time when distance education, video conferencing, and virtual mobility are expected to develop exponentially.

References

Brooks, C. F. (2010). Toward 'hybridised' faculty development for the twenty-first century: blending online communities of practice and face-to-face meetings in instructional and professional support programmes. *Innovations in Education and Teaching International, 47*(3), 261-270. https://doi.org/10.1080/14703297.2010.498177

Narcy-Combes, J. P. (2018). Didactique des langues : de nouvelles conceptions. *Études en Didactique des Langues. De la théorie à la pratique, 30*, 9-34.

Spear, G. E., & Mocker, D. W. (1984). The organizing circumstance: environmental determinants in self-directed learning. *Adult Education Quarterly, 35*(1), 1-10. https://doi.org/10.1177/0001848184035001001

The Douglas Fir Group. (2016). A transdisciplinary framework for SLA in a multilingual world. *The Modern Language Journal, 100*(S1), 19-47. https://doi.org/10.1111/modl.12301

The New London Group. (1996). A pedagogy of multiliteracies: Designing social factors. *Harvard Educational Review, 66*, 60-92. https://doi.org/10.17763/haer.66.1.17370n67v22j160u

Toffoli, D. (2020). *Informal learning and institution-wide language provision. University language learners in the 21st century*. Palgrave Macmillan.

Author index

B
Beaupoil-Hourdel, Pauline v, 5, 167, 267
Berti, Margherita vi, 3, 11, 264, 265, 267

C
Chachkine, Elsa vi, 6, 229, 264
Czerkawski, Betül vii, 3, 11, 264, 265, 267

D
Debras, Camille vii, 6, 199, 264
Dupuy, Béatrice v, 1, 263

G
Grosbois, Muriel v, 1, 263

H
Hashemi, Tara vii, 5, 99, 267

L
Labetoulle, Aude viii, 4, 71, 265

P
Petit, Elyse viii, 5, 137, 264, 267

Z
Zoghlami, Naouel ix, 4, 37, 265

www.ingramcontent.com/pod-product-compliance
Lightning Source LLC
Chambersburg PA
CBHW021836220426